10/05

DAILY LIFE IN
THE AGE OF
CHARLEMAGNE

The Greenwood Press "Daily Life Through History" Series

DAILY LIFE IN

THE AGE OF CHARLEMAGNE

JOHN J. BUTT

The Greenwood Press "Daily Life Through History" Series

GREENWOOD PRESS
Westport, Connecticut • London

Library of Congress Cataloging-in-Publication Data

Butt, John J.
    Daily life in the age of Charlemagne / John J. Butt
        p. cm.—(The Greenwood Press "Daily life through history" series, ISSN 1080–
4749)
    Includes bibliographical references and index.
    ISBN 0–313–31668–6 (alk. paper)
    1. Charlemagne, Emperor, 742–814.   2. France—Social life and customs—To 1328.
    3. France—History—To 987. I. Title. II. Series.
    DC73.B86 2002
    944'.01'092—dc21
    [B]   2002067820

British Library Cataloguing in Publication Data is available.

Library of Congress Catalog Card Number: 2002067820
ISBN: 0–313–31668–6
ISSN: 1080–4749

First published in 2002

Greenwood Press, 88 Post Road West, Westport, CT 06881
An imprint of Greenwood Publishing Group, Inc.
www.greenwood.com

Printed in the United States of America

The paper used in this book complies with the
Permanent Paper Standard issued by the National
Information Standards Organization (Z39.48–1984).

10 9 8 7 6 5 4 3 2 1

CONTENTS

INTRODUCTION

Daily Life in the Age of Charlemagne may seem an odd topic choice in a modern age when we denigrate most prominent individuals. The era of venerating "great men" has passed, at least for the time being. History books written before 1960 frequently focused on an individual as the source of great events. Christopher Columbus, Martin Luther, George Washington, Thomas Jefferson, and Albert Einstein were common titles or themes. However, in the past few decades, the trend has been to find fault with these prominent individuals, rather than to allow one person to stand out almost to the point of worship. For instance, Columbus is said to have been mean spirited and to have brought disease to the Americas. Jefferson fathered children by one of his slaves. Such skepticism is intended to show that these individuals were not that great, yet the criticisms generally miss the point. Columbus is not considered great because of his altruism, but because of his vision, his daring, and his remarkable seamanship. Jefferson is not considered great because of his personal moral purity, but because of his political and philosophical clarity and penetration. The criticisms may point out that after all their greatness they were indeed still human, but do not prove that they should no longer be considered great.

Charlemagne stands firmly in this category. In the sweep of world history, with the need to cover all continents and civilizations equally (even to the point of incorporating cultures that never really developed civilizations), the Age of Charlemagne occasionally is cut or short-changed. However, Charlemagne had as large an impact on history as almost any other individual. Had he not built his empire and encouraged what has become known, for better or worse, as the Carolingian Renaissance, much of the culture of ancient Rome would have been lost and Christianity in the West might have died. Even with the Carolingian Renaissance, many classical texts have disappeared permanently. Many more were on the precipice of disappearing, sometimes down to the last copy in existence before the Carolingian scribes took possession of the text and began the process of copying. In addition, Islam was a serious threat, expanding in nearly all directions. Had it not been for Charlemagne, like his grandfather Charles Martel before him, Islam very likely would have overrun all of Europe, and Christianity consequently could have been wiped out. Had Christianity been wiped out of Europe, it is possible that it might have disappeared elsewhere as well.

The Middle Ages are a modern historical construct, which means that we artificially put dating limits of a beginning and end and call them by a certain name. A person living within the period would not have been aware that he or she was in the Middle Ages. It was only in the Renaissance that the term was coined to refer to the vast era between the ancient classical world and the modern Renaissance or rebirth of those classical ideas. This period was medieval or the Middle Ages (medieval literally means Middle Ages). Modern historians generally date the Middle Ages from approximately 500 C.E. (because of the sack of Rome in 476 C.E.) and usually break the Middle Ages into three blocks: Early Middle Ages (500–1000), High Middle Ages (1000–1300), and Late Middle Ages (1300–1500). The year 1500 is commonly used as an ending because in 1517 the Reformation fractured one of the most important commonalties of the Middle Ages, the single Christian Church in the West. The Early Middle Ages is bordered on one end by the fall of the Roman Empire in the West and on the other by the end of the invasions of the Magyars, the Muslims, and the Vikings. The High Middle Ages was a period of population and economic growth, the height of several of the important institutions of the Middle Ages such as the Church, feudalism, and manorialism, and the rise of new medieval institutions such as the commercial town and the university. The Late Middle Ages was once set apart as a period of decline from the High Middle Ages because population growth began to stagnate and, following the arrival of the Black Death in 1347, plummet along with a decline in construction and production of nearly every agricultural or manufactured good. It is now understood that the Late Middle Ages was a period of decline for overall production because the population declined by one-third to one-half, but in many instances the per capita production increased. The Late Middle Ages were a time of great changes in feudalism, manorialism, economics, and political structure.

The Age of Charlemagne belongs in the Early Middle Ages. The great debate (or divide where most Carolingian historians fall into one camp or the other) is whether the Age of Charlemagne was an important connection with the ancient past of the Roman Empire or a break from the past and a new beginning, the start of Europe. The older histories of this period tended to see the connections with Rome. In the twenty-first century, with less emphasis on classicism and more on the unity of Europe, the importance of the Age of Charlemagne as the beginning of Europe seems to have gained the upper hand. The truth seems to lie somewhere between in that intellectually and artistically the Age of Charlemagne is connected with the past of the Roman Empire. The connections may even be seen in Charlemagne's attempts to emulate the lost power, unity, and cohesion of Rome. But in many other ways, especially economically, socially, and politically, the Age of Charlemagne is a seed, even a foreshadowing, of the High Middle Ages to follow. It is critical as a bridge between the two quite distinct eras. Some historians have argued that there was no renaissance in this era, while others have argued that the real revolution began after the Carolingian era. Although both make credible arguments, the fact that they are built against the strong standing wall of the significance of the Age of Charlemagne also suggests that there is something of great importance here. The traditional claim is that the Carolingian era is the real beginning of a distinctly European history that is neither strongly tied to the ancient Middle East nor to the Mediterranean culture of Greece or Rome. The heartland of the Carolingians was north central Europe, along the modern border of France and Germany. The Carolingians were Germanic in culture and custom, not Latin. Whether the Carolingian era is the real beginning or the seeds of the revolution that takes place immediately thereafter is a question that perhaps has no answer.

CHRONOLOGY

732 Charles Martel, mayor of the palace, defeats Muslims at Tours.

741 Charles Martel dies and is buried at Saint-Denis.

Pepin the Short becomes mayor of the palace.

Royal Frankish Annals begins.

742 Charles (Charlemagne) is born at Aachen on April 2.

Ecclesiastical reforms begin.

744 Council of Soissons is held.

The monastery of Fulda is founded.

746 Boniface is named bishop of Mainz.

751 Lombards capture Ravenna.

Pepin is elected King.

752 Septimania is reconquered by the Arabs.

753 Pope Stephen II visits France.

754 Pepin is anointed by Pope Stephen II in Francia.

Boniface dies.

755 Pepin leads expedition to Italy.

760   Pepin begins conquest of Aquitaine.

768   Pepin dies at Saint-Denis, where he is buried.

Pepin's sons are enthroned simultaneously, Charles at Noyon and Carloman at Soisson. The empire is divided.

769   Son Pepin is born to Charlemagne and Himiltrude (later declared illegitimate).

770   Charlemagne marries Desiderata, daughter of Lombard King Desiderius (Charlemagne is already married to Himiltrude, who is declared a concubine).

771   Carloman dies.

Charlemagne reunites kingdom.

774   Desiderata is sent back to Lombardy.

Charlemagne marries Hildegard.

Saxon wars begin.

The Lombard kingdom is conquered.

778   Charlemagne leads expedition to Spain.

Rear guard of Charlemagne's army suffers disaster at Roncevaux at the hands of the Basques.

780   Charlemagne meets Alcuin.

781   Realms of Aquitaine and Italy are created within the kingdom.

Second son is Pepin born to Hildegard (birth year of Charles, first son is unknown).

782   Paul the Deacon arrives at the court.

In response to Saxon attack, Charlemagne orders execution of 4,500 Saxon prisoners in one day.

783   Hildegard dies.

786   Second Council of Nicaea is held.

788   Charlemagne conquers Bavarians.

791   Charlemagne orders the *Libri Carolini* to be composed as a response to the actions of the council at Nicaea.

794   Palace complex at Aachen is constructed.

796 Charlemagne destroys Avars.

   Alcuin is made abbot of St. Martin of Tours.

   Einhard is at court.

797 Saxony is subdued.

800 Charlemagne is crowned emperor of the Romans on Christmas Day by Pope Leo III.

801 Barcelona is conquered.

   Envoys from Baghdad arrive at Aachen.

804 Alcuin dies.

812 Treaty between Charlemagne and Byzantine emperor Michael I is signed.

813 Charlemagne delegates power to his surviving son Louis.

814 Charlemagne dies on January 28.

   Louis the Pious becomes king.

816 Louis is crowned by Pope Stephen V at Rheims.

819 Louis marries Judith.

   Einhard writes *Life of Charlemagne*, c. 819.

839 Empire is divided between Lothair and Charles, grandsons of Charlemagne.

840 Louis the Pious (son of Charlemagne) dies.

   Lothair becomes emperor.

   Alliance is formed between sons Charles the Bald and Louis the German (grandsons of Charlemagne).

   Einhard dies.

843 Treaty of Verdun divides empire into three parts under Charles the Bald, Lothair, and Louis the German (grandsons of Charlemagne).

   Nithard writes *Histories*.

   Nantes is pillaged by Normans.

845 Paris is sacked by Normans.

846 Rome is sacked by Saracens.

855 Emperor Lothair dies.

Kingdom is realigned into two parts, East and West Franks.

861 Saint-Germain-des-Prés is sacked by Normans.

869 Lothair II, king of Lotharingia, dies.

875 Emperor Louis II dies.

Charles the Bald is crowned emperor at Rome.

876 Louis the German dies.

885 Paris is besieged.

888 Final partition of the empire is made.

889 Hungarians raid northern Italy.

900 Hungarians invade Bavaria

910 The monastery of Cluny is founded.

911 Normans are installed in Normandy.

1

A Brief History of the Kingdom of the Franks and the World around Them

The Carolingian world was transformed within roughly fifty years. When Charlemagne inherited the kingdom in 768, it was, for all intents and purposes, a large Germanic kingdom in northwestern Europe surrounded by other Germanic and Slavic peoples of somewhat lesser power and territory. When Charlemagne died in 814, the Carolingian court was a major player in the world. By conquering the Saxons to the northeast, the Avars to the east, the Muslims across the Pyrenees Mountains, and the Lombards to the south, the Carolingians were safeguarded from immediate threats. This placed them in an entirely different category where the great civilizations of the world, including the papacy of Western Christianity, the Byzantine Empire, and the Abbasid Caliphate, had to deal with the Carolingians as a major power if not their equal. Diplomacy between Rome and Aachen, the site of Charlemagne's court, between Constantinople and Aachen, and between Baghdad and Aachen became nearly commonplace. In the ninth century, along with all the great civilizations of China, Byzantium, and Islam, must be named the Carolingian Empire. This was the first Germanic empire to catapult itself into world prominence and international participation. This upstart state, precarious and unsophisticated, was not to play a major role in world affairs for long, but it was to influence the rest of European history. This Carolingian world, between 732, when Charlemagne's grandfather, not yet king of the Franks, defeated the rapidly expanding and seemingly unstoppable Muslims at Tours, and the disintegration of the vast empire

Carolingian Genealogy

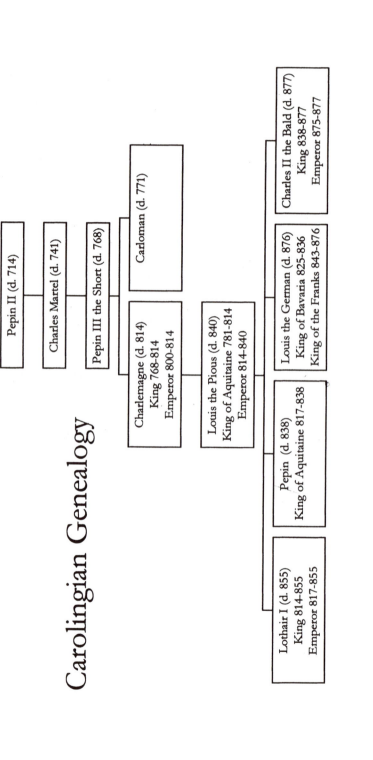

Pepin II (d. 714)

Charles Martel (d. 741)

Pepin III the Short (d. 768)

Carloman (d. 771)

Charlemagne (d. 814)
King 768-814
Emperor 800-814

Louis the Pious (d. 840)
King of Aquitaine 781-814
Emperor 814-840

Lothair I (d. 855)
King 814-855
Emperor 817-855

Pepin (d. 838)
King of Aquitaine 817-838

Louis the German (d. 876)
King of Bavaria 825-836
King of the Franks 843-876

Charles II the Bald (d. 877)
King 838-877
Emperor 875-877

in the late ninth century, was to start Europe down a number of paths that would become distinctive elements of European civilization.

THE CAROLINGIAN EMPIRE

Geography of the Carolingian Empire

The region of the world that comprised the Carolingian Empire covered approximately 600,000 square miles (more than 900 miles north to south and more than 700 miles east to west) from the English Channel in the north to central Italy in the south and from the Atlantic coast of France in the west to the Danube River in the east. Biologically and geologically, this region is predominantly broadleaf forest with some needleleaf forest and has an annual rainfall of 20–60 inches, average temperatures between 30 and 63 degrees, and land elevation ranging from areas below sea level in the modern-day Netherlands to nearly 16,000 feet in the Alps. It was Indo-European speaking except for the Basques, in modern-day Spain and France, but comprised many different languages even in its heartland of western Germany and eastern France. Learned Carolingians would have known the world to be composed of three continents: Europe, Asia, and Africa, with Jerusalem at the center of the world. Within the Frankish kingdom, there were four major regions, Francia, Alemannia (Germany), Aquitaine, and Italy, and the subdivisions of Aquitaine, Neustria, Austrasia, Burgundy, Bavaria, Frisia, and Saxony. Immediately beyond the boundaries of the Frankish kingdom were the kingdom of the Lombards (later known as the Kingdom of Italy), the Kingdom of Galicia and Asturias (northwestern Spain), Brittany, the Slavs, the Normans (Northmen), the Caliphate of Cordova (Spain and Portugal), the Caliphate of the Abbasids (North Africa and the Middle East), lands of the Anglo-Saxons (England), and the Byzantine Empire or Eastern Roman Empire.

The Franks under Clovis

The history of the Frankish people began in the second century C.E. when Germanic tribes entered the Roman Empire from the northeast. They were kept under Roman control during the reign of Marcus Aurelius (161–180), but by the beginning of the third century the Franks had formed a confederation along the lower Rhine in the north, and the Roman borders began to crumble as existing defensive armies could no longer cope with the number and range of invasions of Roman territory. At the same time, external disturbances elsewhere and internal turmoil required the withdrawal of troops precisely when more were needed. By the fourth century, the Franks were employed by the Romans to defend the borders, but instead they occupied the Roman region of northern Gaul (modern France and Belgium).

Merovingians

The first Frankish king of importance was Clovis (481–511) of the Merovingian family. After several successful military battles and the defeat of the Alemanni and Visigoths, the Merovingian Franks established themselves as the dominant Germanic kingdom and controlled a territory consisting roughly of modern France, Belgium, and western Germany. After the defeat of the Visigoths, the Eastern Roman emperor bestowed upon Clovis the title of honorary consul, thus legitimizing his political authority. Most important, Clovis understood the significance of the Church as an effective tool for further legitimization, a source of wealth, and international influence. Clovis converted to Roman Catholicism rather than the Arian movement that had been declared heretical. In doing so, Clovis gained an invaluable ally, while the Church gained a protector against Arianism and against attacks in Gaul. The Gallo-Roman nobility in Gaul, especially below the Loire River, was the most influential group, controlling much of the wealth and also providing the Catholic bishops of Gaul. By gaining their support, Clovis welded together a strong alliance that could influence much of the non-Frankish population of the region. The conversion of Clovis to orthodox Roman Catholicism, as the only Germanic king to do so, has been seen as a decisive moment in history, unifying the wealth and authority of the Church with the military power of the Frankish state. Each defended the existence of the other, and the actions of the Franks took on religious overtones, with military actions becoming religious crusades. Clovis finished his reign in 511 as the most powerful Germanic king.

The Birth of the Carolingian Empire

The Merovingian dynasty lasted for another two hundred years and was a period of rapid social change. Northwestern Europe was transformed from a Roman territory into a Germanic land that assimilated Gallo-Roman and Frankish customs through interaction and intermarriage. Although Merovingian Francia expanded with the conquest of the Burgundians, by the seventh century the Merovingian kings held limited power, while the nobility, both lay and ecclesiastical, held all of the local control. The Merovingian family endured as kings, but in name only, as the kingdom was divided into subkingdoms. The real power lay in the hands of the palace mayor, an office awarded to a member of the Frankish nobility for each of the subkingdoms. Gradually these mayors increased their power at the expense of the Merovingian kings, who in the seventh century were known as "do-nothing kings." In 687, the mayor for Austrasia, Pepin of Heristal (687–714), defeated the mayor of Neustria and was able to unite the royal courts under one mayoral. This union was the beginning of the family to be known as the Carolingians.

Charles Martel

When Pepin died in 714, his illegitimate son Charles Martel (the Hammer, a name given to him only in the ninth century for his military conquests) (714–741) gained the advantage over his two half-brother minors and by 719 was in control of the Frankish government even though he was never officially king. The actions of the Carolingians gradually increased their control over more and more elements of the Merovingian role of kingship. The Carolingians gained control of the granting of land, an extremely important aspect in winning the support of the aristocracy. They gained the right to grant the title of duke, which also helped to displace the focus of power from the Merovingians to themselves. The Carolingians established new religious foundations and endowed existing ones because to gain the support of the Church was to gain the advantage of the only Europe-wide superstructure. They even appropriated the royal role as keepers of the most holy relic in Francia, the cloak of St. Martin, by which men took holy oaths. They also gradually took on the image and status of kingship with the wearing of long hair and the sense of power that could only be gained by success on the battlefield, a power the Merovingians had long since lost.

Muslim Threat to Europe

In 711, the Muslims had crossed from North Africa into the Iberian Peninsula, and by 720 they had swept through to Septimania, just north of the Pyrenees Mountains and at the edge of the Frankish kingdom. In 732, a large Muslim force moved north through central Gaul toward the city of Tours, where the Church of St. Martin was the most important Christian pilgrimage center in the entire kingdom. This was a threat against the kingdom, but also a Muslim threat against Christianity that if unstopped might signal the end of Christianity in the West. Charles marshaled a Frankish army that met the Muslim force in October between Poitiers and Tours and defeated them. One of the traditions has it that Charles's force was heavily armored cavalry (soldiers on horseback), but more recent research has emphasized the importance of infantry (foot soldiers) in the Frankish armies at least until the late eighth century. Another tradition is that this was the forward thrust of an enormous concerted military effort planned by the Muslim Caliphate and that

Charles's victory over this army was stunning, since other armies, including the Byzantines', had been unable to stop the Muslims. Charles has been portrayed in history as having "hammered" the Muslims, hence his name. It is now believed that this Muslim force that Charles defeated may not have been a major part of the Muslim army, but possibly a freelance force of Berbers. Nevertheless, the defeat of the Muslim army stopped any further major advances into France and in effect kept the Muslims bottled up in the Iberian Peninsula. Additionally, the victory brought Charles a considerable amount of wealth—a contemporary source from a Spaniard living under Muslim rule claimed that there were tents full of great treasure taken by the Franks.

Another important development under Charles Martel was the link between the Church in Rome and the Franks. Charles had proven himself a strong supporter of the Church through donations to several monasteries, including the most important foundations of Saint-Denis and St. Martin. In 739, Pope Gregory III appealed to Charles for help against the Lombards, a Germanic group that had settled in the northern Italian peninsula. The Lombards expanded into southern Italy and then threatened Rome itself. Rome's natural ally had been the Eastern Empire in Constantinople, but due to a doctrinal dispute, the Church in Constantinople was in conflict with the Church in Rome. Rome turned to the Franks for support.

Pepin the Short, King of the Franks

Charles Martel's son Pepin the Short (741–768) continued the Carolingian process of increasing the image and power of kingship. Pepin began to use the title *dux et princeps* or duke and principal one—a title that had been used in the Roman Empire since Augustus, and that would normally connote a ruler. In 751, Pepin proceeded to depose the last Merovingian king and with the apostolic endorsement of Pope Zacharius had himself elected king of the Franks. A special papal legate was even sent to the coronation to consecrate Pepin as king, maintaining the sacred element of kingship through what was in actuality a usurpation. Hence the Carolingians began a dynasty as kings of the Franks and also sealed an important alliance between the Church and the Franks that had begun under Clovis and continued through Charles Martel, Pepin the Short, and on to his son Charles the Great (Charlemagne). This sealed alliance proved invaluable for the Church when Stephen II (752–757) became pope and found Rome threatened once again by the Lombards. He personally traveled to Pepin in 754 and pleaded for help.

Frankish Defeat of the Lombards

In 755 and again in 756, Pepin invaded Lombardy, defeated the Lombards, and granted the lands confiscated to the papacy, as had been agreed upon by Pepin and Stephen in return for Stephen having consecrated Pepin king in 754. The Franks also returned home with enormous quantities of treasure and gifts.

Charlemagne's Legacy

When Pepin died in 768, he turned the kingdom over to his two sons, Charles and Carloman, which was the Frankish tradition, but Carloman died in 771, and Charles seized the entire kingdom. The story of the kingdom of this Charles, Charles the Great or Charlemagne, will comprise the bulk of the following text. Suffice it here to say that Charlemagne built a formidable military machine, expanded the territory under Frankish control, pushed the expansion of education, attempted to standardize education and language use, gathered within his realm scholars and artists who created a great stock of material that in some ways acts as a bridge between the ancient and medieval worlds, and built a government that in some ways resembled modern government as much as it resembled the old Germanic personal kingship.

The Fall of the Carolingian Empire

At Charlemagne's death in 814, the Carolingian Empire seemed to be established on a footing solid enough to endure for a long time. His son Louis the Pious (814–840), the only son to survive Charlemagne, succeeded to the throne. Louis continued Charlemagne's political and military policies, although they were more defensive than his father's clearly offensive approach. Louis's own sons were adults when he became emperor, so only three years after assuming power he divided the kingdom, in Frankish tradition, among all three, Lothair, Pepin, and Louis, to take effect when Louis the Pious died. Lothair (840–855) received the middle kingdom and the imperial title, while Pepin received the kingdom of Aquitaine and Neustria to the west and Louis (840–876) the lands to the east, for which he became known as Louis the German. When Pepin died, he was succeeded by Louis the Pious's son by a second marriage, Charles the Bald (838–877). This caused tremendous internal turmoil and a great deterioration in the imperial authority that had been built up by Charlemagne. By 843, in the Treaty of Verdun, the empire was officially partitioned, marking the end of a unified Christian commonwealth in the West. When the middle kingdom continued to be divided among Lothair's sons, the unity of Europe was lost. A series of incompetent kings and emperors, with names like Louis the Stammerer, Louis the Blind, Charles the Simple, Charles the Fat, and Louis the Child, plus internal power struggles, continued to undermine the remains of the great Carolingian Empire. Equally serious were the invasions by the Vikings from the north, the Magyars from the east, and the Saracens from the south. Even Charlemagne might not have been able to stop them, but under the chaos of the political situation in the second half of the ninth century, there was little done to stem the invasions.

Vikings

The worst invaders were the Vikings who could sail into any location in Europe, even up rivers with their shallow-draft longboats, attack, and exit in a different direction, carrying their boats with them. By the year 900, Europe was in ruins, power was highly decentralized, there was little effective economy beyond subsistence farming, and the arts and learning once again deteriorated to a low not seen since the sixth or seventh centuries. Europe would remain divided, to a certain extent, along the lines of division of the Carolingians, with the West Franks becoming France, the East Franks Germany, and the middle kingdom the Netherlands, Belgium, Luxembourg, Switzerland, and Italy.

The Age of Charlemagne was important, but short lived. It rose rapidly and declined and disintegrated as rapidly. Without it, much of ancient culture would have been lost, and medieval Europe would have been very different. The height of the Carolingian age was also a time of some success in other civilizations.

CIVILIZATIONS CONTEMPORARY WITH THE CAROLINGIAN EMPIRE

Byzantine Empire

The Byzantine Empire of the eighth century was the heir or remnant of the Roman Empire. As the Roman Empire began to experience difficulties in the fourth century, a second capital was established at Constantinople in 330 for the eastern half of the empire. As the western half of the empire declined in the fifth century from Germanic incursions, internal dissension, and meteorological (and hence agricultural) deterioration, the eastern half of the empire continued unabated and has become known to historians as the Byzantine Empire. In the sixth century, the Byzantine Empire controlled a large portion of the Balkans and Greece in Europe proper, Asia Minor, Syria, Palestine, North Africa, part of Italy, Sicily, Sardinia, and the southern part of the Iberian Peninsula. Throughout the sixth and seventh centuries, the Byzantine Empire was under assault from Slavs to the northwest, Persia to the east, the Lombards in Italy, and, in the seventh century, the Muslims to the south. Gradually what had truly been the continuation of the Roman Empire became only a remnant in area and entirely different in philosophy and outlook.

The positive side of this diminution of the Byzantine state was that the Byzantine Empire in the eighth century was more homogeneous in language, culture, and philosophy than it had been as a far-flung empire. However, by the beginning of the eighth century, Constantinople itself was under siege by the Muslims, and the Byzantine Empire was feeling seriously threatened. The great siege of Constantinople in 717 and 718 took place by land and sea, but the Muslims were repulsed by a combination of the use of a liquid explosive known as "Greek fire," a great underwater chain that kept Muslim ships out of the entrance to the Golden Horn (the geographical location of the city of Constantinople), and an alliance with the Bulgarians, who brought a land war against the Muslims to draw them away from Constantinople. The use of explosives would return centuries later to haunt Constantinople when the Muslims of the fifteenth century built enormous cannons using gunpowder that battered down the great defensive walls of the city.

The Byzantine Empire of the eighth century was no longer the universal, cosmopolitan, aggressive empire of Rome, but instead became a regional, isolated, defensive, Greek civilization where language, customs, administration, and even the religion were different from those of Rome. Byzantine Christianity, already separated from the Christianity of the West, began to evolve into an indigenous form that widened the gulf between the Eastern Christian Church and that of the West. Yet this territorially reduced empire, constantly on the defensive, would hang on against great odds for seven hundred years more.

The Muslim World

The Muslim world in the eighth century was only a hundred years old, yet it had risen from a largely illiterate nomadic culture into the largest, wealthiest, and most dynamic civilization within the Mediterranean basin. In 600 C.E., the dominant political powers in Eurasia were Christian Byzantium and Zoroastrian Sasanid Persia. These two civilizations had confronted one another for centuries, and it would have been difficult to predict which would eventually predominate. No one would have predicted that both would soon be overrun by an entirely new religion and new civilization.

Although Arabia was not entirely barren desert and nomadic tribesmen, it was certainly not one of the strongholds of civilization. The religion of the region was predominantly pagan with a multitude of cults and deities. Arabia was, however, an important crossroad of international trade between East and West, between overland and sea trade. Mecca was a center of caravan trade in the western Arabian highlands. It was from this commercial center that a man named Mohammad (c. 570–632) claimed to have had a series of visions that laid out a religion with elements of Christianity and Judaism and built on the roots of these two religions. This new religion, Islam, after a rocky start, began to gain adherents throughout the Arabian peninsula. Islam claimed that Mohammad's visions revealed the true and complete word of God, written down later in what would be called the Koran. Like Judaism and Christianity, Islam was monotheistic and highly ethical.

Shortly after Mohammad's death in 632, starting in 634, the Muslim world under the leadership of the caliphs or successors to Mohammad began a course of conquest and expansion. By 643, these Muslim warriors had conquered the Byzantine and Persian lands in the Fertile Crescent, and by 661, nearly all of Persia and Egypt were controlled by Arabs. By 680, Constantinople was besieged and the Byzantine navy crippled. To the east, the Islamic forces pushed all the way to the Indus River in India. To the west, Islam swept across North Africa, and in 711 the armies, replenished and expanded by North African Berber converts to Islam, crossed the straits and invaded the Iberian Peninsula. By 716, most of present-day Spain and Portugal were under Muslim rule. The Mediterranean Sea had become a Muslim lake, and all of the disparate peoples, cultures, and religions of this vast area were unified under one religion, one language (Arabic), and a single proselytizing goal.

The Muslims pushed north across the Pyrenees Mountains into Gaul. In 732, at a battle near Poitiers in west central France (but known as the Battle of Tours), the Muslims were finally defeated by a force of Franks under the command of Charles Martel. The Frankish forces pushed the Muslims back across the Pyrenees, where they were kept at bay throughout the Middle Ages. The Muslims were also defeated in their siege of Constantinople, and this double defeat helped accelerate a shift in Muslim political and cultural structure.

The Umayyad dynasty, in power since 661, had flourished on aggressive militarism and military success. In 750, the Umayyads were overthrown in a rebellion and replaced by the Abbasid dynasty, which reduced the militancy and encouraged cultural and economic development. Muslim society developed into a very sophisticated and intellectually dynamic civilization with flourishing trade, arts, literature, and scholarship. In 762, the Abbasids began to construct a resplendent new capital at Baghdad. Although the military threat to Europe had subsided in the second half of the eighth century, few would forget the recent threats to Christianity. The vast, far-flung Muslim empire was far wealthier and more powerful than the Carolingians. In fact, the Muslim world in the eighth century was greater than any civilization with the exception of the Tang dynasty of China.

The Tang Dynasty

Far from the Carolingian Empire, the great Tang dynasty of China provides an interesting comparison. After the famous Han dynasty that was comparable to the contemporary Roman Empire, China fell into an extended period of division and civil war. China was reunified under the Sui, but the Sui overextended themselves. The Tang dynasty that followed lasted for three hundred years, 618–907, and was contemporaneous with the Frankish empire. The Tang ruled an area more than 1,000 miles wide by more than 1,500 miles long, an area well over twice the size of the empire of Charlemagne. The Tang began a period of internal renewal and external expansion. The Tang took over the Sui capital, renamed Chang-an, and made it the largest and most sophisticated, cosmopolitan city on the face of the earth. It was laid out on a north-south, east-west grid plan with each block of the city administered as a ward. The main avenue through the city from the imperial palace was five hundred feet wide. The central government, which traditionally was stronger and more important in China than in the West, was strengthened and made more efficient under the Tang. A civil service examination was established to select individuals for the bureaucracy. This set China ahead of all other countries in the effective functioning of a bureaucratic government. The Chinese government also tried to equitably distribute land to the peasants and break up the great landed estates. The Tang solidified their hold on the heartland of China and expanded their influence on the surrounding lands, much like the Carolingians, but with greater range and greater efficiency. The Grand Canal was repaired and extended. China became the dominant power in Asia, strongly influencing Japan and Korea.

As part of the Tang plan to increase control of the people, Buddhism was supported. It provided a religion of pacifism and stability. Under the Tang and the influence of Buddhism, Chinese culture flowered, and the Tang dynasty is sometimes viewed by historians as the greatest period of Chinese poetry, sculpture, and painting. The great Chinese invention of paper was passed via the trade route known as the Silk Road to the Muslim world around 750. However, the Chinese were never able to overcome the problems, similar to those of the Carolingians, of over-mighty landed families within and pressure on the borders from nomadic peoples without. In addition, the Tang were always threatened by the Tibetans to the west, the Turks to the northwest, and the Mongols to the north. By the eighth century, the Chinese faced another threat in the Muslims. In 751, a Tang army was defeated by a Muslim army near Samarkand in western Asia. This ended the caravan trade with the West over the Silk Road for five hundred years.

Japan

With no influence even indirectly on the Carolingian Empire, but useful for comparison, Japan in the eighth and ninth centuries was just arising as a significant civilization. In 710, Japan established a new permanent capital at Nara and designed it in grid fashion in imitation of the Chinese capital. In 794, the capital was moved to Heian (later Kyoto), where it remained until it was moved to Tokyo in 1869. Japan was so strongly influenced by China in this period that it became almost a miniature China with the adoption of Chinese institutions, culture, and religion. However, the adoption of everything Chinese was only for the court. Otherwise, Japan was still very backward, poor, and agrarian. The imperial household, on the other hand, was grander and employed a larger number of people in comparison to the population than did the Chinese court. Japan had experimented with a military system of conscription, but because of its inefficiency, in 792, a new system was established with reliance upon local mounted warriors—the beginning of the samurai. They used many of the same weapons as the mounted knights of the West, although the primary weapon was the bow and arrow that was fired from horseback. Gradually, by the tenth century, the samurai became less centralized and more locally controlled, much like the development of feudalism in Europe.

SOURCES ON THE CAROLINGIANS

Because the Age of Charlemagne was successful in bringing about a renaissance in literacy, it was also effective in recording much of its history. Charlemagne himself seems to have been aware of the need to keep good records and have histories written about his reign to ensure a positive place in posterity. Compared to the periods immediately before and immediately after, the Carolingian era has substantial documentation, and fortunately for us, the documentation was written on parchment, sheepskin, a nearly indestructible material. If parchment is kept dry and clean, it can be in as good condition in the year 3000 as it was when it was made in the year 800.

Primary Texts

The *Royal Frankish Annals*, whose author is unknown, must have been written by someone in the royal court who was quite learned and privileged to a great deal of information about the court. However, the author gives us only very brief, very terse comments for each year from 741 to 829, but this at least covers the entire period before, during, and after Charlemagne's reign, 768–814. It also seems quite clear that the author carefully omitted any negative comments such as military disasters. The *Annals* are best at providing positive comments on military expeditions, conquests, and diplomatic missions, both from and especially to the court of Charlemagne.

In addition to the *Annals* Einhard's (lay abbot and courtier) *Life of Charlemagne*, written sometime c. 819, provides the most famous and most complete biography of Charles. Nithard's (layman and grandson of Charlemagne) *Histories* covers the period 814–843, but nearly all of it deals with the period 840–843, during the conflicts among the sons of Louis the Pious (Charlemagne's grandsons). Einhard also left a number of letters, although most of those extant are from the last fifteen years of his life (d. 836) and therefore deal more with the court of Louis the Pious than with the court of Charlemagne.

One of the most valuable sources of information about the Age of Charlemagne is the capitularies or laws issued by Charlemagne orally and in public that were then written down for distribution. Charlemagne seems to have been particularly interested in their compilation for posterity. Capitularies (*capitula*) means chapters, as they consist of a series of chapters of laws. During Charlemagne's reign, they were quite numerous.

The letters of Alcuin provide another perspective on the Age of Charlemagne. Alcuin was an Anglo-Saxon teacher and librarian at York, the famous center of the learned Bede. In 781, Alcuin met Charlemagne for a second time at Parma and was invited to the Carolingian court, where he became one of the intellectual centerpieces and leaders of the educational reform and was put in charge of the palace school. Some of his letters deal with the Carolingian educational reforms.

There are other letters, histories, and annals that relate to the history of the Carolingians, such as Paul the Deacon's *History of the Lombards* or Gregory of Tours's *History of the Franks* and the annals of the monastery of Fulda. There are church records, penitentials (noncanonical guidelines for priest-confessors), Germanic law codes, and lives of saints known as hagiography. Together, all of these sources provide the historian with adequate material to piece together a history, although none of them provides much direct information on life in the Age of Charlemagne. That picture has to be created from bits and pieces in the sources. However, there is always the danger of reading eighth-, ninth-, and tenth-century documents and taking them at their face value. We do not always know what was meant by certain words or phrases. Language was a very difficult issue in the Carolingian world. Not only were there many different languages, speakers of which often could not understand one another, but Latin was not as set and clear as it had been in ancient Rome. Trying to clarify Latin was one of the major issues for the Carolingian intellectual renewal, which should warn us about assuming that we know what is meant in any written document.

Secondary Texts

The secondary literature helps with this process. The early Carolingian historians, such as Leopold von Ranke, François-Louis Ganshof, Heinrich Fichtenau, and Ferdinand Lot, dealt primarily with Carolingian politics, the court, feudal relationships, and scholarship. A later generation of historians such as Peter Classen and J.M. Wallace-Hadrill continued the political studies, and their heirs such as Donald A. Bullough and Richard E. Sullivan expanded the field into art and culture as well as scholarship. Recent historians such as Roger Collins have widened the view by examining some of the civilizations that surrounded the Carolingians, Rosamond McKitterick has expanded the study of culture and art, and Janet Nelson has deepened the work on Carolingian kingship. Suzanne Wemple has written on women in Frankish society, and Pierre Riché on Carolingian daily life.

Archaeology

We have a substantial amount of archaeological evidence for the Age of Charlemagne. However, it always must be kept in mind that archaeological evidence from the eighth and ninth centuries is limited by the chemical nature of substances, as it is for every ancient civilization. Oxidation is the major contributing factor, although there are any number of biological events that can cause destruction of organic matter, such as being eaten by carnivores, rodents, microbes, or fungi. Most organic and some inorganic matter oxidizes because the outer electron ring of the molecules of the substance is not stable. Wood, cloth, thatch, plants, and flesh all rot, and iron rusts. Even copper and silver oxidize somewhat. Consequently, most of these substances will disappear. Even bones decay very quickly when they are exposed in an active biological context, but when they are protected by being buried deeply, the oxidizing flesh around the bones easily absorbs all the available oxygen, and the bones survive. Or the bones may be in an anaerobic context or a calcium-rich one where the bones calcine and in effect are replaced by minerals, leading to fossilization. Wood, leather, hair, and even blood residue can be preserved as bones are, but such preservation is all a matter of the chemical and biological conditions. Salts in the soil can preserve organic matter as they preserve a Virginia ham. What tend to survive are inorganic materials, such as stone, pottery, gems, gold, and silver, and organic material that was valuable enough to be well protected, such as books and other documents, especially if they were illuminated. As was

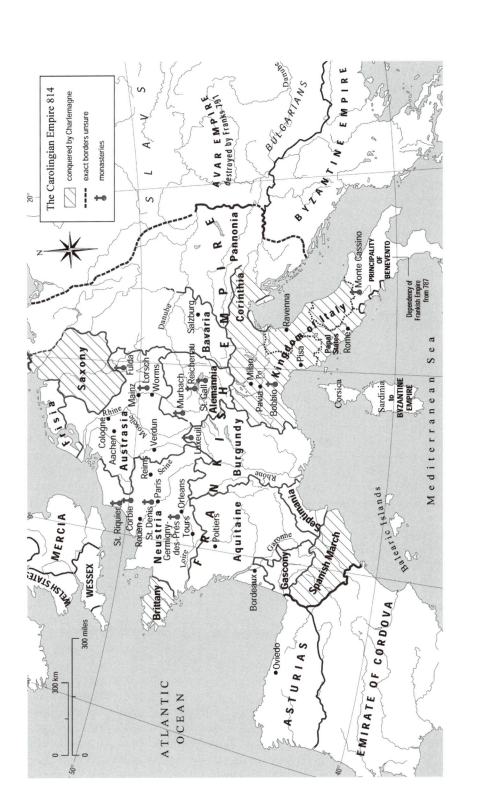

The Carolingian Empire 814

- ▨ conquered by Charlemagne
- ▨ exact borders unsure
- ✝ monasteries

ATLANTIC OCEAN

MERCIA
WELSH STATES
WESSEX

SLAVS

AVAR EMPIRE
destroyed by Franks 791

BULGARIANS

BYZANTINE EMPIRE

Frisia
Saxony
Fulda
Lorsch
Worms
Mainz
Cologne
Aachen
Rhine
Moselle
Verdun
Reims
Austrasia
Murbach
St. Gall
Reichenau
Salzburg
Bavaria
Danube
Alemannia
Pannonia
Corinthia
E M P I R E

St. Riquier
Corbie
Rouen
St. Denis
Paris
Seine
Germigny-des-Prés
Orleans
Loire
Tours
Poitiers
Neustria
Brittany
F R A N K I S H
Burgundy
Luxeuil
Rhône
Kingdom of Italy
Milan
Pavia
Po
Bobbio
Pisa
Ravenna
Papal States
Rome
Monte Cassino
PRINCIPALITY OF BENEVENTO
Dependency of Frankish Empire from 787

Aquitaine
Bordeaux
Garonne
Gascony
Septimania
Spanish March

ASTURIAS
Oviedo

EMIRATE OF CORDOVA

Corsica
Sardinia to BYZANTINE EMPIRE
Balearic Islands

Mediterranean Sea

N

300 miles
300 km
0

50°
20°
40°

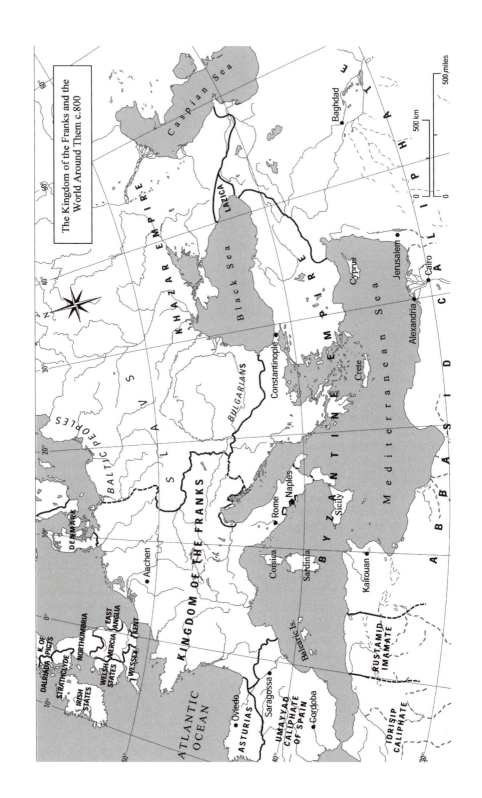

The Kingdom of the Franks and the World Around Them c.800

ATLANTIC OCEAN

DALRIADA
K. OF PICTS
STRATHCLYDE
IRISH STATES
NORTHUMBRIA
WELSH STATES
MERCIA
EAST ANGLIA
WESSEX
KENT
DENMARK

BALTIC PEOPLES
SLAVS
KINGDOM OF THE FRANKS

• Aachen

KHAZAR EMPIRE

Caspian Sea

LAZICA

Black Sea

Constantinople •

BULGARIANS

B Y Z A N T I N E   E M P I R E

Rome •
Naples •
Sicily
Corsica
Sardinia
Balearic Is.

Crete

Mediterranean Sea

Cyprus

Alexandria •
Jerusalem •
Cairo •

A B B A S I D   C A L I P H A T E

Baghdad •

ASTURIAS
• Oviedo
Saragossa •
UMAYYAD CALIPHATE OF SPAIN
• Cordoba

RUSTAMID IMAMATE
Kairouan •

IDRISIP CALIPHATE

500 miles
500 km

pointed out earlier, parchment that is protected from moisture and mice can survive very effectively. Occasionally, other objects survive through unusual conditions. When a person falls into a peat bog, the high concentration of organic matter and the tannic acid of the peat stifle oxidation and preserve the person by turning him into leather. Wood, if entirely waterlogged in a riverbank, for instance, might survive.

The archaeological evidence that we have includes stone buildings and more often bits and pieces of buildings; such as foundations from the Carolingian era under existing buildings because the site was important, as in the case of some churches. Jewelry is also extant, including gold, silver, enamel, cloisonné, bronze, iron, copper, gems, and paste. There is some clothing, usually of high value, that was carefully preserved, such as Charlemagne's imperial vestment cope. The archaeological evidence may be substantial overall, but its weakness is its lack of comprehensiveness and uneven distribution throughout the Carolingian lands and for all elements of Carolingian society. Consequently, the archaeological evidence adds color to what is known about the Carolingians, but leaves it difficult to draw clear conclusions.

2

CHARLEMAGNE'S ROYAL COURT

CHARLEMAGNE THE MAN

We know remarkably little about Charlemagne the man, and we must be cautious about placing too much faith in the writings of Einhard, who wrote during the troubled times of Louis the Pious (814–840). Einhard may have written more with the intention of "how it should be done" than "how it was done." We know that Charlemagne was a large man in size. The sources describe him as huge, but medieval sources often exaggerate. However, when his reputed tomb was opened, it contained a skeleton of a man well over six feet tall, in an age when most men were not more than 5'5". He had unusually large eyes, a short neck, a long nose, a protruding stomach, and a long moustache with no beard. He was known for his military prowess, his keen intelligence, his sense of humor, and his equally fierce temperament.

There was no central government except for the royal court and its household. The functions of most of the officers of the household were primarily domestic. There was a chancellor, a chaplain, a treasurer, a notary, a chamberlain, a seneschal, a marshal, a master of the cupbearers, and a master of the doorkeepers. These individuals did not head branches of government, as we would expect today, but rather performed real pragmatic functions, often doubling as advisors or ambassadors. Many of these same individuals were also nobles who acted as military commanders.

ET SYRIAM SOBAL· ET CONVERTIT
IOAB· ET PERCUSSIT EDOM IN VAL
LE SALINARUM·XII MILIA·

St. Gall Psalter, Stiftsbibliothek St. Gallen, Ms. 22, 0.
140, 890–920. The illustration shows late Carolingian soldiers using stirrups, but still with lances, and a battle
dragon with flames coming out of its mouth.

EARLY GERMANIC GOVERNMENT

Early Germanic government was little more than the king. The king
may have technically owned everything, and all individuals, including
the aristocracy, answered to him. However, by the time of the Merovingians, many of the aristocrats were quite autonomous because there was
limited central government. The mayors of the palace, especially in
Neustria and Austrasia, wielded considerable power with aristocratic
factions constantly haggling for influence. The mayors organized and led
military actions as decided upon at the spring assembly. The Franks
traditionally met annually with all the freemen landholders of the realm
to discuss matters, although in reality that meeting was primarily of the
leading landholders. This assembly was very important to the Franks,

but precisely how it functioned is unclear. The assembly took place in the spring, and new laws were formally proposed, discussed, and agreed upon, although it is also uncertain how democratic these assemblies actually were. There was probably some method of reaching consensus without the king simply commanding it. The other purpose of the spring assembly was to consider and prepare for the annual war. Some of the decision of whom to attack was probably predetermined, for the capitularies that went out to the leading landholders told them when and where to meet with a predetermined number of mounted and foot soldiers and specified what equipment they were to bring and how many months of supplies were needed to support the soldiers. The precise targets seem to have been decided at the assembly.

Charlemagne's Government

Charlemagne changed the structure of government. Whether this was a conscious, planned change or whether it was out of necessity from the scale of the empire that he built is not clear. It does indeed seem that Charlemagne was attempting to alter governance, not so much to imitate the ancient Roman government, as has often been claimed, but rather to imitate Christian theology. For Charlemagne, who was intensely religious, Christianity provided the model of evenhanded justice. In a land where there were a multitude of laws and greatly varied views of justice and enforcement, Christianity called all people equal under Christ. The Church's governmental structure was indeed modeled after the Roman government, for it consciously imitated what it saw around it in the third, fourth, and fifth centuries in the Roman Empire. However, it was not the urban episcopal design that interested Charlemagne, but rather the belief in an orderly cosmos with an absolute benevolent ruler. In many ways, Charlemagne saw himself not so much as the reestablishment of a Roman emperor, but as the earthly manifestation of God ruling God's kingdom in the terrestrial world. In fact, Charlemagne was known as "David," the King David of the Bible, among his friends and advisors. The king held God-given authority to rule in a godly fashion. The Carolingians, or at least those in positions of authority, saw Christ as a king figure fighting for justice and harmony against the forces of evil just as Charlemagne was doing. When the Carolingians saw the city of Aachen as the "Rome of the North," it was more as a parallel seat of Christian authority than as a reestablishment of the Roman Empire. The hope in making Charlemagne emperor was for the establishment of a Christian commonwealth rather than the reinvigoration of the Roman Empire.

No matter what prototype the Carolingian leaders were looking to, the idea that they had in mind was one of a unified whole, a single society. The purpose of government was to rule fairly and justly over all. This was a new concept for the Germanic peoples, and beyond the circle of Charlemagne, his advisors, the clergy, and some of the aristocracy it was probably never understood. The common people expected Germanic-style authority and justice. Because of this expectation, because the empire was so large with so many different laws and systems of justice, and because there were always so many enemies to be dealt with, the Christian commonwealth was never fully implemented. Charles, and Louis after him, attempted to institute a unified legal system and even a unified language in Latin, but the means at hand to effect these changes over so vast a territory were inadequate for the task. If one merely looks at the attempts today to create a unified Europe with a single set of laws, a single justice, and a single currency with the modern means of communication, travel, and record keeping and sees how daunting the task is, one may begin to understand how impossible it was for Charlemagne.

Imperial Coronation

Much has been written about Charlemagne's imperial coronation or crowning as "holy roman emperor." Einhard informs us, and this has remained the dominant view of the event, that Charlemagne knew nothing beforehand about the crowning as emperor. According to this tradition, Charlemagne went to Rome to have his son Charles baptized by the pope on December 25, 800, and was completely surprised by the pope crowning him and declaring him emperor. Furthermore, according to Einhard, had Charlemagne known what the pope was actually going to do, he never would have set foot in the church. This is a lovely view of the event, infusing Charlemagne with great humility and the moment with spontaneity and isolating the responsibility for turning Charlemagne into an emperor entirely in the hands of the pope. Unfortunately, the surrounding evidence does not bear out the same conclusion.

It may always remain impossible to know for certain when the plan was put into effect to turn the king into an emperor, but it most likely began at least a year, if not several years, before 800. When Pope Hadrian I died in December 795, Charlemagne lost an adversary who had become a friend. He was a pope of integrity and honor. Hadrian's successor, Leo III, did not continue the office with the same high moral reputation. Soon after he was proclaimed, Leo was accused of impropriety and sexual scandal. Leo forcefully resisted the accusations, but in April 799 Leo was attacked by a group of conspirators that included some of the highest papal officials. They attempted to blind Leo and cut his tongue out, but instead left him near death, but still able to talk. The pope, with the support of a Duke Winigis, traveled to Francia to gain Charlemagne's support against the conspirators. The traditional position, held by popes since the sixth century, was that there was no one with the authority to sit in judgment of a pope. Charlemagne hesitated, but finally threw his support behind Leo and sent representatives with him back to Rome.

At nearly the same time, several other political developments took place. One was the conquest of the Avars. After having perceived the Avars as a terribly powerful and threatening neighbor, Charlemagne quite easily defeated them in 791 (see "Military Strategy" in chapter 3). The conquest brought with it such an enormous amount of treasure that the Carolingians took several trips to haul it back to Francia, a task not completed until 796. This wealth and the ease with which Charlemagne destroyed this supposedly formidable foe apparently catapulted Charlemagne's reputation into a new level of rulers to be granted respect in world affairs. Also at this time, in 796, the Byzantine throne was left open when Emperor Constantine VI was overthrown and killed in a coup led by followers of his mother, Irene.

It seems very likely that the decision to crown Charlemagne emperor was made at least in consultation with Charlemagne, if not entirely by him, sometime between 796 and 800. Charlemagne was clearly the defender of the faith in Rome. He was also ceremonially granted the keys to the holy sites of the city of Jerusalem in November 800, probably because of the vacuum in Constantinople. There was no sitting emperor in Byzantium, and with the defeat of the Avars and the conquest of the Saxons, Charlemagne had proven himself the most powerful Christian king and one who was no longer ruling a single tribe, the Franks, but many ethnic groups. He had been in diplomatic contact with the caliph of Baghdad, which suggests that the caliph thought Charlemagne someone to negotiate with. Additionally, there was a need for someone with imperial (ruling over a number of different ethnic groups or tribes) authority to make a decision about the justification of the pope. The most logical move was to make Charlemagne emperor.

The title given to Charlemagne on Christmas Day of 800 by Leo III was "emperor of the Romans." This was later changed to "governing the Roman Empire," and he was even later referred to as ruler of the "Christian Empire."

It seems that making Charlemagne emperor had a real and immediate impact on the man and his mission. Charlemagne had everyone take a new oath of loyalty to him as emperor, and the oath was no longer merely loyalty to the man, but for defense of the state. Soon after the coronation, Charlemagne began to turn out legal decrees in an attempt to unify the realm and make laws more uniform. The movement of intellectual and artistic renewal was already under way, but Charlemagne seems to have developed a more unified vision of a single Christian empire.

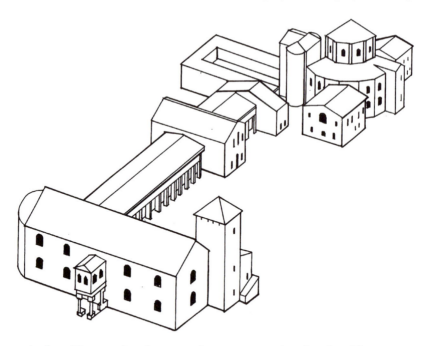

Aachen (Germany), palace complex, reconstruction drawing. The complex, begun in the 790s, was elaborate to demonstrate the preeminence of
Charlemagne as king and then as emperor. It was meant to be a "Rome"
of the north. [G. Lanier.]

THE ROYAL COURT

Charlemagne's court traveled, as had the Frankish courts before him.
There was originally no capital, and the court rarely stayed in town, but
rather moved from rural villa to rural villa. These villas were the great
estates of the king or aristocrats, a holdover from late Roman times when
the leading nobles moved out of the cities and into great landed estates
with huge houses. During the first half of Charlemagne's reign, the court
was often on the move for months at a time. It was constantly moving
from one location to another for a number of reasons. First, one location
for a court of even a couple of hundred people put too much economic
pressure on that locale to support the court. Transporting food was difficult and costly, so, in a sense, the court ate its way around the kingdom.
When the court stayed at a royal palace, the lands held there would
supply food and drink. As the court moved, it would stay at the homes
of great lords or at monasteries along the way. They were required to
support the court, even though that might mean feeding a couple of
hundred people. Obviously the court could not overstay its welcome, or
it would bankrupt the lord or monastery.

Frankish ladies   Charlemagne

A nineteenth-century rendering of Carolingian ladies and a lord. Braun & Schneider, *Historic Costume in Pictures*, Plate 10, Dover Publications, Inc., 1975. Reprinted by permission.

In addition to traveling for reasons of economics, Charlemagne's court traveled to show itself. In an era when laws and loyalty were only as good as the person who enforced them, a king had to show himself to reinforce his authority. As he traveled, the king would renew oaths of loyalty, enforce execution of laws that he had made, and simply let everyone know that the king was present and could and would appear again if there was disobedience or disloyalty. In addition to economics and law enforcement, Charlemagne traveled to perform pilgrimages at any site of relics. This was a tangible way of ensuring one's salvation and of displaying one's religiosity and commitment to Christianity to the public.

Maintaining Justice

Justice on a local level was to be carried out by the count in every county (the smallest district or territory, policed and administered by a count). A court was to meet, presided over by the count, every month. However, there were frequent complaints about both irregularity in the meeting of these courts and their corruption. The counts were also responsible for maintaining local order and for ensuring that all landowners met their responsibilities of supplying fighting men and equipment for the spring assembly. Counts existed at the royal pleasure, not as hereditary offices, as would be the case by the eleventh century, although families of wealth and importance often controlled the office of count almost as if it were hereditary. In other words, the count was appointed, but usually from within the county, which would limit the choice to members of the same family or families.

Above the counts were dukes. Dukes were almost always large landholders and were responsible for the defense of an entire region. All of the military from that region would be under the duke's command, and he would answer only to the mayor of the palace during the Merovingian dynasty and directly to the king when the office of mayor was abolished upon Pepin's becoming the first Carolingian king in 751. Both dukes and counts became hereditary over time and constituted the core structure of the feudal system in the High Middle Ages.

THE TREASURY

Carolingian finances were dealt with by the treasury. Income consisted of profits of royal estates, customs duties, and booty from the conquests of war. The treasury was in actuality the accumulated wealth of the monarchy and was composed more of material possessions than of coins or records of monies owed since coins and monies owed could more easily be used to pay off immediate debts. Consequently, since the treasury was indeed the collection of treasure and was technically owned by the king, the treasurer was often simply the queen as the person most closely in touch with the possessions of the king and aware of what could be disposed of. However, after the destruction of the Avars in the 790s, the treasure that was brought back to Francia was enormous. The treasure was apparently the accumulated loot of hundreds of years of Avar conquests, and it now poured into the Carolingian treasury.

The real functioning income on a regular basis was the total of agricultural production from the royal estates, and most of that was consumed on site. Taxation, as had existed in ancient Rome, disappeared with the Roman Empire. To collect regular taxes required an administrative structure committed to that function and a currency readily available to the people to be taxed. That is why the Romans were very concerned about the production of coinage and why the coins always carried the image of the emperor to show that the coin provided an acceptable standard of value for exchange and for payment of taxes. The Franks, under the Merovingians, certainly had no administrative apparatus to carry out taxation, and in turn, without the taxes an administrative apparatus was impossible. Consequently, Merovingian coins did

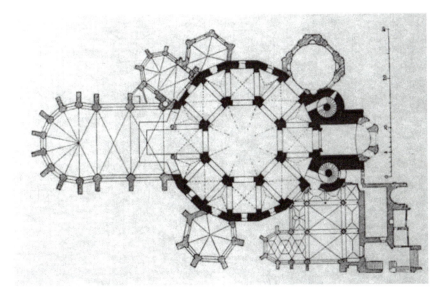

Aachen (Germany), palatine chapel plan. The chapel was derived (not copied) from the Church of San Vitale in Ravenna, Italy. [From Dehio and Bezold, *Die Kirchliche Baukunst des Abendlands.*]

not always carry the image of the king. Under Charlemagne there was an effort to standardize the coinage, although regular taxation never returned.

Another consequence of not having taxes nor an administrative machinery was that there was little purpose for secular education. In ancient Rome, secular education was necessary and readily available to fulfill the need for literate administrators for the government. In Francia, where administrators were not necessary, education was practically nonexistent. The few men required to provide the documents for the royal court were nearly all clerically trained. Therefore, the role of producing the documents was under the authority of the capellanus or royal chaplain until Charlemagne created the office of chancellor near the end of his reign. The chancellor was responsible for all royal writings. The creation of this position removed that responsibility from the Church for the first time since ancient Rome.

CHARLEMAGNE AT HOME

When Charlemagne built the palace complex at Aachen (Aix-la-Chapelle is often used as the translation of the capital's name and refers to the same place) around 790, it became the permanent capital of the expanding empire, and after 794, Charlemagne spent nearly every winter there. It became an entire city by eighth-century standards. The location was chosen as a royal residence by the Merovingians, but not as their capital. However, Charlemagne liked the location because of the naturally warm waters there and built upon the previous palace. The city was built in a glorious fashion, with the church unlike any other in the Germanic West and modeled after the Church of San Vitale in Ravenna, which, although in Italy, was part of the Byzantine Empire. Between 791 and 796, Charlemagne was able to fill the capital of Aachen with tremendous wealth of all sorts from the conquests of the Avars. Wagon loads of treasure were brought in and helped to decorate the church and palace in a fashion beloved by the Carolingians with elaborate, colorful, and gem-encrusted surfaces. The Carolingians even covered books with colorful gems.

When Charlemagne was in residence at Aachen, it resembled a true capital. There were grand feasts, especially to celebrate the arrival of any important personage such as a diplomat from afar. Charlemagne loved to eat, especially meats, but was not known for excessive drinking, although he, like everyone, drank wine or ale. He was opposed to drunkenness. He saw every occasion of socialization as an opportunity to advance his views, and inebriation would only interfere with this.

Carolingian Dress

In dress, Charlemagne was not extravagant, but preferred to dress as all Frankish nobles did. In fact, their clothing was not far different from what the common people would have worn. There were linen undergarments and a tunic over them. Legs were wrapped in cloth strips, laced boots, or shoes with leather strap leggings. In cold weather, an otter or ermine jacket was worn along with the typical Frankish cloak made from two large squares of heavy cloth, so that it covered the person entirely from ankles to shoulders. This is the great cloak that Charlemagne complained was going out of fashion with the Franks. He also complained that the other cloaks were small and ineffective at protecting the wearer, and yet the tailors were charging as much as for the large Frankish cloaks. Charlemagne hated foreign clothing, would not wear it himself, and recommended that other Franks not wear it. On great feast days, he dressed in embroidered clothes and shoes decorated with golden buckles. Charlemagne was also always outfitted with a sword, usually one with a gold or silver hilt and sometimes a bejeweled sword.

This traditional Frankish clothing had not changed much in two hundred years. In 1959, an extremely important grave was discovered under the floor of Saint-Denis of a Merovingian lady of aristocratic status. The woman was about forty years old and had a ring with the inscription "Arnegunde Queen." The only Frankish Queen Arnegunde was the wife of King Chlotar I, and so the burial has been dated from around 570 C.E.

However, some of the gold jewelry and other artifacts seem to be from circa 600 C.E., and so her identity is uncertain. She was lying in her stone coffin on a bright red blanket and was clad in a linen shift under a violet silk knee-length tunic. She wore stockings wrapped in crossed leather straps and had a gilt leather belt. Over the tunic she wore a dark red silk gown with wide sleeves embroidered with gold. She also had gold brooches with cloisonné, a large gold pin, the gold ring, gold pins holding a red satin veil to her blond hair, earrings, and silver buckles and strap ends on both her belt and her slippers. All of the jewelry is indicative of a queen or highborn individual, but the style of clothing was not unlike the type worn by most women of the day.

We know from other graves, including two discovered during renovations to the choir of Cologne Cathedral, also in 1959, one of a princess and one of a young highborn boy, that jewelry for women and weapons for a male were highly revered, as they were usually included in the burials. The princess had an array of gold jewelry including earrings, brooches, and a necklace. The boy's grave contained a small helmet with chain mail on the back, a two-edged long sword, two spears, a battle-ax, a bow and arrows, and a shield. Since the weapons were adult sized, it has been concluded that status was clearly inherited and that it was important that it be designated even in the grave.

Charlemagne's home and court setting (between which there would have been no distinction) were lively. Charlemagne's personality must have kept everyone on his or her toes. He was noted for his affability and his encouragement for everyone to participate in conversation at gatherings, but conversely he was a fearful tyrant when he chose to be, and as a huge domineering king, it is likely that when Charlemagne was angry, everyone cowered and looked for cover. There was usually a large number of people in attendance at the court, and that alone would liven things up. In addition, Charlemagne had an enormous brood of children.

Charlemagne as a Father

Pepin, the hunchback, born in 769 to the concubine Himiltrud, was always trouble for Charlemagne. Illegitimate children were not a terribly significant problem for the Frankish aristocracy, but this particular child was. In 792, Pepin plotted against his father and paid for it by being imprisoned at Aachen to keep him out of further trouble. The objective seems to have been to produce as many heirs as possible, and for many Frankish aristocrats, having a concubine as a young man was considered appropriate. In 770, Charlemagne married a Lombard princess, but in the melee of political machinations she was sent back to Lombardy in 774. Charlemagne then married the thirteen-year-old Swabian princess Hildegard, who bore Charlemagne nine children before her death in 783.

Six reached adulthood, Charles, Louis, Pepin (a second son named Pepin), Rotrud, Berta, and Gisla. Charlemagne then married Fastrada and had two daughters, Theodrada and Hiltrud. Fastrada died in 794, and he married Liutgard. After he lived with her for several years, she died in 800. Charlemagne must have then decided that it was easier to have concubines than wives, for he never again married, but by several concubines bore daughters Adaltrud and Ruodada and sons Drogo, Hugo, and Theoderic. In addition to his own children, other relatives and grandchildren were often present.

When the family was attendant, Charlemagne's daughters enlivened what must have been a predominantly male court. They were, by all accounts, quite beautiful. With their refinement, education, and natural audacity as daughters of the king, they entertained the court. Charlemagne adored his daughters, to the point of not readily allowing them to marry. When Charlemagne's son Charles was to marry the daughter of King Offa of Mercia, King Offa insisted that Charlemagne's daughter Berta marry Offa's son. This so enraged Charlemagne that he called off his son's marriage and ordered a prohibition on English merchants in Francia. Two of Charlemagne's daughters had illegitimate children of their own, although this does not seem to have caused much consternation.

TRADITIONS OF WOMEN

Traditionally, women were chiefly bearers of children, but the Frankish social structure gave aristocratic women some importance since kinship was determined by both male and female sides of the family. Aristocratic women in the Merovingian world played an important role in kinship connections, especially in marriage, since women could marry across ethnic and class lines, and in bearing and raising the children who would provide the next generation of connections. Women were visible and powerful in their influence, although they did not have direct control of political power.

This role began to change in the Carolingian era. As power was consolidated into the hands of a smaller elite and means were designed to pass this power on within that elite, the role of women was narrowed. The duties of aristocratic women were defined more as those of a housekeeper and mother and were removed from political concerns. Women in Charlemagne's court were respected and, according to the sources, even consulted on some issues, but this became increasingly rare because the new model woman was a professional housekeeper and childbearer. With the need to narrow the number of people in power, there was an increased urgency to ensure that these limited families perpetuated themselves. Therefore, the aristocratic woman's main job more than ever

Aachen, palatine chapel interior, octagon toward nave.
To provide a moving aesthetic experience, the interior
was constructed of rich stone- and bronzework. [From
Pinder, *Deutsche Dome des Mittelalters.*]

was to produce heirs. Aristocratic women often married as early as age
twelve. The penitentials preached by the clergy condemned contraception, and by use of wet nurses aristocratic women could get on to bearing
another child soon after the previous one. Charlemagne's Queen Hildegard bore him nine children, including a set of twins, before she died at
age twenty-five.

CHARLEMAGNE'S SOCIAL LIFE

Charlemagne surrounded himself with people whom he found interesting. People from all over the Frankish kingdom, as well as from England, Spain, Italy, and Ireland, were commonly present. At the same
table might be found scholars, military commanders, abbots, bishops,
and administrators. All were expected to participate in the conversations.
Alcuin (the Anglo-Saxon court scholar), Theodulf (the poet who became
bishop of Orléans), Angilbert (friend and son-in-law of Charlemagne,
and abbot of the monastery of Centula), and Einhard (biographer of

Charlemagne) all wrote about the royal banquets and how entertaining they were. Charlemagne expected something to be read during dinner, and apparently anyone might be put on the spot to perform the reading. Since Charlemagne himself did not read or at best read poorly, this custom provided a way to have material read to him. It also provided a source of conversation. Charlemagne's intellect was great, and he certainly recognized and understood the significance of learning. His surrounding himself with intellectuals and interesting people was an indication of what he considered important. Charlemagne took a court that was Germanic and provincial, where even the nobles of the land paid only limited attention to the court, and turned it into a significant center of intellectual and political activity, where decisions affected the world and where intellectual directions were set that influenced Europe for the rest of its history.

3

FEUDALISM AND THE MILITARY

FEUDALISM

The Roman Empire was a highly centralized state. As the Roman Empire in the West began to crumble in the fifth century, Europe disintegrated into a highly decentralized civilization. The invasions by Germanic groups such as the Franks of the third and fourth centuries that brought the Roman Empire to its knees left Europe to reestablish some form of political, economic, and social structure. Unlike the Abbasids in the Middle East or the Tang and Song of China, the Europeans did not rebuild a powerful centralized society. It remained politically fragmented and socially and economically disorganized. Each Germanic group established its own petty kingdom, and within most of these there was little centralized authority. Europe also lost most of its contact with the rest of the world with little to trade, no security for travel, and no central authority to dispatch diplomatic missions.

The Franks continued a process that had begun in the late Roman Empire of a relationship between lord and underling. Roman political and military authorities often established ties with individuals as bodyguards or military recruits by offering protection or even land. The *scara* was the palace or royal guard, the men who were prepared to fight at any time and who often formed the leadership of other military units formed for specific campaigns. These men were the backbone of the Carolingian military and needed to be well protected and well rewarded. A promise of protection from above and a grant of land were the logical rewards. Even though feudalism in the Age of Charlemagne was not the classic model of the twelfth century, it contained many similar characteristics.

Under the Carolingians, this protection and reward relationship was refined into a lord-vassal relationship. It is not clear exactly how this transformation came about. Originally, the term *vassus* seems to have been used to designate someone of humble status. During the course of the eighth century, the term came to mean someone who was of free birth, but dependent upon a more powerful man. The vassal took an oath of loyalty and military service toward the lord, and the lord reciprocally vowed protection of the vassal. The bond was symbolized by the vassal kneeling and putting his hands together as in supplication while the lord put his own hands around the hands of the vassal. It symbolized that the vassal was literally and figuratively in the hands of the lord. This process made the vassals not men of low or humble origin, but freeborn and even of highborn origin who "surrendered" to men more powerful than they in a relationship of service and protection. This would gradually change the entire social structure of Europe by replacing a system of freeborn men of nearly equal status and of equal legal standing into one of severe hierarchy that over time would become increasingly complicated and multifaceted. Originally the benefice of land or fief was not a part of the structure, but during the course of the eighth century this became commonplace. This benefice or fief would not have been necessary in an earlier Frankish social structure where most free individuals had access to necessary lands, and it would not have been possible without a constant increase in lands, through warfare, available for distribution as fiefs.

THE MILITARY

Military Exploits

In early 772, when messengers arrived at all Frankish nobles' estates with the word from King Charlemagne to assemble in May 772 at Worms, the command would not have been unexpected. The noblemen had been through this many times before. They had assembled at Worms two years previously and at Valenciennes in 771. All of this was summarized in the *Royal Frankish Annals*. The noblemen now had to settle affairs on their lands for the next couple of months and prepare for a campaign. Each nobleman would prepare his equipment and gather his supplies. His horse was his major piece of equipment. It had been fed all winter on hay and oats, but now that spring had come, the horse could feed on grass in the field. This made it much easier to travel long distances, for much less food had to be carried for the horse. The nobleman's other equipment included lances that had been prepared by his workmen during the slow months of the winter. The custom-made sword that he cherished was cleaned, sharpened, and lightly oiled to protect it from rust. The same was done for the short dagger. The shield was checked for damage. Extra clothing and food supplies were packed into the small wagon that would be pulled by another horse.

Worms was the destination for the staging point, for it was Charlemagne's residence on the middle Rhine close to the frontier, where the campaign would be continued. When the nobleman arrived at Worms, hundreds of other noblemen were also arriving, each with his horses and supplies. From Worms the army, then led by Charlemagne, marched into Saxony and captured the castle of Eresburg without much of a fight after the defenders saw the power of the assembled army before them. The army then proceeded to the Irminsul, the column that symbolized the mythic Universe Tree and served as a Saxon pagan temple, destroyed this idol, and carried away all the gold and silver that they found there.

Charlemagne decided to stay there for a few days to destroy the temple completely, but there was no supply of water to drink for the men or for the horses. Suddenly, at noon, by the grace of God, according to the *Annals*, a stream of water appeared that was plentiful enough to supply all the army and its horses. After meeting with the Saxon leaders and agreeing to terms, the Saxons offered twelve hostages to ensure the agreement, and the Frankish army returned to its homeland to disperse in October in time for Charlemagne to head to his court at Herstal for the hunting season.

The next year, however, the Saxons broke the treaty, and while Charlemagne and his army were in Rome, a large Saxon army attacked Frankish lands, burning houses and churches. Charlemagne returned and in 774 sent four military detachments to Saxony. Three of these units fought the Saxons, while the fourth took as much booty as it could gather.

In 775, Charlemagne decided that the treacherous and treaty-breaking Saxons should be defeated entirely and forced to accept Christianity or be entirely exterminated. He moved into Saxony, captured the castle of Hohen-Syburg, restored the castle of Eresburg that he had captured in 772, and confronted the Saxon army on the banks of the Weser River. The Franks killed many of the Saxons, put the rest to flight, and took control of the Weser. Charlemagne then divided his army in two, leaving one part to guard the river while he moved forward with the other. A large contingent of Saxons came to Charlemagne, handed over hostages and swore oaths of fealty (fidelity) to him. On returning to meet the other half of his army that had remained behind to hold the river, Charlemagne discovered that the Saxons had attacked this part of the army while the men were asleep, and that many of the Franks had been killed. Charlemagne took the combined Frankish army and counterattacked the

Saxon army, defeated it, and slew large numbers of Saxons. The Franks inflicted as much damage on the Saxons as possible, collected a large amount of booty and large numbers of hostages from the Saxons, and then began the trek back to Francia believing that a serious-enough blow had been dealt the Saxons that they might be subdued.

But that was not the end of the Saxon treachery, according to the *Annals*. In 776, while Charlemagne was celebrating Easter in Italy, a messenger came with news that the Saxons had rebelled again. They had broken their oaths of fealty, had deserted all the hostages who had been handed over to the Franks to ensure compliance with the treaty, had retaken and demolished the castle of Eresburg, and had the castle at Hohen-Syburg under siege. The Saxons built siege machines to storm the castle, but the catapults caused more damage to the Saxons than to the Frankish defenders. The Saxons were preparing to storm and burn down the castle when a miracle reportedly unfolded. Viewed by many people both inside and outside the castle were two shields, red with flame, wheeling over the church of the castle. The Saxons interpreted this as a sign that God was protecting the Franks, and they were thrown into confusion and began to flee. In the stampede, many of the Saxons were killed by their own men, and when the Franks saw that God was on their side, they were encouraged and pursued the fleeing Saxons, slaughtering them in great numbers. When Charlemagne arrived in Worms from Italy, he assembled his warriors, marched into Saxony, broke through the main lines of the Saxon defense, and utterly defeated them. Saxons from all directions came, including women and children, to surrender their lands to the Franks, to convert to Christianity, and to take oaths of loyalty to Charlemagne. Charlemagne ordered the castle at Eresburg rebuilt and another, Karlsburg, built on the left bank of the river Lippe to hold this territory permanently for the Franks by installing Frankish garrisons.

The Art of War

The military was one of the most successful features of the Carolingian Empire. This success was built upon good leadership, good supplies, and superior numbers. There has been debate among historians over whether Charlemagne had a long-term strategy. There is no documentary evidence of a long-term strategy until after the fact, but the approach and policies toward surrounding territories have some consistency to them. Under Charlemagne's rule and even under his father's and grandfather's rule, the expansion seems to have been directed toward enlargement of the realm rather than wars of personal gain or economic plunder. There is no doubt that Charlemagne's reputation was aggrandized by his success and that the military victories sometimes brought with them great treasure, but this does not seem to have driven the military campaigns. The Carolingians made certain that their armies were superior in nearly every way. They used the doctrine of overwhelming force by ensuring that they had a far larger army than the enemy. They tried to ensure high morale among the troops in a number of ways. They made certain that the armies were well supplied with food and clothing and were well led by experienced commanders. They used preparatory speeches and prayers to work up the spirit of the troops immediately before going into battle, and they widely publicized the successes of the Frankish armies so that both the enemy and the Carolingians were well aware of who was expected to win the confrontation.

Wars were fought nearly annually from Charles Martel's time onward. The *Royal Frankish Annals* records a large military confrontation nearly every year. In fact, it was noteworthy in the official and unofficial records when a year went by without a war, as the *Annals* records in 790 and 792. Occasionally more than one war was fought in the same year. Wars were fought in the summer when weather permitted, although if the campaign season started early enough, as in 767 when it began in March, then another could take place in August. To have an army slogging through deep mud and sleeping in freezing temperatures would have made the fighting force ineffective. Even more difficult would have been the supplying of the army since loaded wagons cannot easily be pulled through mud. Only in the summer could the horses of the army feed off the land as they went. In the spring, the military was gathered, and a campaign began against some neighboring foe. If the campaign could not be successfully wrapped up by autumn, it was discontinued until the next spring.

Spring Assembly

The annual assembly of the spring was a Frankish tradition that served two major purposes. The first was to gather all the leading landholders together to propose new laws and have them agreed upon. The second was to gather for the military campaign; hence the assembly was known as the *Campus Martis* or "Field of Mars." Because the assemblies often took place in March, it has sometimes been called a "Marchfield" because of the mistaken similarity with *Campus Martius*. Capitularies were sent out to the landholders specifying where and when they were to meet. The number of men was probably predetermined, but the exact equipment and the amount of supplies would be specified according to the terrain and the estimated length of the campaign. A single campaign might last for up to six months, requiring several wagons per warrior. When the assembly of landholders met, the specific targets of the campaign may have been decided, although it is not clear how much input

even the dukes, the military commanders of regions, had in these decisions. A duke commanded the military of a region, but counts were
responsible for each county's proper allotment of troops and equipment.

Wars were fought for several purposes: (1) to pacify or eliminate opposition and interference by a neighboring people; (2) to collect the booty
that came with conquest (this was often quite substantial and kept the
Carolingian coffers filled); (3) as a religious war against real or perceived
non-Christians. This was the psychological motivation, often mentioned
in the *Royal Frankish Annals*. Military expeditions aimed to destroy enemy strongholds such as castles or palaces, but also farmlands and villages that would supply the enemy forces. The *Royal Frankish Annals*
mentions missions that devastated regions to suppress opposition. Sometimes the opposition was internal, as when groups such as the Saxons,
Bavarians, or Basques revolted.

Forts and Castles

Castles were not terribly common in the Carolingian age. The great
age of castle construction was the eleventh and twelfth centuries during
the social, economic, and political revolution that strengthened the aristocracy and handed control of the lands to its members. Castles became
essential to maintain this inequitable structure, but in the Carolingian
age there were some castles and heavily defended towns that required
siege methods to overcome. In the Saxon campaigns in the 770s and 780s,
the Franks built some castles or forts, and there was a sprinkling of
castles built throughout the realm, but especially in frontier areas. They
used the standard building techniques employed by all since the Romans. The castles were built in stone with crenellation (indented battlements), round and square tower construction, and interior battlements,
often built of wood. The Carolingians did not have a fortification style
all their own, but seemed to borrow readily from others. A fortress at
Heisterburg Deister was built in a Roman style, nearly square, while a
fortress at Pipinsburg was built in a Saxon style, nearly circular with a
series of curved earthen mounds.

Siege Machines and Artillery

The Carolingians were equipped for sieges to take the occasional fortified town or site. Armies at this time used siege machines such as catapults. The *Royal Frankish Annals* tells of a Saxon revolt in 776 in which
the Saxons took one Carolingian castle, Eresburg, by talking the guards
into surrendering, but when they tried this at a second castle, Hohen-
Syburg, the Franks put up a valiant defense. The Saxons, in turn, set up
war machines to storm the castle, but the catapults did more damage to

the Saxons than to those in the castles, for the machines were complex and needed skilled practitioners to handle them. The most common artillery was a relatively small (1,000 pounds) machine using a torsion system of flexed material to throw small objects such as stones. This would have been an antipersonnel device rather than a true siege machine to batter down fortified walls. Paul the Deacon notes that one of these was used to throw a severed head over the walls of a fortress. This technique was purely for intimidation. The records, however, also refer to throwing rocks that had been coated with a flaming substance. This would intimidate and wreak havoc. The Carolingians did have true siege machines, probably constructed with a level mechanism, that could throw large stones to batter down walls.

Occasionally the Carolingians had to resort to more coercive measures, as in 782 in the Saxon campaign when, after repeated defeats of the Saxons and treaties with them and repeated disregard for these treaties and the hostages given to enforce them, Charlemagne marched against the Saxons, drove out their leader, and then took 4,500 surrendered Saxons and massacred them at Verden. Even so, the Saxon resistance was merely inflamed. It took three more years before the Saxons were finally subdued, and then only by using forced conversions, imposition of the death penalty for the practice of pagan rites, and the emplacement of Frankish political institutions and Frankish nobility to maintain control of Saxony. Church dioceses were established, and bishops and clergy were imported. Only through a rule of iron was Saxony incorporated into the Carolingian Empire.

Military Service

By tradition, the king of the Franks, as in many of the Germanic groups, had the right to call on any and all freemen for military service. But in a realm of some eight million people, there would have been more than two million men between the ages of fifteen and fifty-five, the ages considered available for military service. The largest numbers of men were those least suited and therefore available for defensive purposes. Since the Carolingian armies were very successful during Charlemagne's reign, there was little need for defensive armies. After Charlemagne, during the later ninth and tenth centuries, the general levies of defensive armies became important. But during Charlemagne's era, the select levy was called repeatedly. This provided the rank and file of the expeditionary forces who were able to be sent to distant lands for weeks or occasionally for months at a time. The select levy was drawn from those men who possessed a *mansus* or landed estate of between twenty-five and forty-five acres or those who had an income equivalent to a *mansus*. If one qualified and was eligible for the select levy, one had to provide the fighting equipment necessary and the supplies for the duration of the campaign. If a person owned a landed estate equal to more than one *mansus*, he might be required to provide more than one infantryman or a mounted warrior. A corporate lord, such as a monastery, which might own thousands of manses, usually had its quota determined in an alternate fashion so that the burden was not too heavy on it. Even so, a monastery might owe dozens or even hundreds of men. Hiring professional soldiers, men who trained for warfare, but might not have the landed estates to support them, fulfilled this burden.

Beyond the determination of select levy service by ownership of land, the wealth of the individual might determine what equipment he was expected to provide. The poorest provided merely a short sword and shield, while the wealthier might be required to provide a long sword, a lance, even a bow and arrows, mail armor, a helmet, and a horse as well as the short sword and shield.

Numbers of Troops

Some historians have claimed that the predominant element of the military was noble mounted warriors. There has been debate about the numbers of both the mounted warriors and the infantry within the Carolingian army. It seems quite clear now that the bulk of the Carolingian army was infantry. Early Carolingian historians thought that the Carolingians were able to raise a total of not more than 5,000 men. More recent historians have begun to raise the estimates, one claiming that there were between 2,500 and 3,000 horsemen and 6,000 to 10,000 infantry, while yet others claim that the Carolingians could have raised as many as 35,000 mounted and 100,000 foot soldiers. These are potential figures, however, and not representative of what was actually raised for any particular campaign. The greater likelihood was that early in Charlemagne's career, an army would have been composed of between hundreds of men to a couple of thousand men. By the latter part of Charlemagne's reign, there may have been much larger armies in the thousands, but considering the logistics, it is less likely that armies in the tens of thousands were regularly raised.

The Song of Roland, written around 1100 as an inspirational poem to encourage valiant participation in the Crusades to the Holy Land, tells the story of Charlemagne's campaign in the south, crossing the Pyrenees into Spain against the Muslims. In this story, Charlemagne was leading an army of 350,000, including twelve nephews, each with 3,000 men. In reality, the army might have been 3,000 men altogether. Mounted warriors were too costly and rare, and even infantry soldiers were too rare, to be able to raise an army of 350,000.

Technically, all men who were physically able were eligible for military service, but in reality, that would happen only if a region were invaded. By the ninth century, many of the men who served were closely attached to the king through the aristocracy and vassalage. Even so, in 796, Charlemagne's army had 15,000 to 20,000 eligible horsemen, some of whom must have been drawn from beyond the aristocracy. This would have been a dramatic change from Charlemagne's early days or from the time of Charlemagne's grandfather, Charles Martel. The total number of warriors was certainly much smaller then, and historians have revised the importance of horsemen versus footmen. The position that historians had long held that the Battle of Tours in 732 was comprised primarily of mounted Muslim warriors versus mounted Christian warriors is now believed to be unlikely.

It was once believed that the innovation of the stirrup by the Carolingians won the day at Tours, or alternatively that the Muslim cavalry was the stimulus for the Franks to switch to a predominantly cavalry force that won the day. In fact, the Muslims did not fight as a predominantly cavalry force until after 750, and there is no proof of the introduction of the stirrup in the early eighth century. There are no written or pictorial sources to indicate that the stirrup was used in the early eighth century by the Franks. It is true that pictorial representations might follow the ancient Roman model of showing riders without stirrup, so the lack of a stirrup in any given depiction is not proof that they were not being used, but that they do not show up at all is worrisome for this theory. The other "innovation" that has been related to this period is that of the horseshoe. For the military, horseshoes were invaluable, for without iron shoes horses would split and damage their feet when they were ridden hard over rough surfaces. For the use of horses in agriculture, where most of the work was on soft fields, the horseshoe was probably of lesser significance.

Horses

Carolingian mounted warriors were noblemen. It took a lot of land to provide for the maintenance of a horse. All of the grazing land and arable land for oats generally would otherwise have been available for production of food for human use. Only a nobleman or a very wealthy freeman would have enough land to allocate its use for horses, and to have multiple horses for war that were not productive themselves (they were not used to pull the plow or cart) wasted enormous amounts of land. Charlemagne worked to ensure the supply of warhorses by requiring an annual payment or tax in warhorses from those who owned estates. This encouraged the specific breeding of warhorses as opposed to plow, riding, or cart horses. There must have been a constant need for additional horses with their losses in combat. In the Avar campaign of 791, 90 percent of the horses died from some virulent equine disease.

In addition to all the land necessary to produce warhorses, tremendous amounts of time were required for training to fight on horseback. Only someone free from other work obligations would be able to commit this kind of time, and that again meant that only large landholders, with others doing all of the farmwork, could afford to become warriors in mounted warfare. This point has been somewhat modified in recent research that suggests that boys did not start training as youngsters. Boys may have played warrior and certainly learned to ride, but formal training may have been minimal. In fact, it has been suggested that formal training only took place on the field in the heat of combat. Even if this is true, it does not detract from the point that a boy or young man had to be free from other work obligations to be able to learn to ride a horse well enough to be able to fight on horseback. This was only possible for the sons of large landowners. There is evidence, however, that "live" combat training on horseback was done. One document talks about dividing horsemen into two groups and having them charge at one another with untipped lances, pulling up at the last second to practice wheeling about.

The Infantry

The infantry was composed of common freemen, who were more plentiful and cheaper to outfit than mounted warriors. Estimates of the number of infantry in the Carolingian army run, as stated earlier, from a few thousand to as many as 100,000. Of course, the total number of infantry available would never have been drawn up at one time. Such a massive force would have been impossible to supply and to coordinate. Warfare on the eastern front may have used more infantry and fewer cavalry since fewer horses would have been available in these regions. The infantry would rarely have worn any type of uniforms. As the term indicates, a uniform meant that all were dressed alike, which served two purposes: to simplify outfitting and to demarcate units. There is some evidence that common apparel was used on occasion, but it was quite unusual.

Formation of the Infantry

The Carolingian infantry was trained to march in set formations. Some historians have disagreed with this as too complex for a primitive culture such as the Franks. But moving a large number of infantrymen into position, keeping them from overrunning their own ranks, or losing the value of the tight formation would have required training in movement.

Utrecht Psalter, University of Utrecht, Ms. 32, fol. 14r. Note the military emphasis on infantry with spears, shields, and bows and arrows.

This seems to have been one of the Carolingians' advantages when they faced less well trained infantry. When infantrymen are trained in marching, it becomes possible to quickly alter the direction of a unit without losing its cohesion. Men could move from column to line upon command.

Weapons of the Infantry

The weapons of the infantry were spears, swords, axes, and bows and arrows. Spears were always the cheapest weapons since they were simply wooden poles with a limited amount of metal, iron or even copper, for the blade. They could be made quickly and with minimal skill. The traditional Frankish throwing ax, which is probably the most famous of the Frankish weapons, had already been replaced for the most part by the *seax* by Carolingian times. The *seax* was a cross between an ax and a short sword. It was single edged, made of iron, and used for hacking rather than piercing. The early Frankish bow was a very long (five- to six-foot) yew bow. By the ninth century, a shorter bow was more typical. Unlike the late Roman double-convex bow, which was very much like modern bows, the Frankish bow was straight and flat, for this was much simpler, cheaper, and faster to produce. This type of bow could have been used on horseback, as was done by Asiatic warriors such as the Mongols. Some historians believe that the Carolingian armies increased the use of the bow after their war with the Avars in the 790s because they saw the effect of these weapons. That is certainly possible, but according to the evidence the Avars put up only a limited resistance to the Carolingian armies, and it seems that the Carolingians would not have "learned their lesson" on weaponry from an enemy army that was not terribly successful. It is true, though, that the Carolingians increased their use of archers during Charlemagne's reign. They were used both by the infantrymen and by the cavalrymen. It would not have required tremendous additional training to turn infantry into archers, but to turn cavalrymen into archers must have required a great deal of training.

The Carolingian sword was the most personalized weapon. The sword of the average soldier was made of iron, but was still his most valuable weapon and symbolic of the warrior's place in society. The noble's sword, however, was usually of much greater significance. The process to make a good sword was known only to certain blacksmiths. (See the subsection "Iron" in the section on trade in chapter 5.) Swords were made by taking thin rods of wrought iron and twisting them together to form the core of the blade. Then two strips of iron that had been carburized by being heated red hot for an extended time in a charcoal fire were placed on either side of the twisted core. The pieces were then heated again and hammer forged into one welded piece for the blade. The carburized strips were primitive steel and very hard. By forming the edge from a rod of metal, the steel could hold sharpening and resist chipping or dulling. If the twisted core was hammered through the outer strips and the metal was pickled in acidic juice, the twists showed through, sometimes making a herringbone effect or other beautiful and completely original designs in the blade. No two swords were alike, even when made by the same swordsmith. A sword made in this fashion was highly prized, extremely valuable, and protected with one's life just as the sword protected the warrior's life.

The Cavalry

Even though the bulk of the Carolingian army was the infantry, the core of Charlemagne's army was the cavalry. A mounted warrior had an extraordinary advantage in speed and weight. In shock combat (even infantrymen are shock combat troops, hitting with their lances, swords, or axes), the heavier the object causing the impact and the faster it is moving, the greater the actual effect. Therefore, a warrior mounted on a thousand-pound horse has a tremendous advantage. The battle horse of the Carolingians was not the huge, heavy, and relatively slow horse of the High Middle Ages. That horse was bred to carry the warrior with heavy armor. The horse of the Carolingians was smaller, lighter, faster, and more mobile.

The evidence seems quite clear that during Charlemagne's life the Carolingian cavalry was not using stirrups. We find no stirrups in Carolingian graves until the ninth century and no representations of stirrups in art of the period. If the Carolingian cavalry did not use stirrups, riders could not hold themselves in place on the horses as they could if they had stirrups to push down into with their feet. With stirrups, a rider can couch a lance (hold it tightly under one's arm or even have a permanent holder on the warrior or the horse's saddle) and charge into the enemy. This is the style of mounted warfare developed later in the Middle Ages, but not that of the eighth and early ninth centuries. The stirrups also made it easier and more likely for a warrior to remain on the horse when he used his sword or ax against an enemy while mounted. Without stirrups, the usual form of attack was to fling the lance or thrust it into an enemy, overhand or sidearm. The speed of the horse still adds to the impact, but there is no corresponding reaction to the rider to unseat him. Using a sword or ax or, for that matter, wielding a shield in defense against a hard blow would necessitate fairly slow motion on the horse so that the rider could hold tightly with his legs since both hands would be occupied.

The Carolingian cavalry was trained to fight in formation just as the infantry was. Cavalrymen could apparently wheel at command from a single in-line formation (column) to a massed frontal-line formation (line). There is some evidence that the Carolingian cavalry even used the feigned retreat by cavalry to fire arrows from the back of the horses, similar to the methods later used effectively by the Mongols.

Military Strategy

Charlemagne's great success with his armies was often obtained without going into combat at all. In many instances, the enemy merely surrendered without a fight. Charlemagne encouraged division among the enemy and tried to gain some support from within the enemy numbers. But part of the reason for this success was that Charlemagne's armies were organized with leadership of loyal and battle-hardened officers and with armies of large numbers of mounted warriors. This formidable offense would often split or undermine the enemy's defense. When the Carolingians invaded Avar territory, along the Danube, in September 791, they had spent a great deal of time preparing for the campaign, indicated by the late arrival (the Carolingians preferred to begin a campaign in May or June). The reputation of the Avars was that they were powerful, numerous, vicious, and highly experienced warriors. The Byzantines were very afraid of the Avars, and the Carolingians clearly took this seriously. The Carolingians attacked with two divisions, one led by Charlemagne, with a fleet of boats on the Danube carrying supplies. After all the preparations, the Frankish army met with little resistance, and few battles with the Avars ever took place. The enemy simply collapsed in the face of superior forces. The Avars were totally defeated by 796.

Charlemagne's armies were composed of warriors from all walks of life, including great lords drawn from all over his kingdom, although the core of the officers was generally central Frankish lords. Units were often composed of regional, even ethnic, groups commanded by a Frankish lord since most confrontations were localized and the mobilization would have been from a limited area.

The central core of the army was composed of professional warriors called the *scara*. They formed the personal following of the king and also of other leading magnates and provided the leadership for other units. A palace army was prepared to fight at almost a moment's notice, whereas the larger army would have to be raised by levy. After 790, even this part of the army was designated and prepared so that when the order to join the army arrived, the force could be assembled within days. All noblemen or counts were required to come and fight for the king and to raise an army. If a count did not come, he was fined so substantially that the amount was greater than the total cost of outfitting a mounted warrior. This would reduce the truancy and pay for replacement if a man did not attend. If a nobleman left the scene of a battle, all of his lands were confiscated and he was executed. The purpose of confiscating the lands was to ruin the family forever. This was as serious a threat as, perhaps greater than, that of taking the warrior's own life.

The form of combat in the early Frankish era was aristocratic (sometimes called heroic) warfare in which there was a massed army, but when the army went into battle, it was really every man for himself. However, under Charlemagne, the units of the army were more organized and coordinated. That the army was drawn together in the first place and that there were so many mounted men put Charlemagne's armies far ahead of any of his opposition. The units practiced with mock battles to rehearse coordinated attacks and even retreats, for a cavalry retreat had to be planned and warriors had to learn to ride with their shields to their backs. To locate one's unit or to know the direction of the charge, Carolingian armies used banners. The representations of the banners suggest long, thin, waving cloth banners on a pole. Sometimes the armies would have an animal's head stuck on a pole with burning oil in its mouth and a cloth tube or hose banner waving behind that would fill with the hot air from the burning oil, looking a little like a dragon representation in a Chinese parade. These must have inspired the Carolingian soldiers and intimidated the enemy. The Carolingian armies also used horns to signal commands to units.

To maintain morale, the Carolingian armies sang or chanted as they marched. This also served a double purpose in providing the rhythm to maintain an orderly step to keep the lines of the infantry in formation. Also for morale, before the army went into battle, numerous priests went around the troops to absolve them of their sins and to pray for them. When the Franks campaigned against the Avars in 791, they spent three days in prayer and absolution before going into combat.

Cost of Weapons and Armor

The cost of equipment for a cavalrymen was exorbitant, averaging about forty to forty-five solidi, which would be the equivalent in cost to twelve to fifteen cows, a very considerable sum in an era when a cow was of great value itself. The most expensive item was, of course, the horse. This alone would have cost the equivalent of four cows, which explains why only a very wealthy individual with large landholdings could afford to become a mounted warrior and why most mounted warriors were barons. The other expensive item was the tunic. It may have cost as much as the warhorse because of its elaborate construction and because it was made of iron, always an expensive substance. The construction of the tunic has caused almost as much consternation among historians as the use of stirrups. There were probably two types: the mail hauberk made of tiny interconnected rings of iron, and the scale byrnie made of small plates or scales of iron, bronze, or even horn sewn onto a leather or cloth tunic. Some were waist length and some longer to protect the legs, but split on the sides for mounting a horse.

The helmet cost the equivalent of two cows and probably also varied according to the region. The Carolingians were influenced by the Lombards, the Byzantines, the Avars, the Saxons, the Muslims, and others. Some of the helmet designs followed that of one or the other of these groups. One style was to have a ring around the crown of the head and another going across from front to back, while the frame was sheathed in leather or metal strips drawn together at the top. Two additional pieces were attached to hang down and protect the sides of the face. These helmets would not have protected a man against a direct blow of a sword or ax, but might have helped deflect a glancing blow. The man receiving the blow would be seriously injured, but might at least survive.

In addition to the helmet, the shield afforded protection. It was made of hardened leather on a wooden frame with a metal boss in the center for added strength and protection of the hand and arm immediately behind it.

Utrecht Psalter, University of Utrecht, Ms. 32, fol. 35v. Besides the military of spearmen and archers, there is a man sharpening a sword on a grindstone.

The main weapon for a mounted warrior was the lance, made of a wooden rod and an iron head and intended to be jabbed or thrown. The iron head or blade often had crossbars or lugs at the base of the blade. Some historians assume that this was to prevent too deep a penetration upon impaling a victim. However, it seems more likely that these bars served the same purpose as those on a knife, dagger, or sword, which is to protect the holder from being hit on the hands with a counterblow from a blade of some sort.

The most expensive weapon was the sword. The real sword, as opposed to the *seax* or short sword, was carried by the nobility, that is, the cavalry. It was very costly to produce because, described earlier, it was made by a time-consuming method of twisting several rods of iron together and hammering them flat. The process of heating and hammering to flatten and meld the bars of iron together caused a certain amount of carbonizing and driving out of impurities that made the swords harder. This method was slightly similar to the Japanese method of making samurai swords, although the Japanese method kept up the process by flattening, folding, flattening, and folding many times. This process turned the Japanese iron into a very high quality close to steel.

The Frankish method of sword making was never as careful or well understood, so that their swords were inconsistent in makeup. Yet because the construction took hundreds of hours, and because a warrior's life might depend upon this weapon of final defense, swords were often decorated with fine metalwork or even gems. They were also cared for like no other weapon. All of a warrior's weapons were closely guarded and maintained since his life and occupation depended upon them, but the sword especially would have been kept in a sheath or scabbard made of leather and lined with oil-soaked fur to keep the sword from rusting. In a damp region, with inadequate heating even in the palaces, iron weapons' worst enemy was rust.

Supply Lines

The Carolingian armies were also effective at constructing bridges to cross a river to pursue or attack an enemy. Most bridges were built of wood; only rarely were they made entirely of stone or even with the base of stone. Wooden bridges were faster to built but rotted away in a few years or could be burned down or chopped apart by anyone wanting to interfere with the movement of Charlemagne's troops into or out of a region. Stone would avoid these problems, but the immediate need more often than not necessitated wooden structures. In one year's campaign, Charlemagne's army built two bridges across the Elbe. One was a fortified bridge with bulwarks of wood and earth at both ends. To cross the Danube, Charlemagne's army built a movable bridge on floating pontoons with anchors. In other instances, when bridges were unavailable or washed out by flooding, boats were tied together to form an impermanent, but quick bridge.

Another very important component of the Carolingian army was the commissariat. Whole wagon trains of supplies and support staff followed the Carolingian army. Each soldier was supposed to bring enough food to last for the entire campaign, which could be as long as three months. This would have necessitated one wagon per soldier, especially when extra weapons and clothing were added. By order of Charlemagne himself, all royal demesnes (lands held by the king) were to provide special oxcarts of standardized size, waterproofed, and constructed with leather coverings well stitched to be made watertight so that the wagons could be floated across rivers, since bridge building was a very time-consuming process. Besides, it was faster to look for a possible ford across a river than to move to the location of the rare bridge. Additionally, siege equipment, tools, and supplies were carried if necessary. The carts or wagons moved very slowly because there were no wheel bearings, and so the wheels turned roughly and broke frequently. Packhorses carried light supplies, and cooks, blacksmiths, personal servants, women, and even merchants followed along. At the rear would have been the herds of cattle for food. Fighting during the summer reduced the need for supplies for the oxen and horses that grazed when they could, and any supplies that could be confiscated from the region were taken. However, all of these supplies must have made the thought of an attack on the rear of the army attractive to an enemy and feared by the commanders. In 778, the Basques attacked the rear guard of the Carolingian army, which was led by Count Roland. This was a great coup for the Basques and a terrible blow for the Carolingians.

Conquests and Defeats

Prior to Charlemagne's time, the military strategy was raiding and conquering of towns, but Charlemagne attempted to destroy an enemy's ability to continue by destroying a capital and the main army and eliminating the opposing king or leader. Additionally, Charlemagne often reduced the threat of an enemy by drawing the nobility to the side of the Carolingians. This was usually possible because of the numerical superiority and military advantage of the Carolingians. Within a short time of conquering a foe, these people were usually incorporated into the Carolingian military system. Many of the units of the Carolingian armies were Lombard, Breton, Burgundian, Bavarian, Provençal, Gascon, Goth, or Saxon.

In *The Song of Roland* referred to earlier, the Carolingian army was on a campaign to destroy the Muslims of northern Spain. After driving the Muslim forces out of the Pyrenees and besieging the city of Saragossa, according to tradition, Charlemagne did something unusual and made a deal instead of destroying the Muslim foe entirely. As his army retreated to France, the Bretons were put at the rear to guard the retreat and protect the supply wagons. In *The Song of Roland*, the rear guard is attacked, as part of a planned deceit, by a massive Muslim force. In reality, the Breton rear guard was attacked by Basque Christians who were enraged by interference in their territory by anyone, including the Christian Carolingians. The Basques apparently attacked and massacred the rear guard, plundered the baggage train, and then quickly disappeared into the mountains of the region before Charlemagne could counterattack. The Bretons were led by a nobleman named Roland who was Charlemagne's nephew or close ally. Roland, along with Charlemagne's steward, his count of the palace, and many men, was killed in the confrontation in August 778. *The Song of Roland*, written three hundred years later, claimed that this was an enormous loss, but the sources of the time did not make much of it. The *Royal Frankish Annals* did mention it and admitted that the Franks were defeated by the Basques, but only because of "unfavorable terrain and the unequal method of fighting," even though the Franks "were obviously their betters in arms and valor." The question is whether the contemporary sources are the most accurate because they were closest to the event or whether they were downplaying the loss to minimize the defeat for Charlemagne. Since at least three counts were killed in this confrontation, and it went unavenged, it was probably a major blow militarily and psychologically.

This brings up the problem of the use of literature in understanding history. In the case of *The Song of Roland*, there are several inherent problems with reliability. The first is that the poem was written more than three-hundred years after the event. It is surprising that there was even that much known about the battle. Another problem is that the poem was almost certainly written at the time of the First Crusade to the Holy Land as an inspirational work. Therefore, the story had to be told with details that would serve the purpose, rather than to be historically accurate. Clothing, weapons, and attitudes are more closely aligned with those of the eleventh century than with those of the eighth century. Yet the fact that the story was transmitted across many centuries with even a modicum of accuracy is remarkable and tells us something about the events, whereas the supposedly more objective sources of the Carolingian period may have been seriously biased for other purposes and are therefore partially unreliable.

From the *Royal Frankish Annals* we know of numerous skirmishes. For instance, in the spring of 808, Charlemagne was informed that the Danish king Godofrid had invaded the lands neighboring the Saxons, who were at that time allies of the Carolingians. Charlemagne sent his eldest son Charles with a force of Franks and Saxons with orders to resist if Godofrid invaded Saxony. After setting up quarters, the Danes took several castles and booty, but lost many of their best men and nobles. Charlemagne quickly built a bridge across the Elbe River, moved his force into the territories of tribes that had defected to the Danes, and destroyed their fields, recrossing the river untouched.

In 806, three campaigns are mentioned in the *Annals*. One was commanded by the eldest son Charles (Pepin "the hunchback" was imprisoned and disowned) against the Slavs. After the Franks killed a Slav duke and built two defensive castles, the Slavs were pacified and the Franks returned. A second was of an army of troops from Bavaria, Alemannia, and Burgundy sent into Bohemia to lay waste the lands that returned "without serious losses." The third was a naval confrontation when a fleet was dispatched under Charlemagne's son Pepin to attack the Moors who had pillaged Corsica. Before the fleet even arrived, the Moors retreated.

In all of these cases, the Carolingian forces were victorious with little or no actual fighting. Apparently the Carolingian army was feared enough that most enemies were unwilling to fight them, or more of the defeats of the Carolingian army were simply not recorded.

Navy

The Carolingian navy was not nearly as effective or as feared as the army. In the early years of Charlemagne's reign, there was increased trade on the seas and increased importance of seaports. In the latter part of his reign, some of these ports and their trade were already being threatened by Vikings. In 810, a Danish fleet attacked and ravaged the coast of Frisia. Charlemagne organized a navy that included a flotilla in the Straits of Dover, but his approach toward the Vikings seems to have been defensive, not offensive. Charlemagne ordered the old Roman lighthouse at Boulogne put back into working order. He also built up the shore defenses, and towns began to build walls around themselves again. Many towns had torn down the circumference walls during the ninth century because they needed growing room and the Carolingian armies seemed to provide all the protection that would be needed in the future. The Carolingian navy had some successes against the Muslims in the Mediterranean, both along the Catalan coast, where the navy captured the Balearic Islands, and out of Pisa, where the navy captured Corsica in 816 and in 826 even raided the North African coast. It was not long, however, before the Muslim naval forces retook the Balearic Islands and even began to harass the coastal region around the Rhone River delta. The Carolingian navy under Louis the Pious added a fleet in the Atlantic along the shores of Aquitaine, but by the 830s, the Carolingians abandoned their navy and resorted to land defenses. Compared to Alfred the Great's English approach in the latter part of the ninth century, to emphasize the navy and take the war to the Vikings at sea, the Carolingian approach may have been a major mistake.

4

LIFE OF THE COMMON PEOPLE

THE WORLD OF THE COMMON PEOPLE

Obstacles of Nature

Life for the common people in the Age of Charlemagne was, in a word, awful. Nature itself was a forbidding challenge. More than 90 percent of the population lived in the countryside in small villages and depended upon what they could grow, hunt, and gather. Famine and malnutrition were always present. Survival against the barriers of nature was a life-long challenge, and each season brought new hurdles to overcome and terrors to face. In the spring, when people might think that they had made it past the worst season, there were the dangers of floods, late frosts, or inadequate rainfall. The summer brought fears of drought, or too much rain, especially as crops were ripening, or storms of hail that would beat down the grain in the fields so that it could not be cut. Insects could destroy the entire crop, as grasshoppers several times did. Autumn weather determined how much of the crops could be harvested and whether the family would survive the upcoming winter. Winter was the hardest season, with the unrelenting cold that could kill people or the animals that the people depended upon. If the winter was mild, it might bring more severe cases of pestilence that wiped out large numbers of people.

This was a world of vast forests. The darkness, the isolation, and the silence of the forest scared most people. Going beyond the immediate clearing was risking one's life. Wild animals, especially wolves, plagued the Carolingian world. As scary as the vast forest was, night was even scarier. Once the sun set and light faded, darkness descended upon the Carolingian world, and most people could afford to light their world artificially for only a short time. Beeswax candles or oil lamps could light a room, but they were too expensive for the average person to use and provided very ineffective lighting for the out-of-doors. Generally, when the light of the sun was gone, people went to bed. In the summer that might mean 10:00 P.M., but in the winter it could be 5:00 P.M. In people's minds in the Carolingian age, night brought with it the evil spirits of the woods and evildoers among humans.

This was a world of few roads and little contact between villages. Information traveled slowly, even for the royal court, and moved almost not at all for the common people. The old Roman roads were to be maintained by order of the king, but with limited use and limited resources, many of the roads deteriorated to the point of nonexistence. Most roads were little more than dirt tracks that turned into quagmires in rainy weather and when dry were hard-rutted paths that would break the axles of the wagons. Most people moved on foot, and that pace has always been the same from the beginning of humans to the present: about four miles an hour over long distances, if the terrain is flat. Horses only move at about five miles an hour over long distances, since a trot or gallop can be kept up only for a short distance. When information needed to be sent to a specific location, a letter was sent either with a traveler or pilgrim or with a professional courier. Thieves and brigands always made the transmission of the letter risky. Some people would hire a courier and have him memorize the message since it was easier to steal a letter than torture the information out of a person.

Superstition

Superstition, mystery, and tradition predominated. Christianity had a foothold on the Carolingian world, but not much more than that. Charlemagne himself posed a question in 811 to his bishops, abbots, and counts: "Are we really Christians?" Most of the common people understood the theology of Christianity very little. Superstition and magic were probably closer to their hearts, and natural explanations of physical events were rarely sought. Instead, magic or witchcraft made more sense. If someone's infant died, or if a cow or sheep sickened, it was easier to believe in curses than in natural disease. Witchcraft, the practice of black magic by compact with an evil spirit or the devil, could explain ill fortune better than Christianity could, especially in a world surrounded by ill fortune and darkness. Darkness was feared. The night was a time of mysterious and evil actions. Wild animals and evil men were believed to be the only creatures roaming the forests at night.

Freedom

For all the struggles, obstacles, superstition, and fear, most of the common people in the Age of Charlemagne were at least free. In fact, the word "Frank" meant "free." But over the course of the tenth and eleventh centuries, more and more of the free peasants fell into serfdom as a means of protection and as a means of consolidation of landholdings to strengthen the aristocracy. It is this structure that is often presented in the history books as typically medieval, but it was really a social, economic, and political revolution of the tenth and eleventh centuries. In the ninth century, free men could commend themselves to a lord and gain that lord's protection. But more frequently, free men worked their own piece of land or *mansus*. The important social and political structure was the clan or extended family unit, not a feudal structure. There were slaves in the Carolingian Age (the word slave comes from Slavs, whom the Carolingians thought very lowly), but even slaves could be freed and contracted to work part of the lord's domain. They could even be granted a *mansus*. A *mansus* varied in size tremendously, but the average was twenty to thirty acres, large enough to support a peasant family. In addition to the free men, there were men who were less free and worked the lord's domain as less free serfs, but in the Carolingian age neither slaves nor unfree serfs were very common. Only by the end of the eleventh century did unfree serfs become the norm. In the Age of Charlemagne, most common people were free to contract their own work arrangement, their own obligations, and their own marriages. They were free to raise their family within all of the limitations of disastrous weather, ignorance, and superstition.

MARRIAGE AND THE FAMILY

Family and Kinship

Family was extremely important in the Age of Charlemagne. The extended family or kindred was the social, economic, and legal unit. Kinship was bilateral; that is, descent was traced through both the mother and the father, although usually not very far back. This is different from the Celtic clan, which is a large group of individuals of unilateral descent, often with a common name, and tracing their descent to a distant common male ancestor. In kinship, the kindred could serve as coswearers in court or provide moral or financial support if a member of the kinship was in conflict with someone outside the kindred group. It was not until the social and political revolution of the tenth and eleventh centuries with the consolidation of power and authority into the hands of a few that primogeniture (all wealth and authority passed to the eldest son) became the norm. With that revolution, only the eldest son mattered, and all subsequent sons were driven into celibate holding pens such as the clergy, monasteries, universities, and knightly apprenticeship. Women became less free and were considered significant only as transmitters of wealth and power into that consolidation. But in the Carolingian world this revolution was already beginning.

Women

In Merovingian society, the mother's family may have been even more important than the father's. The uncles and brothers of the woman were of great significance in providing protection and determining the status of the woman's children. If the woman's husband died, the woman's family would normally take the family in. Because the Merovingian political structure was so loose, women played a more significant role. Political connections were important for noblewomen, and for nonnoblewomen it was tremendously important that women could marry across class lines. This meant that women could raise the social status of a family much more rapidly than men could. In addition, since primogeniture had not yet become established, and no highly centralized male governance had developed, the kinship group was of greater importance. Since women played a greater role within the kinship group, they also played a more important role in the political structure in general. Women were participants in the political discussions and, when a husband was killed, could even replace the husband in the negotiations. Women could manage property, act as guardians of their minor children, inherit and donate land, and run businesses.

By the middle of the eighth century, however, several institutions were working to change the status of women. The Church, in its first several centuries, was a revolutionary institution proclaiming equality among its participants, and the communities of women were treated under the same standards as the communities of men. But after Christianity became the official religion of the Roman Empire, it began to reflect the male-dominated, hierarchical, and authoritarian society in which it existed. As this happened, women were increasingly disqualified from ecclesiastical functions. Eventually, in the West, women were excluded on the grounds of impurity (the monthly menstrual cycle had provided a source of uncleanliness claims in Judaism and in Greek culture as well), and celibate males dominated the Church's administrative structure. Deaconesses and priests' wives disappeared, and the only remaining place for women in the Church was in convents, which were gradually put under the supervision of males. In the Carolingian era, the Benedictine Rule was imposed on most of the monastic communities, giving the bishops the opportunity to bring these communities under episcopal control, and the entire church structure became state controlled.

At the same time, the political structure was being reformed under the Carolingians with greater centralization and a narrowed group of aristocrats who controlled the state. Property was increasingly concentrated in the hands of these nobles. Women saw their role reduced to management of the household and rearing of children. These roles could still provide women with some influence on Carolingian society, but their influence was reduced from that of Merovingian times. A new image was created for women as chaste, pure, and faithful. The alternative image for women who failed to maintain the new standards was of an impure social outcast. Women became more dependent upon men and had less control of their own lives.

Marriage

The kinship of the woman was of great importance because a family's status derived from both sides equally. Gregory of Tours tells us of great kindred feuds that occurred in the sixth century when a woman was wronged in marriage or despoiled before marriage. Brothers and sisters remained close and protective of one another throughout life. Women also shared in inheritance of property and money, if not always equally with the men.

Exogamy (marriage outside the same kinship group) was looked down upon in the Germanic tradition, as well as incest (sexual relations with a relative). The Church imposed its policy encouraging exogamy and discouraging marriage to close relatives. The definition of how close the relatives could be varied over time. Roman law had allowed marriage to first cousins, but by the sixth century, church law forbade marriage to first cousins, and by the eleventh century the restriction had become so severe that it was nearly impossible to find a mate to whom one was not related. The purpose of this seeming obsession with marriage to a relative and with incest was to break the monopoly that the wealthy Germanic males held over women. Since polygamy and concubinage were acceptable within the Germanic tradition, wealthy males were often able to accumulate a number of females, thereby reducing the availability of females for the rest of the male population. Even though the Church tried to encourage exogamy, the Germanic tradition of marriage within the kindred pool often took precedence, especially for the Carolingian nobility. Marriages within the extended kinship group were extremely useful for political purposes.

For the common people, kinship demands probably superseded

Church rulings, and marriage to first cousins was not uncommon. However, there is evidence that the Carolingian family in peasant settings married not only outside the kinship group, but outside the immediately marriageable estate group. There was some movement of males from one estate to another, and the evidence suggests that frequently the newcomers had better luck marrying, while some of the marriageable males in their own estate remained unmarried. This apparently took place because family units became rigid about expectations of family expansion and a sort of stalemate developed where families refused to allow one of their members to marry if it meant losing that member to another family within the estate. When outsiders entered the community, they could more easily marry, for they were added to the family unit and no loss was suffered. Those moving in were probably forced out of another region by political or economic turmoil or by the same rigid marriage requirements.

Stories of multiple marriages sequentially or at the same time were often true for the nobility, especially the royal family, since there was little anyone could do to stop the practice. When a king tired of one wife and preferred another, he divorced and remarried. If he wanted to marry a second wife before divorcing the first, he did so. For the common people, however, marriage to more than one woman, without death ending the first marriage, was probably unusual. Since it was popular for the nobility to take concubines (a woman taken as a mate without marriage) before marriage, we might assume that the common people participated in sexual relations before marriage, as was common in the Late Middle Ages, but we do not know for certain.

Girls were considered nubile (of marriageable age) at age twelve, although both Pepin and Charlemagne passed legislation prohibiting the marriage of girls or boys before the age of puberty. Since the age of menarche (puberty for girls) was apparently around age thirteen (similar to the age of menarche in the twentieth century and earlier than in the nineteenth century), most aristocratic girls married between age thirteen and fifteen. Peasant girls may have married somewhat later since there was no pressure to produce as many male heirs as possible. Fifteen was considered a marriageable age for both boys and girls among the peasantry. Within the aristocracy, while the age of first marriage for girls remained fairly constant, the age of first marriage for boys increased in the ninth century so that it was not uncommon for a male to be in his twenties or even in his thirties. Whereas virginity for life was highly esteemed in the Merovingian era, it was no longer held in such high regard in Carolingian times, and marriage became the accepted model type.

Marriage included three steps: betrothal, settlement of terms, and marriage. Betrothal for the common people, at least in later centuries where marriage was not arranged by the family, was the promise of marriage made between two people after courting or even after sexual intercourse. A gift, sometimes a ring, was given by the man to the woman as a sign of the promise. The terms required an agreement of gifts to be given to the bride and to the bride's family. Whereas in ancient Rome the dowry was a gift from the female to the male, the dowry in the Carolingian era had become a gift from the male to the female. This is sometimes described as compensation for the female's family losing her as she joined the male's family or even as compensation for the loss of virginity of the female. The marriage was not the elaborate ordeal of modern times. The bride and groom declared their vows, but this did not necessarily take place in a church. The Church was insistent that marriage was to be monogamous and indissoluble. Many of the aristocrats in the Merovingian era had been polygamous, but polygamy was being effectively eliminated by the Age of Charlemagne, although divorce and remarriage were still common, as was concubinage. Divorce was allowed by the Church in cases of adultery, lack of consent (abduction was commonplace, especially for the aristocracy), impotence, leprosy, and a few other reasons. Among the lower classes, polygamy was not as frequent, nor was divorce, and probably few could afford a concubine. In the 780s and 790s, Charlemagne, under pressure from the Church, enacted legislation that severely limited divorce.

In the eighth and ninth centuries, because the purpose of marriage among the aristocracy was increasingly to produce as many male heirs as possible, sexual relations were for procreation. The penitentials (directives to parish priests for instructing the laity) condemned contraception even though the methods of contraception were not very effective anyway. There has always been a belief that nursing of an infant acts as a form of contraception, although the reduced rate of pregnancy has probably been caused by suppressed sexual interest on the part of women and possibly even men when a woman is nursing. Even so, aristocratic women often used wet nurses to remove this chore and enable the woman to work on becoming pregnant again.

Sexual relations outside of marriage were strongly discouraged by the Church. Many of the penitentials were directed toward what was considered inappropriate sexual activity. Homosexuality (both male and female), bestiality, masturbation, incest, adultery, and even lustful thoughts were condemned in the penitentials. What that tells us, however, is that these actions existed. Homosexuality was most often spoken of in the context of the monastery because of the all-male setting. The military in many societies also provided the conditions for this practice. In both cases, however, the problem was less often homosexuality than pederasty (sexual relations between adult men and boys). There were special provisions made in the Benedictine Rule for boys as they were reaching puberty to ensure that they were not taken advantage of sexually.

Family Structure

Family size and structure in the Carolingian world have been examined, but with very limited evidence, clear conclusions are still uncertain. The studies suggest that most families were conjugal or simple families with a husband, wife, and children living under one roof. The manse provides strong evidence for the conjugal or nuclear family since the acreage of the typical manse would have been sufficient for the support of only a nuclear family. There were also solitaries or individuals living alone and extended families of more than two generations (typically with one or more grandparents or with brothers or sisters with their spouses and children) under the same roof. The assumption that families would have included several generations in one household is not substantiated. There were also multiple families with more than one married generation together, such as parents with married sons or daughters living in the house.

While the evidence is limited, information available indicates that mean family size was around six, although many families had many more than six. Some historians have suggested that female infanticide existed, claiming that this phenomenon occurs in agrarian cultures where boys are more valuable than girls, but there is no proof of this, and the penalties for death of children, including girls, would indicate that it was not practiced. Since contraception does not seem to have been common and any form that was used would have been only marginally effective, most females by the end of their childbearing years, between the ages of fifteen and thirty-five, would have had many pregnancies. Queen Hildegard bearing Charlemagne nine children by the time of her death at age twenty-five is partly a statement of the royal need for heirs, but also indicates the pressure on the childbearing years of womanhood. Miscarriages, stillbirths, and infant deaths within the first year normally kept the number of children produced per family limited. Approximately three out of ten children born alive would have died before age one. Almost as many would have died before reaching puberty. On average, only one out of two children lived to reproduce, and even among the Carolingian kings only about two-thirds survived. Noble families tried to overcome the inherent limitations by replacing wives who were not productive and by providing wet nurses to suckle infants so that the wife could go back into reproduction more quickly. The Church spoke out against both practices, claiming that they were done out of lust on the part of the male rather than for procreation.

Women in the ninth century, on average, died younger than men. It is not certain why this was so. Childbearing alone does not necessarily shorten one's life. It has been suggested that women suffered from iron deficiency because of diet and that menstruation and childbirth both reduced iron levels and may have shortened women's lives.

Children

Children of the Carolingian era left little evidence. We know from Germanic law codes of the centuries preceding the Carolingians that children were given very little value. Within the old Germanic wergeld system of fines imposed if someone was killed, the value of male children remained a fraction of that of adults, increasing very slowly each year until adolescence, when the value increased rapidly and reached greatest value at age twenty. The highest value was retained from twenty to fifty and then declined until age sixty-five, at which time it declined again to the value of a ten-year-old child. Female children followed a similar pattern, but with lesser value. The female reached greatest worth when she entered childbearing years between fifteen and thirty-five, at which point she was worth nearly the same as an adult male.

If the figures of a survey of the estates of Saint-Germain-des-Prés are to be believed at face value, the ratio of male children to female children was remarkably weighted toward males, while the ratio of children to adults was nearly equal, which in any society would be extraordinary. This could suggest that infanticide, especially female infanticide, was practiced on a large scale, in which case the ratio of male to female adults should have expressed this as well. In addition, Christianity has always condemned infanticide, and there is no evidence of the Church speaking out against the practice of female infanticide in particular even though it was speaking out against a great number of other practices that it thought unacceptable.

The one logical explanation is that children were severely underreported and that girls especially were not reported for the survey, which was to list all humans (as chattel) on the estate. This would be supported by the Germanic wergeld system, in which children were considered of little value and girls were of lesser value than boys. The more likely explanation of the disparity in the ratio of males to females is that some males were counted twice if they had landholdings or responsibilities in more than one place.

Children began their formal education at around age six or seven, whether this education was geared toward being purely vocational, providing a minimal level of literacy, or an extensive education intended for the priesthood. Children of the aristocracy were often taught reading and writing, and in addition, girls were taught household crafts, while boys were taught the art of war.

The best conditions for children were probably within the monastery. Children were occasionally accepted as oblates (offered up or dedicated) into monasteries at a very young age, from toddler onward, although typically monasteries and convents would not accept a child until age six or seven, the same age considered appropriate for beginning education. Aristocratic Frankish families normally sent at least one girl into a monastery, often around age six or seven. According to the rules governing monasticism, children were to be treated well and especially cared for as more tender and needing more encouragement and nourishment both bodily and spiritually. Most monasteries kept separate quarters for the children and provided greater warmth, more food, and longer sleep and expected less physical labor than from the adult monks. They ate three or four times a day, and at least one meal usually included meat, unlike many of the adult monastic meals. This would indicate that at least within the monastic world it was recognized that children were special and not merely incomplete adults, as many historians have suggested was the case for medieval society.

In the monastery, children were still expected to follow the monastic offices of the day. They rose at about two or three in the morning to recite the first prayers. They then went to school, where they read and chanted. Children were forbidden to speak, as were the adults in the monastery. Children were constantly supervised, even when using the toilet. Their day ended back at the dormitory sometime after six in the evening. Children were given occasional times to play, including any number of activities such as running, swimming, horseback riding, and games. Girls would receive instruction in sewing and embroidery as well as in reading and chant. Life in the monastery was very rigorous, but it was probably the best life available for children. The organized life of the monastery allowed for more time off to relax or play than would have been possible on the manor.

It has sometimes been argued that for children of the peasantry, play would have been an unknown concept; that play is a modern concept that made no sense in a setting of severe conditions of bare survival. However, play is a natural developmental element for children, and if modern societies are examined where conditions are extremely harsh, children still find some time and some means to play.

HOUSING

Housing for the common people was crude and rudimentary. Some of the rural manorial housing was probably little more than huts. Construction would have been with whatever local materials existed. In the northern regions of the Carolingian Empire where woodlands surrounded nearly all clearings, wood was plentiful. Rough beams would have been cut and pieced together with notching and pegs. Walls were made from

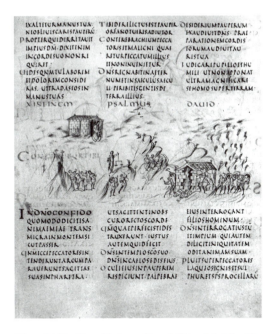

**Utrecht Psalter, University of Utrecht, Ms. 32,
fol. 6r. Construction methods are roughly
represented by hewn (ashlar) stone and by
corners of buildings constructed before the
walls. Notice also the trade scales in the
center of the drawing.**

wicker or lathe. Between the upright corner beams, small rods were stuck in the ground and flexible thin green sticks as laths were woven through these uprights to make a basketlike wall. Laths were often included in manorial payment quotas. The wickerwork or lathwork was then plastered with a mixture made of mud or clay and lime. Once hardened, this was fairly durable, although brittle.

Lime was an extremely important substance in Carolingian society, as in most societies. It was produced by mining limestone, burning it (which causes the loss of carbon dioxide), crushing it, and then mixing it with water. When water is added to this material, it becomes cement-like. If it is thin, it can be painted onto a surface and serves several purposes. First, it will harden and protect the surface from weather. It is also much more durable than mud. Second, lime kills nearly anything it comes into contact with. In more modern times, whitewash (lime wash) has been used to disinfect farm buildings. Whitewashing the walls of a building, both inside and out, eliminated infestation of insects and reduced the growth of molds and mildews. Third, the white interior made the space much lighter and magnified the use of artificial lighting. If the lime and water mixture had sand added, it became the mortar used to hold together most stone structures. Sometimes other materials were added to increase the durability of these mortars since dried lime mortar has a tendency to crumble.

Roofing would have been of wood or thatch. Thatching was usually made from reeds or tall marsh grasses, although it could be made from straw. Bundles of the grass were bound tightly and then were tied to the horizontal roof poles. Good thatching from marsh grasses was very durable. If the bundles were made thick enough, were tied tightly, and were attached close together, thatching was waterproof and would last up to sixty or seventy years.

From the few references we have to Carolingian houses, the houses themselves probably would not have lasted that long. They were described as dark, cold, creaky, leaky, and uncomfortable. In the southern regions of the empire, it was more common to have stone houses, as stone was more plentiful than wood.

Houses of the peasantry ranged from about nine feet square (eighty-one square feet) to rectangles of two hundred to three hundred square feet or more. The interior often was just one room, sometimes subdivided into compartments, but where the main central room served all accommodation purposes such as cooking and sleeping. The other compartments were for storage and for animals, so the building served as house and barn. The chimney had not been invented yet, so a fireplace was simply a flat hard surface in the center where the fire was built. Cooking was done in pots or frying pans hung or held over the fire. The smoke from the fire filled the house, although with open beams the smoke would rise to the roof, where there would be small crevices in the beams and thatch for the smoke to exit. That still would make for a very smoky existence.

Furniture

Furniture within the common house included benches or stools and a table. Benches are easy to construct, and stools, when three-legged, are the easiest to level on an uneven beaten dirt or flagstone floor. Benches were sometimes laid with a cushion. Chairs were considered to be somewhat extravagant and were uncommon, perhaps because the construction for a chair is much more elaborate than for a bench. Chairs, like benches, might have a cushion or be upholstered. For the truly fortunate, chairs might have arms. The table would probably be a form of trestle table that was easy to construct and could be taken down when not in use to make that space available for other activities such as sleeping. It requires little more than a pair of X legs with a crossbar to stabilize the legs and a top surface made from one or more wide boards. The well-off might have a form of dresser to hold clothing, but for the poorest there would be little extra clothing to hold.

Sleeping Arrangements and Patterns

Since many houses had only one room, not only would everyone sleep in the same room, but several would sleep in the same bed. Usually the youngest children would sleep with the parents, and as they grew older, they would move out to beds with other siblings. Any sexual activity on the part of the parents in a house would have to take place in the presence of the other members of the family.

Beds for the common people were probably little different from common beds throughout European history, a sack filled with straw or other dried grasses. Each year this sack would be emptied and refilled with fresh straw. For the more fortunate, the sack might be filled with down from ducks or geese. In some of the records, Charlemagne instructed that his villas be equipped with eiderdown and beds, covers, and sheets. There are inventories of mattresses, pillows, and sheets. An infant would have its own cradle (a wooden box is necessary to contain and protect the infant), but once a child left the cradle, often because a new infant needed it, the child would move into the bed of the parents.

It has usually been assumed that prior to the advent of artificial lighting, people slept more. Most modern historians have assumed that people went to bed when it became dark outside and slept until it was light again. If this were true, people in the Carolingian Empire would have slept approximately seven hours in the summer and more than twelve hours in the winter. Recent studies have discovered that in fact, people did not sleep through the night, nor did they necessarily sleep any more than people sleep currently. Prior to artificial lighting, people had segmented sleep. They slept for approximately four hours and then woke up. This was called first sleep. When they woke, they might simply lie in bed for some time, or they might get up and putter around the house, check the coals of the fire, start preparations for the next day, or even go outside. After being awake for a while, often an hour or more, they would go back to sleep for approximately another four hours, known as second sleep. Individuals' sleep patterns and length varied then as now, but most people did not sleep much more than eight hours total. Even with the hour or so between first and second sleep, this suggests that people did not immediately go to sleep at the onset of darkness nor wait until morning light to awake. This helps explain why many of the sources for medieval life, both in the church and on the manor, refer to getting up before dawn to begin activities. This also explains how monks could have been expected to arise in the middle of the night for prayers.

One of the interesting points that becomes significant from understanding this sleep pattern, according to sleep specialists, is that people must have been much more aware of their dreams. If people awaken naturally, especially in the middle of the night, and have time to meditate, they will recall dreams much more effectively than under modern twenty-first-century conditions. This suggests that dreams would have played a much more prominent role in Carolingian society. Charlemagne kept lamps and wax tablets at his bedside so that he could record his dreams when he woke in the middle of the night.

Heat and Light

Darkness was something that was almost tangible. Medieval people talked about darkness closing in around one and of the need to move indoors as darkness approached. Night air was also viewed as threatening. People closed themselves to the night by moving inside and shutting doors and closing shutters.

Heat and light in the average household were provided by a central fire. Since fireplaces with connected chimneys were as yet unknown in the ninth century, in the more elaborately designed buildings, such as major buildings of monasteries or palaces, holes were cut in the ceiling to take away the smoke from the central fire. Most of the Carolingian Empire was in territory that became very cold and damp during the winter, and Carolingian people would have suffered from this cold every year. Huge amounts of wood were gathered from the great expanses of forest to burn continuously during the winter and for much of the day during other times of the year. Cooking was also done over these open central fires. Even baking could be done in a heavy pot, lidded and covered with hot coals. Monasteries had separate ovens heated by contiguous fireboxes, but most homes would not have had ovens.

Lighting was very costly and hence very rare. Peasants went to bed when it became too dark to work on chores in the house. The light from the fire would provide the ability to see, but not enough to perform most fine motor-skill activities. Fat or oil lamps existed, but peasants could not afford to burn them. Animal fat, whale oil, and oil from olives, walnuts, or poppies were used in different locations in Charlemagne's territory, but only by the more well-to-do. Candles made from beeswax seem to have been most commonly used by churches, while torches and lamps were also used. From the fact that churches comment on their candles and sometimes mention their cost, they must have been beyond the reach of many of the peasants or at least costly enough that they were used sparingly.

When people did have to move around outside in the dark, and they did, especially in the winter when darkness came early each day, most movement was probably done without artificial lighting. When one is adjusted to natural lighting, it is remarkable how much light is provided by the moon and even the stars. On a clear night, even without the moon, starlight makes it possible to see a little. On an overcast night, the darkness would have been forbidding and nearly impenetrable. However, in a small village, before the advent of artificial lighting, people also would have memorized the location of every ditch, tree stump, fence, or hole for the regular route that was traversed at night.

Generally people feared fire more than they feared darkness or cold. The fear of fire at night was real and serious. Without a fireplace and chimney and with thatched or wooden roofing, the possibility of fire was great. A fire for heat and cooking within a house could never be left unattended even as people slept. Houses were frequently destroyed by fire. In winter, when fire was the most needed, a house fire could be disastrous for the occupants. To avoid house fires, during the summer, cooking was probably done outside.

FOOD

During an era in which many people were barely able to survive, every household had its garden. The Carolingians were great vegetable eaters. Foods were not yet composed primarily of grains in one form or another, as they would be by the twelfth century. The same revolution of the tenth and eleventh centuries that strengthened the aristocracy by consolidating land into their hands also increased the cereal production by intensifying land cultivation. This enabled the aristocracy to skim the surplus from the agricultural production, but it forced most of the agrarian population into cereal production and away from hunting and gathering and specialized agriculture such as viniculture (grape growing for wine). However, the Carolingians began to cerealize northern Europe to a great degree and were becoming more dependent upon grains. Of the cereal grains, rye, wheat, barley, and oats were all grown. Any grain could be ground into flour and baked into bread, which was an important and probably primary, if not completely dominant, component of their diet.

Ale

Grain could also be brewed into ale, which, along with wine, was the major source of fluid and calories. Once a child was weaned from its mother's breast, the child drank weak ale or diluted wine. Milk was cooked or turned into cheese, and the only juices were ones that were fermented into powerful drinks. Few drank water because it was considered unsafe (justifiably so, because of inadequate human and animal waste disposal). Brewing (the word has the same origin as boiling) made the water safe. The drink that was made was not technically beer since beer is made from the addition of hops to the brewing process. Hops also make the drink clear and slightly bitter and act as a preservative. Therefore, ale would have been slightly thicker and much cloudier than modern beer and with a slightly sweet taste. Without hops, the drink was highly perishable. Housewives would have brewed regularly, commonly once a week, just as they would frequently bake bread. According to Einhard, Charlemagne was temperate in his drinking, hated to see anyone inebriated, and would not tolerate drunkenness in his household.

Stew and Meat

In addition to being used to make bread and ale, grain could be boiled into a gruel somewhat like modern oatmeal. Another almost ubiquitous meal was a stew of nearly anything that was edible thrown into a pot that was kept cooking, and as some was consumed, other vegetables, grain, or meat were added in. Meat was more frequently eaten by the common people in the eighth and ninth centuries than it would be after the eleventh century. Hunting rights were held by everyone in the Carolingian world, but after the eleventh century those rights were confiscated and consolidated in the hands of the aristocracy to force the masses of the population into production for the aristocracy.

Meat was popular with Charlemagne and probably everyone else, although it was most likely a rarity in the diet of the poor, based on success in hunting rather than production of flesh animals. Rabbits were the easiest to hunt, but any animal that could be killed or trapped would be welcome. Pork, beef, mutton, goat, chicken, duck, and goose were all eaten, but animals were valuable enough that they were not eaten every day except by the well-off. Bacon, sausage, and smoked meats, salted meats, and partially salted meats were popular. Fish was common and eaten on all fast days, which were frequent in the Church. Both saltwater and freshwater fish were eaten, although the saltwater fish probably were never known very far from the coast because of rapid spoilage. Freshwater fish were caught in rivers and streams with both nets and hook and line, but fish ponds were also built for fish farming. During Lent, meat could not be eaten, and the fishmongers had a monopoly.

Other Foods

Other foods would have included eggs, onions, leeks, radishes, beans, peas, lentils, cabbage, turnips, beets, cheese, butter, and honey. Butter and cheese were not eaten in large quantities, so animal fat made up a relatively small proportion of the average diet. Honey was the only "sweet" available and was therefore quite popular, although the wax from the beehive was just as valuable. Fruit may have been more popular in this era than it was later in the Middle Ages. Pears, apples, peaches, mulberries, and quinces were all grown, as were filberts and walnuts. Herbs grow nicely in the climate of Europe (spices, on the other hand, do not and were little known in the eighth and ninth centuries in Europe), and according to inventories of the ninth century, mint, parsley, rue, celery, lovage, sage, savory, juniper, garlic, shallots, tansy, and coriander were all grown in herb gardens. Vegetables were eaten daily, especially by the poor, while fruits were eaten less.

Wine

Wine was important enough that there were royal proclamations regulating its production. Whether one drank ale or wine would have been determined primarily by location since more wine was produced in the central and southern regions, while ale was more common in the north. Other drinks included mead (fermented honey water and a drink that can be sweet or dry and very powerful), cider (drunk fermented), perry (fermented pear juice), garne (made from fermented grain), and the very popular mulberry wine.

Charlemagne and Food

Charlemagne tried to be temperate in his eating, but according to Einhard, it was difficult for him to abstain from food. He is described as having had a large belly and a matching appetite. He rarely gave banquets, but ate four courses each meal, not counting the roast, which was his favorite part. This was brought to him on a spit not by the cooks but by his huntsman.

One of the most remarkable statements about food to be found in the records of the eighth century is from a capitulary (directives from Charlemagne that acted almost as laws) known as *De villis* (Concerning manors). It ordered that people on the Carolingian estates take care that whatever was prepared by hand, such as lard, smoked meat, sausage, salted meat, wine, vinegar, wine, mustard, cheese, butter, malt, beer, mead, honey, wax, and flour, all be prepared with the greatest cleanliness. This indicates that they understood that lack of cleanliness caused a problem, although the capitulary does not specify why the cleanliness is to be followed. It is also quite likely that rules of cleanliness were not followed by most people in the eighth or ninth centuries. By the Late Middle Ages, washing hands before eating was common among the nobility, but whether it was common in the eighth or ninth centuries is unknown.

Tableware

Most tableware was made of wood. Rudely carved wooden bowls would have served the purpose for nearly all foods. Food would be eaten with a spoon and the hands. Pottery was made in the Carolingian age. We have remains of several distinct types of glazed pottery, but local unglazed pottery was almost certainly made for common use. Drinking vessels could have been constructed of wood, pottery or leather or from gourds. Leather cups, sealed with pitch, are very effective and durable. Pitchers existed, but seem to have been rare enough that common people may not have had them. The same is true for bottles and other types of pottery containers. Glass was known in the Carolingian age, but it was a rare and highly valued product. There is mention of glass kilns and of glass products, but usually of such value that the mention is in a will or testament indicating high cost, taking it out of reach of the average person.

CLOTHING

Not a great deal is known about the common clothing in the eighth and ninth centuries. All of the materials for the clothing of the common people would have come from their manor and have been readily available. Cloth was made of linen and wool. Cotton, a plant and cloth of India, was as yet unknown in Europe, although it would be grown in some Mediterranean regions by the later Middle Ages. A tunic of coarse linen, which came down to the knees, was worn over an undershirt if one was lucky enough to own an undershirt. The tunic was generally girded at the waist with rope or a leather thong that would also hold a knife. Legs were wrapped in narrow strips of cloth. Shoes were most commonly a form of sandals since leather boots were very expensive (Charlemagne sometimes wore boots). Shoes or sandals did not have left and right versions, but simply were one shape made to length. After being worn for some time, the shoe would form to the foot and become left or right. A type of hood was worn for a hat. Hooded capes of wool were worn in colder weather.

Cloth Used

Although exotic cloth such as silk was occasionally imported for the wealthy, the common people not only used materials that were close at hand, but very often manufactured the clothing themselves as well. Women took sheared wool, washed and combed it, and spun it into thread that they wove into woolen cloth to make into clothing. Or they soaked and beat flax, combed it into thread, and wove it into linen. The advantage of wool is that in its washed but unbleached state it still contains lanolin, which is oily and repels water. If wool clothing is woven tightly, it is relatively waterproof. Wool also dyes easily, is quite elastic, and insulates very effectively. Additionally, wool dries easily, so that clothing that becomes wet while it is worn will dry from body heat. The most common dyes were woad, madder, and vermilion. Woad, an herb grown commonly in northern Europe, provided blue dye, madder, the root of which was used, produced a red dye, and vermilion, a pigment of mercuric sulfide, known as the crystal cinnabar, produced a bright red.

Linen is finer and smoother than wool and better as clothing against the skin, so if possible, the people of the Carolingian age wore undergarments made of linen. Linen also dries quickly, even better than wool, and therefore does not chafe. Linen does not dye easily, but for undergarments color was not important. Flax grew easily in the northern areas of the Carolingian Empire. In fact, northern France would become renowned for its linen manufacture. Flax could also be used to make a much heavier cloth, canvas.

Animal Skins

Since hunting was allowed in the Carolingian Empire, animal skins and furs would also have been used for clothing and would not have been restricted to the aristocracy as they would have been in later centuries when hunting rights were held by the few. This means that leather may have been more readily available to the common person in the eighth and ninth centuries than it was in the twelfth century. Deer were plentiful and were hunted for their meat as well as for their skins. Deerskin provides a particularly fine leather that was valued for shoes and gloves, although it was also used for any type of clothing. Fur was more often used as a lining for outer garments because it provides a high level of insulation. Bear, fox, weasel (ermine in the winter when it turns white), marten, rabbit, and squirrel fur were all used, although bear was so heavy that it was probably used mostly as an outer fur cape. Sheepskin or, even better, lamb was used as a lining on any piece of clothing from booties for indoor wear to gloves and coats.

Bathing

The Frankish nobility traditionally changed their clothing and bathed once a week. Some of the evidence for this comes from the tradition's disallowance for monks at the time. Monks were specifically forbidden to bathe regularly as an ascetic practice for fear of them becoming indulgent or intemperate. It is not clear what the average person's hygienic practices were, but it is unlikely that regular bathing and clothes washing were common since supplying large quantities of water and heating it for these activities would have required a substantial outlay in work. Washing of hands and face was probably more common than full bathing. There are occasional references to cleanliness, but how far it was taken is unknown.

DEATH AND BURIAL

The Age of Charlemagne brought about a fairly important change in the practices and ceremonies attached to death and burial. In pre-Carolingian times, especially among pre-Christian Franks, the celebration of birth was more important than that of death, although the commemoration of the dead had roots in pagan antiquity. With the coming of Christianity, the focus was on death as the moment of rebirth in Christ, as experienced in Jesus' resurrection. The New Testament emphasized this with Jesus' statement at the Last Supper "This is my body, which is for you; do this as a memorial of me" (1 Corinthians 11.24). It was believed that the death, not just of Christ, but of all, should be memorialized. Commemorative meals were often held. St. Augustine in the *City of God* (426 C.E.) accepted the practice of commemorative meals and prayers.

The Merovingians celebrated death with a heavy measure of paganism, for they buried their dead with objects that showed their status and might be needed in the afterlife. Consequently, Merovingian graves are wonderful archaeological finds. Under the Carolingians, burial became more uniform within the Christian context. Bodies were buried without objects. More and more focus was directed toward the dead. Pope Gregory III wrote to Boniface in 732 that the Church believes that everyone should offer prayers to the dead. The recitation of prayers for the dead became common. By the eighth century, there was an increased focus on dead saints. Recitation of saints' names in prayers during the Mass became standard practice, and by the ninth century entire masses for the dead were performed. At the same time, a new focus on saints' relics expanded in the Frankish empire, and entire saints' bodies or pieces of bodies were transferred from their original burial sites to churches or monasteries in Francia (see "Saints' Relics" in chapter 6).

As Charlemagne tried to extend a uniform practice of Christianity throughout his realm, the Roman form of the Mass was brought into the Carolingian Empire. This practice was described as more cold and less personal, with fewer references to specific dead persons. However, just before Charlemagne's death, bishops and abbots from the province of Lyon gathered at the council of Chalon-sur-Saône in 813 and decreed that the prayers of the dead should be included in the masses and in all

**Utrecht Psalter, University of Utrecht, Ms. 32,
fol. 28r. Burials take place in the foreground.**

prayers so that all the dead would be prayed for by all living Christians. Alcuin himself promoted the celebration of the feast of All Saints on November 1. As this holy day became more common and more important in the Christian calendar, gradually the belief in Hallowed Eve (Halloween), the night before All Saints, arose.

5

THE ECONOMY: WORK, AGRICULTURE, TRADES, AND MARKETS

WORK

Carolingian Work Policy

Charlemagne did not have a clear economic policy, but he did understand that the more wealth produced on the land and in the towns, the better off he and the kingdom were. This meant that in a sparsely populated land he wanted as large a population as possible, and he needed it settled on land or in the towns and working. Charlemagne sent out capitularies ordering that beggars be settled on land, that unsettled manors be populated, that newly conquered territories be repopulated by moving people in, and that nobles who received benefices use the workers on that land and not move them to privately held lands. He supported marriage and procreation, for they would provide a renewable workforce.

Charlemagne encouraged work in a number of ways. He discouraged the old Roman noble idea of leisure while emphasizing and rewarding work. Charlemagne himself was what we might call a "workaholic." From his travels alone, travels intended to inspect, supervise, and inspire, we know that he spent enormous numbers of hours performing his kingly tasks. His legislation and capitularies supported work, trade, and agriculture and even criticized the nobility for their ruthless attitude toward their workers. As a model, Charlemagne concerned himself with the royal domains. The vast lands under his direct control were ordered to be built up, put in better working order, and made self-sufficient. He tried to build up long-distance trade, but was most concerned about the internal infrastructure of roads and rivers and safety for commerce. As far as we can tell, Charlemagne's attempts at economic recovery were at least marginally effective. The economy may have been recovering even before Charlemagne's reign, but certainly during the eighth and ninth centuries there was a buildup in the economy in the West. However, at the lowest level, life probably continued much the same as it had long been, a dreary succession of long days, weeks, and years of arduous work with no respite in sight.

Work Patterns

The nobility and upper echelon of the clergy did not have to work because they owned enough land to rent out that as rentiers they could have others do their work for them. Otherwise, everyone had to work. From the time a child was old enough to walk, that child would be put to work. Even fairly responsible jobs were given to young children who would have worked and learned responsibility from the time they were old enough to carry out a task. Everyone rose from bed at dawn or before. The women would stir up the fire in preparation for cooking, or this job might be allocated to one of the girls in the family so that the mother could begin other preparations. In the summer, the men and boys would eat a light meal of bread and cheese and drink some ale or wine and be off to the fields for work. If they were working any distance from the house, they would carry with them food and drink for the noon meal.

The females baked and brewed and tended the garden that was near the house, fed the fowls and gathered eggs. Since poultry were not penned, but roamed the village, collecting eggs was an everyday Easter-egg hunt. Children would be assigned to this duty and would have to look in bushes and trees, corners of buildings, and clumps of grass, all favorite spots for fowls to nest and lay. Once a nest was established, the hen tended to lay in the same spot, so the hunt was not a complete guessing game. The females would also gather wood, cook the food for supper, and tend the sheep and pigs. Pigs needed the least attention, for they are smart and durable. Pigs will make mud to cover themselves (pigs are one of the few animals, along with humans, that suffer from sunburn and therefore need to cover themselves), build their own nests for a litter or merely for warmth in winter, and very effectively search out their own food. Acorns are one of their favorites, and the woods of much of the Carolingian Empire were filled with oaks. For all of these reasons, pigs made the ideal animal for raising as a source of meat. Sheep, on the other hand, need tending. They are not intelligent and will get themselves into trouble if they are not watched. Sheep were also easy targets for the plentiful wolves of the empire, so at night sheep would have to be watched by a shepherd or folded (put inside a fenced or hedged enclosure) near the house. Females were responsible for the care of most of the animals and were often required to work in the fields alongside the men as well. For the farming family, no job was beyond the women.

The males at dawn went out to the fields, as mentioned earlier. Work was certainly hard, as farmwork is at any time, and the conditions to survive were not advantageous, but the work obligations to the lord for the average peasant were not as onerous as they would later become. Many peasants, free or not, owed work obligations to the lord. In addition to the rent payment in coin or in kind such as two sheep, four dozen eggs, and three sacks of barley, the peasants often had to work the lord's land. However, a wide range of obligations might exist on the very same manor. One family might owe two weeks a year, while another might owe two days a week. This work obligation could be a burden if it was frequent, for the peasant's own work had to be put on hold while the lord's field got plowed or harvested. However, the image that most people have today of serfdom and its work obligations comes from the High Middle Ages when the population had risen dramatically and therefore the pressure for lands played into the hands of the landlords. They kept increasing work obligations whenever possible, and the peasantry had little choice but to fulfill them. In the Carolingian era, the work obligations were usually not so heavy as to break the peasantry.

AGRICULTURE

Agriculture was the way of life of almost everyone in the Age of Charlemagne. More than 90 percent of the population lived in the countryside farming. But even those who lived in the few towns or remnants of cities would have been closely connected with agriculture. First, the towns were small enough that the countryside was never far away. Second, the people living in the towns would usually have had gardens and livestock. The small plot of land surrounding a house would have contained a garden to grow as many foods as possible, including onions, radishes, peas, and beans. Chickens and pigs would have roamed the town, and people could recognize their pig as well as someone today could identify his dog among others.

The Agricultural Year

Since agriculture was nearly synonymous with the economy, Charlemagne tried to support and encourage agricultural production throughout the empire. He renamed the months using Germanic names, many of which were taken from agricultural activities of those months: June was "Plow-Month," July "Hay-Month," August "Ear-Month" (as in ears of grain), September "Wood-Month," and October "Wine-Pressing-Month." Charlemagne also encouraged landholders in many ways to build up their manors, to make them self-sufficient, and to treat the laborers well. When the Church ordered that people not work on Sundays, Charlemagne supported this right down to the lowliest swineherds for two reasons. One, it drew all his people into a unified and universal Church, but second, it gave the laborers—the people doing all the work—a break. In reality, when essential work had to be done, such as milking the cows or harvesting the ripe grain, attendance at church was surely ignored by the laborers, by the landowners, and even by the clergy for everyone knew what jobs could not be put off. If the grain was not harvested when it was ready, families could end up starving later.

Grain

All grain (the European term is corn; American "corn" is maize) was scarce, yet it was by far the major source of food for people in the Carolingian world. Harvests, at their best, were marginal successes. Grain heads (the actual ear of grain such as wheat, oats, or barley) were much smaller than today with fewer seeds per head and smaller seeds. That meant that for every seed planted, the number of seeds produced was much fewer than today, known as low yield rates. From those harvested, some was lost in the harvesting and threshing process, some had to be saved for planting the next year or there would be no next harvest, some was given as rent payment to the lord of the land being cultivated, some was given to the Church, and what was left was what a family had to survive on until the next harvest.

During a good year, there was enough to survive. During a bad year, there was starvation, or a family ate its seed corn (planting seed) and then had nothing the following year. Two bad harvests in a row were devastating. Any weather changes might bring about a bad harvest. Too little or too much rain, too late or too early a freeze, and especially a storm with wind or hail just before harvesting could make for a poor harvest. Add to this the dangers of marauding armies, floods, and other disasters, and it is no wonder that Carolingian society was always on the precipice. Charlemagne also worried about this and wrote capitularies forbidding anyone from taking advantage of bad harvests to hoard grain or to buy up land at below-market prices because of hardship. In 794, Charlemagne set maximum prices for grain and then found that he

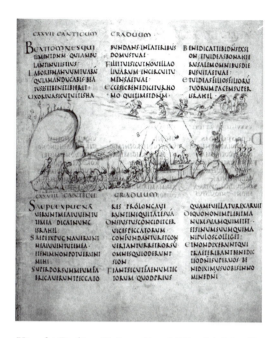

Utrecht Psalter, University of Utrecht, Ms. 32,
fol. 74r. Agricultural activity on the left
includes haying with scythes.

had to follow this with standardized measures for grain since each region and sometimes each farm had a different measure.

The grain fields of the empire were not only the breadbasket, but the basis of the entire economy of the empire. Farming techniques varied according to the region, but in general, fields were either square or strip. The square fields often dated from Roman times and worked particularly well in the southern regions of Europe where there was light soil and scratch plowing was effective. In this method, a small plow, little more than a pointed stick, was pushed and dragged by human or animal traction to scratch the ground open. After the entire field was plowed in one direction, it was plowed in the other direction at a right angle to the first plowing. Because of this, the square field, with width and length approximately the same, made sense. However, in the north, where the soil was heavy, strip fields worked better, especially after the fourth century C.E. when the weather became wetter. Prior to this, the square field might be surrounded by a stone wall that protected the field from animals, but also kept needed moisture from running off. After the fourth century, when retaining moisture was no longer as much an issue, the fields were less often walled and a different plowing technique was found to be much more effective than the scratch plow.

The Plow

This new technique was the use of the large wheeled plow that required a team of two, or preferably more, oxen. This plow has a large frame that rests on wheels and carries a coulter that cuts the sod, a share that deepens and widens the cut, and a moldboard that turns the slice of sod to one side. Turning this plow takes time and space (although it is not quite as cumbersome as some have claimed it to be), and because of this, it is better to keep the plow going in a straight line as long as is practical. Therefore, fields where the width to length ratio was 1:20 were more common. The wheeled plow with a fixed moldboard meant that the farmer plowed from the center in each direction, folding the sod in toward the center. This tended to create a mounded or convex shape to the fields that helped with drainage, running water to the edges of the field, in an era of greater moisture, although by the eighth and ninth centuries the climate had turned. Starting in the eighth century, Europe moved into a period now called the "little climatic optimum" with weather warmer and drier, which was optimum for growing grain.

Oxen versus Horses

In the Roman period, oxen (bovines domesticated for work, especially an adult castrated male) were most often used as draft animals. That continued to be true in the Carolingian era because oxen were cheaper than horses, could be kept by grazing on pastureland, and when past their prime could be eaten. Oxen were also easier to yoke than horses. They were fitted with a wooden yoke that was fastened to the head and horns and attached to a shaft between a pair of oxen that was attached to the plow or cart. This type of yoke was unsuitable for a horse since it pressed against a horse's windpipe and cut off the horse's breathing. In the ninth century, a horse harness was developed with a fixed padded wooden head collar that made it possible to use a horse for traction, although oxen continued to be the predominant form, while horses were used for warfare. Horses were costly for work since they had to eat oats and in rough work areas had to be shod. Horseshoes and the new harness or head collar came into use by the ninth century, from which we have some specimens. The horseshoe was unknown in the Merovingian period, but appeared in the West and in the Byzantine Empire at about the same time as the head collar. The real significance of the horseshoe was for the military, where horses would be ridden hard over various terrains. The iron shoes protected the horse's hoof from wearing and from splitting. Under some circumstances, in agricultural use horses as well as oxen would be shod. Iron could be produced locally fairly easily,

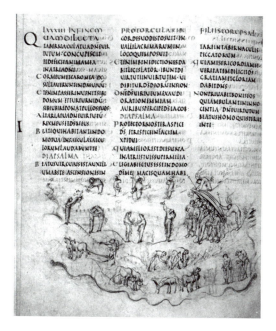

Utrecht Psalter, University of Utrecht, Ms. 32,
fol. 49v. Ox-drawn plow, harvesting with
sickles, and sheep and goats.

and so most estates or locales would have a full- or part-time blacksmith
to produce the horseshoes, nails, and other iron products.

The advantage of the horse for traction over the ox is not in power,
since they are about equal in that, but in speed. A horse can pull a load
approximately 50 percent faster than an ox and therefore can accomplish
the same amount of work in less time. In fact, in measured analysis, if
a horse produces 1 horsepower (500 foot-pounds per second), an ox produces 2/3 horsepower. A human, in comparison, produces approximately
1/10 horsepower. Horses also have greater endurance than oxen, being
able to work approximately two hours longer on the same job.

The plowing process was difficult and labor intensive. The oxen were
yoked and connected to the plow. Two men worked the team and plow,
with one leading the oxen by standing to their left and using a long
switch or rod to urge the lumbering animals on while the plowman
directed the plow itself. Additionally, another man or boys would walk
along with bats or clubs to break up the clods of soil as they were turned
over by the moldboard. After plowing the entire field in one direction,
if it was square, they might plow again in the other. If they were plowing
a strip, the team might be used to drag a log, after plowing, to help
break up the clods and to smooth the soil. Plowing was done in the

spring and in the autumn, and on the fallow (unplanted) soil additionally in summer to keep down the weeds since they were one of the greatest enemies of the farmer.

Planting

After the field was plowed and the soil was as finely broken and smoothed as possible, the planting could begin. Until the seventeenth century, seeds were not planted mechanically and in rows. In the eighth and ninth centuries, as throughout most of history, seeds were broadcast (literally cast abroad). An adult would carry a sack or tightly woven basket with the seeds and carefully step and toss a handful of seeds in a spreading motion across in front. The trick was to get the seeds spread as evenly as possible so that there were not too many plants coming up in one spot and too few in another. Because of this method of seeding, plants were never in rows, and weeding, therefore, had to be done by hand with a hoe. Only when the plants are placed in rows can any mechanical device such as a harrow be used to weed.

Field Rotation

Crop rotation was critical to agriculture. Much of Europe traditionally followed a two-field rotation in which half the land was planted with a crop and the other half was left fallow to rejuvenate itself for one season. The next year, the two fields were switched so that the rejuvenated field could be planted and the other could be allowed to remain fallow. In some areas of the Carolingian Empire, a variant was followed in which a field was tilled for one year and left fallow for two. This would be useful either where arable land was plentiful or where the fertility of the land was low. It is believed that sometime in the Carolingian era three-field rotation came into use, in which the land was divided into three units and two were planted while the third remained fallow. This increased the amount of land under cultivation by approximately 16 percent (66 percent of available land planted instead of 50 percent). A winter crop such as rye or wheat was planted on the first third, a spring crop such as oats or barley was planted on the second third, and the last was left fallow. Each year the fields were rotated. It was not yet understood, and would not be until the seventeenth and eighteenth centuries, that legumes could be planted on the area previously left fallow, increasing fodder for the animals and increasing the quality of the land by adding nitrogen to it.

Another advantage of the three-field rotation was that it increased the spring crop of oats, which are necessary for horses that are being worked. Working horses burn large amounts of calories and need the high-calorie diet of oats. In a civilization that depended on mounted warriors, horses were essential, and therefore oats were essential. Oxen can be almost entirely grazed on common pasture.

One thing that cannot be claimed for the development of three-field rotation is Charlemagne's support. One famous historian claimed that the idea of changing from two- to three-field rotation was one of Charlemagne's major concerns in his later life and that he should be credited for many of the changes that took place in the ninth century. There is little doubt that Charlemagne would have encouraged the changeover from two- to three-field rotation for economic development if he had understood this, for it strengthened the overall empire, yet there is no evidence that he was ever specifically interested in the change of rotations in agriculture.

Livestock and Crops

In the Carolingian era, small livestock, such as pigs, sheep, goats, chickens, ducks, and geese, predominated. These animals were turned loose to graze on the wasteland that was covered with all the wild plants and forests. This wasteland provided unlimited grazing because it stretched across much of Europe. These animals foraged for whatever food they could find. Often these animals, especially pigs, were little different from wild animals, and finding and killing them would have been almost as difficult as a wild hunt. Some might have been penned and fed as they were fattened for butchering. As more large animals came into use in the Carolingian era, the peasants had to begin to use the arable lands as pasture after the crop had been harvested or during the field's fallow season.

In addition to the grains of wheat, oats, barley, rye, and spelt, other crops were grown. Barley, spelt, and oats were the most important grains. We know from the records of four great estates in northern France from about 810 of a variety of crops. Other foods included beans and peas, onions, leeks, radishes, horseradish, cabbage, and fruit. Apples and pears could be eaten fresh, dried for storage, or crushed and fermented into hard cider or perry. Other crops included gold of pleasure and olives for oil (cooking, lighting, and industrial), herbs for cooking, flax and hemp for cloth and rope, woad and madder for dyes, honey for sweetening and the wax for candles and waterproofing, fruits and nuts, and grapes for wine.

Harvesting

Harvesting grain was a critical activity. The great scythe, called the Hainault scythe, which could be used for reaping, did not come into use until the fourteenth century. A sickle was used, and the heads of the grain were cut off a short way from the top. This made harvesting the grain quicker since the entire stalk was not cut at first. However, it was labor intensive since harvesters had to come through a second time with sickles or crude scythes and cut the stalks for the straw that was an essential component of the farming process. Straw was used for bedding not only for animals, but for humans as well by stuffing it into a sack.

Most farming implements were made of wood except for cutting edges, which were iron. Rakes, pitchforks, and even most shovels were wood. Only spades (which dig into the soil, as opposed to a shovel, which is used to move substances), plowshares, scythe or sickle blades, axes, hatchets, augers for boring holes in wood, and blacksmithing tools were made of iron. If a farming implement was not used for cutting— cutting wood, plants, or sod—or for forming the cutting implement, as in the case of blacksmithing tools, it was made of wood. Very little metal was used for peasant implements in general. Most metal was used for the military or for the nobility.

Farm Setting

The typical agricultural setting was to have one to several families per farm. The population density of the Carolingian lands was extremely uneven. In the ninth century, there were regions that were severely underpopulated and declining, with many empty farms. At the same time, there were regions close by that were overpopulated. The curious part of this is that there was only limited movement, and that movement does not seem to have been from overpopulated areas to underpopulated ones. In fact, the evidence suggests that the opposite direction of migration took place. The second curious element is that there was not an appreciable expansion of arable lands in the overpopulated regions. The explanation for both these odd features is that security was more important to the Carolingian peasant than expansive lands. Maximizing security rather than advancing economic conditions would explain the lack of expansion into the wild. Additionally, sources make it clear that the policy of Charlemagne and of the nobility was to limit destruction of forests for the expansion of arable lands.

TRADES

Trade and manufacturing were not the strengths of the Age of Charlemagne, but both trade and manufacturing took place, and Charlemagne realized that the well-being of the empire was partially dependent upon the success of trade. Charlemagne in his capitulary *De villis* ordered that each district have workers in iron, gold, and silver, shoemakers, turners, carpenters, shield makers, fishermen, bird catchers, net makers, and soap makers. That Charlemagne would order these trades to be established indicates that they were well known and recognized as important, but it also indicates that they often did not exist, or the order would not have been given. Since the Carolingian Empire was a rural empire with few cities of great size, the amount of specialized trades would have been limited. For every specialist artisan there have to be agricultural workers feeding him, for the artisan makes a living producing a product and not growing food. However, it is this specialization that makes a city different from a village. In the Carolingian world, many of the artisans were to be found at the monasteries as often as in the towns and cities. The larger monasteries such as Fulda, St. Riquier, Bobbio, and Corbie had a number of artisans, some from the monks themselves, but more often as employees of the monastery. There would be blacksmiths, carpenters, masons, shoemakers, weavers, pelterers, harness makers, and occasionally goldsmiths, silversmiths, and parchment makers. The plan for St. Gall that was never fully realized called for an entire quarter of the monastic complex for the artisans.

Mills

Water mills existed, and although they were not terribly common in Roman times, they spread across Europe during the fifth to ninth centuries. In 845, on the monastery of Montier-en-Der's twenty-three domains, there were eleven water mills on the Loire River. Around the same time, the monastery of Saint-Germain-des-Prés had at least fifty-nine water mills. While many of these were small, they indicate a substantial increase in mechanical power in Europe that foreshadowed the dramatic increase in machinery during the course of the Middle Ages. For instance, by the time of the Domesday Book in 1086, there were more than 5,624 water mills in England. But water mills have several drawbacks. In flat areas such as the Low Countries, there was not enough flow in the rivers to power mills, and even in hillier land the water flow could dry up, especially in summer, or freeze in winter.

Some water mills in this period were undershot wheels where the water flowed under the wheel to turn it. With this type of construction, a deep-enough stream is needed for the wheel to sit in the water, and it requires a fairly substantial flow to turn the wheel. Installing any water mill was a costly and delicate job, but if it was to be an overshot mill, installation was even trickier. An undershot mill required a mill race to clear an area for the turning wheel and direct water as much as possible toward that race. An overshot mill has water poured down onto the wheel, increasing the power of the water by adding to the flow the action of gravity. The overshot mill also could run with a limited water supply, which meant that it could run longer into the summer as the stream or river withered to the point where an undershot mill could no longer run. But to make an overshot mill required building a sluice to direct the water from the stream to the top of the wheel. Any mill was a substantial investment because it included the machinery, the millstones, and the maintenance necessary to keep a mill running.

Even though a mill was a substantial investment, it was considered an excellent one. If we consider the vast amount of human power needed to grind anything by hand, it can be seen how important a mill was in releasing all of that previously wasted human power for other productive work. A large water mill could grind in one hour what would take forty people the same time to grind. Water mills were used to grind grain, to press oil from olives, nuts, and poppies, and to grind mustard seed, woad, or oak bark, which was used in the tanning process. Even with the spread of water mills, hand-operated mills still existed throughout the Carolingian world.

Windmills are not mentioned in Europe until the end of the twelfth century, indicating that the idea was probably brought back from the Middle East by the crusaders. When they did appear, they were often best suited to the very areas that could least use water mills, such as the Low Countries or modern-day Netherlands.

Cloth Production

Cloth production was extensive and important among the Carolingians. Both wool and flax were woven into cloth. Wool first had to be clipped from the sheep. Although this sounds easy, it requires a great deal of experience and expertise to avoid cutting the very thin and soft skin of the sheep. Once a lamb was eight to twelve months old, it could be sheared, this first shearing producing a finer and softer wool; adult sheep were normally sheared once a year in the spring. Once the wool, or fleece, was clipped, it had to be washed to remove dirt and dung. The washed wool was then carded, a process in which it is combed both to remove foreign objects and to begin the straightening out of the wool fibers. The cleaned and carded wool was then spun. The spinning wheel was not invented until the fourteenth century, so wool was spun into yarn with a distaff and spindle by twirling the spindle with wool caught on a hooked end. The yarn was then woven into cloth on a loom. The woolen cloth was pounded to full it, or force the fibers to mesh with one another, making a fairly solid surface, and the surface was clipped to make an even cloth. After fulling, the cloth could be dyed, usually blue, orange, or red. Because of the lanolin in wool, once it was woven and fulled, it was water repellent and very durable.

Flaxen cloth, or linen, required slightly more work in that the flax first had to be harvested in late summer. Flax grew very effectively within the Carolingian territories. At harvesting, the flax stalks were tied into bundles and dried in the sun. Then they were retted or kept moist for weeks to begin the rotting process to break down the matter around the actual fibers in the stalks. Then the stalks were steeped, washed, and beaten before the fibers could be combed out and spun. Once spun, flax was woven like wool, but into a dense, very durable cloth, since flax fibers are extremely strong. Linen was sometimes dyed, but it does not take dye very well and was more usually left white or even bleached to a greater whiteness. Flax was also used to make thread, nets, and a heavier canvas cloth.

Pottery

Carolingian pottery is not extant in large quantities. In the seventh century, a pottery industry of some significance developed in the Rhine valley. Primarily domestic pottery, it was decorated red clay, which was the common form of pottery in the Roman Empire, although Roman pottery was nearly always glazed. It is not clear whether this Rhineland pottery had continued ever since the Roman era or whether it was a reintroduction. Some incision decoration was used. During the ninth century, a better form of kiln was developed that enabled potters to fire at a higher temperature and produce a harder and more durable ware known as stoneware. Because the local clay often contained some sand and because of the higher-temperature kilns, the pot vitrified (changed into a glassy substance) into a hard dense pottery that was often produced without glaze because the dense hard surface was already impervious to liquid. This pottery was of sufficient value that an export business developed. Although in the Rhineland the Romans used several glaze techniques with great success, including lead glaze that is very hard wearing, it is not certain how common this was in the Carolingian Empire. Lead-glazed pottery was the most common form in Byzantium, and tin-glazed and lead-glazed pottery was common in the Islamic world and was also known in Francia. But in the Rhineland in this era, stoneware was the predominant form of pot, although lead-glazed pottery was certainly used. Pottery did not play quite the role in the Carolingian civilization that it did in Islam, where the ban on the use of gold and silver vessels for domestic purposes shifted the emphasis onto pottery. This meant that pottery was more important to the Islamic civilization than it was to Byzantium, for in Byzantium there was no prohibition against the use of gold and silver, and therefore the wealthy used these instead of pottery.

Glass

Glass was produced in the Carolingian age, although we do not know a great deal about its production. Glass kilns are occasionally mentioned, and small amounts of Carolingian glass are extant. It takes considerable skill to make glass into any usable shape, and therefore glass was an extravagance, not a necessity. In addition, the Church, the one institution with the resources to encourage the craft and ties to traditional crafts-manship, forbade the use of glass vessels for the Sacrament, probably out of fear that glass vessels could shatter, dropping the wine or host on the floor, a desecration. There were some glass bottles, drinking beakers, or containers, and glass was used for windows in important buildings. Glass was also ground into powder to be used in enameling and cloi-sonné (enamel produced within an area set off by tiny wires soldered on a metal background).

Glass production, though, was low during the Frankish empire. Good-quality glass had been produced in the region in the fourth and fifth centuries and was still being produced in the Byzantine Empire, Muslim Spain, and the Middle East in the eighth and ninth centuries, but not in Francia. The practice of burying glass in pagan tombs was dying out, and with it the art of glass making. In the ninth century, some glass-makers were persuaded to emigrate to an area near Genoa. Most of the known glass of the Merovingian and Carolingian periods is dull, imper-fect, and lacking in purity of color. The art of making a foot for a vessel seems to have been lost during this time. Drinking beakers were shaped like horns, which they certainly imitated and which had some religious significance in the Germanic tradition, or were small cups with widened bases, but pointed bottoms. This allowed the cup to sit angled upright. These shapes would suggest that the drink they contained was to be drunk before setting the vessel back down.

The primary materials necessary for glass production are silica, alkali, and fuel. These are readily available in many areas in the form of sand, soda, and wood. In the fourth and fifth centuries glass produced in Gaul, for which it was renowned, used soda imported from the natron lakes in Egypt. By the seventh century, this import trade disappeared, and the alkali was supplied by potash made from beechwood, which was readily available in the Frankish regions. Potash produced a heavier and sturdier glass than soda glass. The sand available also affects the outcome of the glass. The local sand produced a characteristic green color since it had a high iron content.

To produce glass, knowledge of the process is necessary, for it must be heated in a kiln to the correct temperature. As with firing pottery, making enamel, or doing precious metalwork, no temperature gauge of any sort was known, but experience in watching the material enabled the artisan to know when the proper temperature was reached. At this time, the procedure to produce a glass container was to repeatedly dip a sand core attached to a metal rod into molten glass. It was then rolled and smoothed so that a thick layer of glass adhered to the core. After cooling, the core was removed.

Glassblowing had been known since the first century C.E., in which the glass was heated to red-hot temperature and then could be blown into a bubble through a long pipe. This procedure expanded the range of glassmaking dramatically. A flat sheet of glass could be formed by blowing the glass into a bubble. Then it could either be rolled into a cylindrical shape, split open, and unrolled into a flat piece or could be spun rapidly into a large flat disk, called a crown, and the flat portion cut away to form a flat piece. These could be used for glazing. Glazing, or the use of glass for windows, had been known since Roman times, but had become quite rare by the sixth century. In the seventh century, Benedict Biscop, abbot of Monkswearmouth in England, according to Bede, sent for glaziers from Gaul. This indicates that the practice was alive and well in Merovingian Francia. In the East, pieces of glass were set in stone, but in the West, the glass was normally set in metal, usually lead, sometimes copper, and pieced together, made more rigid with iron bars since the glass is brittle and the lead soft. Even a small glazed window could not take the pressure of the wind without the iron bars. Stained glass is made by mixing ground metal such as copper or iron into the molten glass. Because of the iron content of the sand used for glass in the Carolingian realm, stained glass would have been impractical, so any glazed windows, unless the glass was imported from outside the empire, were grayish-green in color. Some glass was "painted," which is actually an enamel, or colored powered glass, which was ground, mixed with oil, painted on the glass, and then fired to fuse the two glasses.

Iron

Iron production was of the utmost importance in the Carolingian Empire because of its use for the military. In the Roman Empire, metal production was a nationalized affair carefully controlled by the state. The state provided the organization and capital for large-scale production in mining and smelting. With the destruction of the Roman Empire, the organization and capital necessary to carry on large-scale production in metals also disappeared. Metal production of all sorts declined, and many sites faded into oblivion. Iron production became localized and quality highly variable. Quality weapons were usually imported during the sixth and seventh centuries. During the eighth century, new sources of iron ore were discovered, providing the Carolingians with the needed metal.

The Carolingians were renowned for their military partly because of the extent of the use of iron and steel. According to the records, other armies trembled at the show of iron and steel weaponry by the Franks and commented on the fact that there was little comparison in the military forces because of this. The Frankish swords (see "Weapons of the Infantry" in chapter 3) were formidable weapons because they were constructed of a primitive form of steel. Steel has a high content of carbon that determines the hardness of the steel, while wrought iron has only about .1 percent carbon content and is quite soft. For a cutting edge, the metal should have approximately 1 percent, or ten times that of wrought iron. Modern steel, which has only been made since about 1740 and only on a large scale since the Bessemer process was developed in 1856, is made by melting and casting. Carolingian sword construction was quite elaborate and required a forge, heavy iron hammers, and blacksmithing tongs and charcoal. Bellows had been known for hundreds of years and were used to oxygenate the fire to higher temperatures for the forging of the iron. Charcoal was used, for the iron needs to be heated for a long time in contact with a carbonaceous material such as charcoal in order for the iron to absorb some of the carbon. This carburized the surface layer of the iron. This steelwork for swords was time consuming and costly, but the results were often more valuable than gold. In fact, a sword was worth the equivalent of three cows. Therefore, most weapons were probably not made of steel, but of iron. The nobility may have been armed with steel swords, although of highly variable quality, but the average soldier's sword was iron as well as the heads of lances, axes, adzes, daggers, and knives.

Iron, of course, was not used solely for weapons. Horseshoes were made of iron, as were plow points, scythes, sickles, bill hooks, and knives for agricultural work (see "Agriculture" earlier in this chapter). Even oxen were sometimes shod to keep their hooves from splitting under difficult working conditions. Among artisans, smithing hammers, knives, chisels, adzes, saws, scissors, and other specialized tools and implements were made of iron. One of the most common uses of iron was for nails. Wooden pegging was sometimes used in building construction, but so were nails, as well as iron bands, clamps, and hinges. Church bells were also made of hammered iron rather than bronze or brass. Only after approximately 900 C.E. were bells usually cast in bronze.

Interestingly, iron production increased during the Carolingian era from the preceding centuries, but most other metal production did not. All of the other metals of gold, silver, copper, bronze, and brass required costly production plants. Consequently, as new supplies of iron were produced, the supply of some other metals declined dramatically, and a great deal of the metal worked in this period was probably reused from treasure confiscated during conquests.

Gold and Silver

Gold- and silversmithing were of significant interest to the Carolingians. Gold, silver, and copper mines that had been closed since Roman times were reopened, and new ones were brought on line in the regions of Saxony, Bohemia, and Silesia beginning in the 780s. In western Neutria, successful silver mining took place at a location now known as Melle, but in Carolingian times as Metalia. Along with iron, gold and especially silver supplies increased marginally over the amounts available in the preceding two centuries. Even so, it has been estimated that the amount of precious-metal money in circulation dropped by more than 90 percent between 14 C.E. at the death of Augustus and 800 C.E.

Other Metals

Other metal or related crafts that were plied during the Carolingian age included cloisonné, inlaying, niello, filigree, engraving, embossing, and lifting. Inlaying is the process of casting metal with insets or etching into the metal or forming compartments by soldering onto a back piece of metal tiny wires of metal into shapes and then filling in the spots with another metal to produce geometric designs with different colors or even images of animals or humans. This was often done with niello work, which is a metal alloy of copper and lead that when used creates a black metal that is attractive when it is inlaid in silver or gold. Cloisonné was produced by much the same method of soldering small wires to a metal back to form enclosed shapes and then filling the enclosure with ground glass. When the object was fired in a kiln at the proper temperature, the powdered glass would melt and, when cooled, would harden into glass in the shape of the wire containment. When the openings or compartments in the metal are created by casting or gouging, and the glass is poured in as a liquid, the product is properly called champlevé, although it is often referred to as cloisonné. This process was used extensively in Europe from the sixth to the ninth centuries and reached extraordinary heights in some of the Germanic lands, such as Anglo-Saxon England. Stunningly beautiful champlevé pieces were found among the Sutton Hoo burial objects, which date from the seventh century C.E. In many of the pieces of jewelry from the Carolingian Empire, decorations were created with a combination of inlay of gold, silver, niello, cloisonné, champlevé, and gems.

Utrecht Psalter, University of Utrecht, Ms. 32, fol. 6v. In the upper right is a blacksmith at his forge heating metal to be hammered.

Bronze

Bronzework was done in the Carolingian Empire, although sophistication was lacking in the work. Bronze is an alloy made from combining copper and tin and requires more elaborate production works than for iron. Therefore, bronze weapons and armor virtually disappeared in these centuries. Around 800, Charlemagne had bronze doors made for the royal church at Aachen. They were probably one of the largest projects in bronze in many years, but the doors are very simple in design, with a cast molding that forms three square or rectangular panels. The handles, which could also serve as knockers, are of lion heads.

Brass

Brass was a relatively new development among metals; the Romans contributed this discovery. Brass is an alloy of copper and zinc, but it was not until the nineteenth century that it was made by melting pure copper and zinc together. From the Roman days throughout the Middle Ages, brass was made by melting copper and then adding calamine, which is zinc carbonate, to the molten metal. Although zinc vaporizes at the temperature necessary to melt copper, if it is added to molten copper, enough of the zinc is absorbed into the copper to form brass. It is a durable metal, and with its almost goldlike color it was popular, especially in the Roman Empire. Even though brass production had one of its major centers near Aachen in the third century, production seems to have disappeared during most of the Carolingian era.

Parchment

One of the important trades for the Carolingian era was parchment making performed by a professional known as a *percamenarius* or parchmenter. Parchment as a writing surface was usually made from the skins of sheep, goats, or calves, although parchment could be made from any mammal skin, including rabbit, deer, or pig. For a particularly fine writing surface, calf, kid, or lamb was preferable and is today usually known as vellum, although experts sometimes use the words *parchment* and *vellum* interchangeably. For especially valuable codices, stillborn or newly born calf, kid, or lamb was used because the skin was thinner and softer.

The skin had to be carefully removed to avoid tears or cutting holes in the middle, so the job of the parchmenter was to look over available skins and select only the best. The skin was washed in cold water for a day or more and then dipped into a solution of water and lime (made from baked limestone that was then crushed) for up to a week to help in the removal of fat and hair. The skins became limp and slippery and were then stretched slightly and scraped with a knife to remove all hair and impurities. The knife had a curved blade to make it easier to scrape without cutting, tearing, or piercing the soft skin and a wooden handle parallel to the blade for the parchmenter to stand over the skin and use two hands while scraping. After all of the hair had been scraped away, the skin was turned and the flesh side was scraped to remove all flesh and fat. The skins were washed thoroughly a second time and then stretched on a special frame that enabled the parchmenter to continually adjust the tension by turning pegs. Any tiny hole or tear would appear at this point as the skin was stretched. These might be repaired by fine stitching or, if small, might be left to become tiny holes in the finished parchment, reducing its quality and value. Scraped again, this time to pare the surface to an even thinness and smoothness, the skins were kept wet during this process. Finally they were allowed to dry and then were scraped again. When this process was finished, the skins were dusted with powdered chalk and rubbed with a pumice stone to make the surface as white and smooth as possible.

If the skin had not been pared away adequately in the process, the finished parchment might have a glassy, shiny surface (seen today in some of the less valuable manuscripts) that was difficult to write on, for the ink would not "take." Sometimes this shiny surface was preferred for the look and because it resisted oils and dirt. Properly finished parchment was thin, soft, and very flexible. If it was prepared properly, a very creamy white surface of great smoothness and evenness could be produced, although the original hair side is always slightly different in color from the flesh side, usually a little darker or yellower. The surface at its best was as good as paper, more flexible, and, most people have claimed, more durable. The slightly softer parchment was preferable for most codices. Sometimes, for very expensive codices, the entire page of parchment was dyed, often purple, and then the writing might be done in silver or even gold.

The number of sheets that could be cut from one skin depended on the size of the skin and the size of the desired page, although since skins are oblong, most books were made oblong. That is the reason that books, even today, tend to be longer than they are wide. From a sheepskin only two pages of the larger size might be made since the sheet was a double page, creased down the center and stitched at this center crease to form two pages, called a bifolio, which would be added to other bifolios in the codex. To make a smaller book, the parchment sheet might be folded in quarters or even in eighths, and then the edges would be cut free and the center crease stitched. This is called a gathering. Then groups of gatherings, as many as needed, could be stitched together into a codex of many pages. By folding the sheet this way, pages in a codex always have skin side to skin side and flesh side to flesh side.

If the quality of the parchment was good, a piece could not be cut too close to the edges or leg holes or near a tear or hole created during processing. This meant that as demand increased during the Carolingian era, more parchment was needed, and quality sometimes declined, with parchment that was not as white or smooth or parchment with nicks or rough edges.

Wine and Ale

Ale and wine were often produced in the home, although there was also a need for commercial production. Grapes grew then, as now, very well in most of the territories in the Carolingian Empire. Vineyards were highly prized and cared for. For wine production, the grapes were harvested in late summer or early fall. The grapes were then crushed and left in great tubs to naturally ferment the juice into wine. It is not known whether the Carolingians produced various kinds of wine such as red and white or sweet and dry, but certainly the process was very ancient and would have been known by their civilization. Most wine at the time was mixed with water before consumption, so the quantity of water mixed in would determine the alcoholic content of the drink. The Church was a major consumer of wine for the daily communions as well as for the priests and monks.

Ale was made from any grain available, although barley, which grew well in the Carolingian Empire, made the finest ale. The barley grain was first steeped in water to begin the germination or sprouting of the barley. This process naturally transformed the starches in the barley kernels into sugars. Once this process reached the proper point, the germination was halted by mildly roasting the grain over a fire using a hair sieve, often made from horsehair, to hold the grain. The grain was then slowly heated in a vat with water to form what is known as mash. Yeast was added, and the grain sugars fermented into alcohols. The mash was occasionally stirred with a broom, which after each brewing was hung up to dry since the yeast that dried onto the broom would accelerate the process the next time it was used. At least in later years of the Middle Ages, the brewer might hang the broom outside the front door to dry and to act as a sign that a new brewing had just been completed. After the sugars had turned to alcohol, the yeast was removed and could then be used to bake bread, and the liquid or wort was drained off and cooled. One way to test the ale's alcohol content, to ensure that the sugars had all been converted, was to pour a little on a seat and sit in it while drinking a tankard. If the person upon rising stuck to the seat, then there was still too much sugar in the ale, and yeast might again be added. When the product was finished, it then was barreled and was ready for drinking. The difference between this drink and the modern beer or "ale" is that modern drinks are made with the addition of hops. Hops clarify the liquid and add a slightly bitter taste, but most importantly, act as a preservative. The ale of the Carolingian age would not have had a preservative factor and in warm weather would have spoiled quite quickly. Consequently, ale production was never terribly large on a commercial basis since it could not be produced for long-distance shipment or for storage. Ale often had flavorings added during production, but unlike wine, ale was drunk without watering it down. The alcoholic content would have varied dramatically from brewer to brewer and from batch to batch. Later in the Middle Ages, special ales were made for holy days with higher alcoholic content, and March and October ales were also made with higher alcoholic content because these months had the best temperatures for the ideal cooling of the wort. Hence the finest ales were generally produced during these months. Whether special ales were produced during the Carolingian age is not known, but March and October would still have been the best months for producing ale. This fact accounts for the Octoberfests of later days.

MARKETS

The vibrant economy of the Roman Empire had crumbled along with its political, legal, and military structures. Recent archaeological studies have proven that most of the Roman towns within the Frankish empire, as well as towns in Italy itself, were severely reduced in size, sometimes merely continuations of the Roman towns in name only. Many of these towns disappeared entirely, only to be revived in the tenth or eleventh century. Even those locations that were cities in the Roman Empire were generally reduced by the seventh century to small markets with limited commercial production and almost no export to distant locales. There was clearly a discontinuity with the economic conditions of the ancient past. Charlemagne probably did not have a coherent policy of town building the way he did for monastic renewal. Nor did Charlemagne look to ancient Rome as a model for his town building the way he did in his revival of education and learning.

The markets of the Carolingian Empire included local and regional markets as well as long-distance trade. Pepin the Short ordered designated market days in the cathedral towns, for specified markets were the best way to control trade, and regulated trade provided taxes. It was for this reason that markets of certain goods were set for specific days, and toll gates were erected on roads and into towns. Any goods carried into or out of a market town would be taxed. In 802, Charlemagne forbade the sale of goods after dark or anywhere other than in public locations, again because the trade of goods needed to be seen to be taxed.

Long-Distance Trade

Some long-distance trade existed in Europe even during the low points of the sixth and seventh centuries. Even though precious-metal currencies declined as dramatically as by more than 90 percent between 14 C.E. and 800 C.E., as mentioned earlier, they did not disappear completely. As long as there was currency, there was long-distance trade. There had long been substantial trade between Francia and the surrounding civilizations. One of the long-held historical theories was that the rise of the Muslim world in the seventh century cut off the European West from its trade contacts with the rest of the world. That theory has been proven untrue in that it was not the rise of Islam that broke the ties with the past and with the rest of the world. However, it is true that much of the long-distance trade disappeared, but it never became extinct. Even in the seventh century, a lively trade must have existed between the Merovingian Empire and Anglo-Saxon Britain. When the Sutton Hoo cenotaph burial (it contained no human remains) of circa 650 C.E. was opened in 1939, it contained thirty-seven gold coins, all Merovingian.

Coinage and Currency

There has been debate about the significance of coinage in eighth- and ninth-century Europe. Coins serve five basic functions: a medium of exchange, a means of noncommercial payments such as taxes and fines, a standard of value, a standard of deferred payment, and a means of stored value. Some historians have seen the main purpose of coins in the eighth and ninth centuries as stored value because many of the coins that have been discovered have been in buried hoarded collections and because many of the Carolingian coins look relatively new and unworn. However, the coins that are discovered are often likely to be ones buried in a hoard. It is less common to find individual coins and unlikely that bog people will be discovered with pockets loaded with coins. Second, Carolingian coins were struck or minted very carefully and very heavily, meaning that the dies for casting were cut deeply. This produced coins with high and sharp relief. Therefore, they often still look in mint condition. These coins were not meant just for the nobility nor as a means for saving value, for they were minted in a number of locations around the kingdom, including Aachen, Amiens, Quentovic, Rheims, Rouen, Paris, Lyon, Strasbourg, Verdun, Melle, Milan, Pavia, Dinant, Maastricht, and Dorestad. Charlemagne tried to consolidate minting to the royal palace at Aachen, but was unsuccessful in doing so.

The existence of so many mints indicates that coins were needed regularly and continuously around the kingdom, and there could be no other purpose than trade that would require such continuous supply of coins. Some historians have suggested that the purpose of coins was for hoarding of treasure or that they were used solely by large-scale merchants, but the number of coins in circulation proves that coinage was primarily for regular trade. There has been a great deal of debate about the number of coins that were in circulation in the Carolingian Empire. An estimate has been made for the number of coins minted in Mercia (England) under King Offa, a contemporary of Charlemagne, of 6.7 million. Estimates would suggest that the number of coins minted during Charlemagne's reign was considerably larger than this, perhaps several times this. Even 10 million coins would provide numbers far beyond savings of treasure and even beyond use by a few large-scale merchants. Numbers such as these would suggest that many people were using coins on a regular basis for everyday trade.

The second part of this premise about the lack of use of Carolingian coins is based on the belief that barter (exchanging goods or services for other goods or services) was more common than money exchange. Barter can work and certainly did exist in the Carolingian economy, just as it has always existed in every economy. But anyone who has tried to barter goods for services or even goods for goods knows that the ability to exchange in an equal and standard value acceptable to both sides is often extremely difficult even between friends. Trade in the marketplace and trade over long distances would be nearly impossible without a medium of exchange, a standard of value, and a standard of deferred payment. Again, the number of coins that were minted in the Carolingian Empire suggests that coins were available for trade to large numbers of people. If so, the need for barter would be reduced.

Carolingian currency is difficult to track, yet it can reveal a great deal about the economy and about government policies toward the economy. Changes in weight or metallic composition are as important as the supposed value of the currency that is struck. To be able to know the influence of coins, one has to know the date that they were struck, and although that would seem to be an easy task, it is notoriously difficult. Almost none of the coins of the Carolingian era can be dated to a specific year, and more often they cannot even be dated to a decade. Some coins can only be located to within a sixty- or even eighty-year period. Even though the inscription on a coin should locate it to a reign, that has not proven to be true in the Carolingian era, and none of the Carolingian coins had dates on them. Sometimes coins continued to be struck after a monarch's death. Sometimes the son of a monarch would begin to mint coins before his father's death. Sometimes a monarch would mint more than one type of coin simultaneously. Coin finds rarely help in dating the coins. Coins were usually buried without other objects that might help in dating, and without any explanation of why or when the coins were buried.

Charlemagne began a new mintage along with his new monetary reform around 790. Monetary reforms were begun by his father Pepin in 755, who tried to clarify the value of the Carolingian currency, but the reforms were only brought to full effect by Charlemagne. The documents refer to the new coins or the reforms in the early 790s, but the dating cannot be much more precise than that. It is clear from the records that Charlemagne was trying to formulate a coherent economic policy. Clarifying monetary issues was at the root of this.

When Charlemagne established a new system of currency around 790, he hoped to gain greater control over the minting of money and to produce a more consistent currency whose value would not be questioned. It is also quite possible that the catalyst for the reform was a falling out between Charlemagne and King Offa of Mercia. They had agreed to a marriage of Charlemagne's son Charles to Offa's daughter. Offa would only agree to the marriage if Charlemagne's daughter Berta was also given to Offa's son. Charlemagne was so infuriated by being pressured, especially to hand over his beloved Berta, that the marriage was called off and Charlemagne decreed that no Anglo-Saxon merchants could land in Gaul. King Offa then decided to reform his currency, minting a new silver penny at his mint at Canterbury, and to set a new and higher standard for coinage.

Charlemagne decided to proceed with the reform that he had been working on at least since 787 and to set an even higher standard. To heighten the value of the new pound, so that it would replace any old currency, the weight of the pound was increased. The new standard had twenty solidi to the pound and twelve denarii to the solidus, making 240 denarii or pennies to the pound. (This arrangement was soon copied by England's King Offa and was so sound that it continued to be used until it was dropped by the United Kingdom in 1971.) He ordered the minting of new silver denarii, the coin most important for everyday trade. Minting of all these new silver coins was possible because of the new silver mines that had been opened up in the East and the West. Increased trade between England and the Carolingian Empire eventually resulted after the rift between Charlemagne and Offa was resolved.

Economic Standards

Capitularies were issued that indicate that the Carolingians were concerned about economics and understood that the strength of the economy was at the root of the strength of the empire. Charlemagne's reforms in the economy, including his monetary reforms, were as substantial as the artistic and literary reforms that have become known as the Carolingian Renaissance, but their endurance was not always as great. However, the standardization of currency was extremely important. Charlemagne also tried to do the same with weights and measures. Citing Proverbs 20.10 from the Bible, "A double standard in weights and measures is an abomination to the Lord," Charlemagne ordered that all weights and measures should be equal, exact, and just both for buying and selling in the towns, monasteries, and manors. Charlemagne complained to King Offa of Mercia that the bolts of English woolen cloth coming into the empire were of varying lengths and needed to be standardized.

One example of how Charlemagne may not have understood economics, especially for long-distance trade, was his position on usury or lending money with the charge of interest. Charlemagne defined usury as getting back more than one originally gave. The Church had forbidden interest-bearing loans on the grounds that one was charging for time and that God gave everyone time equally and freely. Receiving interest in money or in kind for a loan incurred a severe fine. Part of the concern was that the security on repayment of a loan plus interest was the borrower himself, and when the loan came due and had to be repaid in full, the borrower, as security, might be forfeit to the lender. However, loans, which were necessary to fuel trade and commerce, were possible only if repayment included interest or some additional payment above the amount originally borrowed. If this were not the case, there would be no reason to lend money, or land, or goods, and trade would stop functioning on speculation of profits to be made in the future.

Travel for Markets

The great markets for which people traveled long distances were a feature of the twelfth century, not the ninth. Travel was too difficult and uncertain. Charlemagne tried to have the old Roman roads maintained, but this was too large a task even for him. Under the best of conditions, humans walk four miles per hour over long distances. Much of the time the roads would not be in the best condition, so that rate would be slower. Any up-and-down travel, which one is bound to have except in Flanders, decreases the rate even further. Horses, which were too expensive to be common in travel or commerce, only walk at about four to five miles per hour over long distances. A horse can canter at twenty miles per hour or more, but it can maintain that rapid pace for only a few miles, perhaps as many as six or eight. When a horse is exhausted, it will simply stop running and drop to a trot or walk or stop altogether. At a trot, a horse can travel for twelve to fifteen miles if it is well conditioned. For longer distances, until the invention of the railroad in the nineteenth century, humans could generally travel at five miles per hour or less, and a day's walk normally would be anywhere from six to ten hours according to the conditions of the terrain, the weather, and the walker. To travel from Ghent to Mainz took fifteen days, from Rome to Pavia twenty-one days.

Not only were the roads bad and the terrain uneven, but bridges across rivers were extremely rare and often dangerous when they did exist. There were bridges at major points, and when they decayed or burned, royal orders were usually given to replace them. At Mainz the wooden bridge crossing the Rhine burned in 813 and was replaced with stone. Charlemagne ordered the maintenance of bridges across the Seine, the Marne, the Oise, the Elbe, and the Rhine. In some places ferries were used to cross rivers. Fording a river on foot is difficult, and even though the roads would route to a normally fordable location, high water would change that. Fording on horseback is a little easier, but still dangerous, and fording with a cart or wagon is always perilous. Charlemagne's armies had specially built wagons with waterproofed bodies and tightly sealed leather covers to make them as waterproof as possible and floatable. Most wagons, however, would not have been so well made. Hauling a cart or wagon was also nearly impossible when the roads were muddy, for the wheels would quickly get bogged down all the way to the axles. It was for this reason that the Carolingian armies moved in the summer, and the same was true for the movement of wagons of goods. The other factor in the speed at which goods could move overland was the source of tractive power. Horses can pull a lightly loaded cart or wagon at about three miles per hour on a smooth, level surface, while the more common oxcart moved at approximately two miles an hour.

Bandits and other roving peoples also made life on the road dangerous. The Carolingian government tried to eliminate banditry on the roads, but with such a vast empire and such limited resources, policing the roads everywhere was impossible. When the likelihood of successfully carrying goods to a distant market is low, people tend not to attempt it at all. The rate of success needs to balance the risk as well as the profit. Extremely high-value goods that may make a great profit can stand a greater risk, but not one where there is little chance of ever realizing the profit.

It is always easier to move goods by water, although moving by water is generally slower than moving by land. Moving upriver can be slow going, while floating down is rapid and relatively easy. There is also the advantage of floating weight as opposed to rolling it. With a well-built boat, a large amount of weight can be floated without much effort, while that weight being rolled requires a great deal of force. For that reason, goods moved overland lost their value quickly since the cost of transport soon equaled the value of the goods for sale. On water, more weight for less effort meant that goods could be moved longer distances without losing their value. Thus in the Carolingian Empire, goods did not move very far overland unless they were extremely valuable. The Carolingian Empire was very much a land-based empire, but the Carolingians certainly recognized the advantages of floating goods. Large amounts of goods were moved by river by individual merchants and by monks. Merchants carried grain, salt, iron, and many other goods on all the major rivers of the empire. The monastery of Saint-Germain-des-Prés had four ships plying the Loire.

By following the finds of coins from the Carolingian Empire, trade routes can be discerned. There was very clearly a line of trade between northern Gaul and Italy. In fact, the line can be extended to southern England. Trade moved in both directions along this north-south axis. From Italy, it connected to the rest of the Mediterranean, the Middle East, and North Africa, and from the north, through both Frisia and England, it connected eastward to Denmark, the Baltic, and Scandinavia. Within the Carolingian Empire, the trade routes tended to follow the rivers, such as the Loire, Seine, Meuse, Rhine, Rhone, and Danube.

Overseas Trade

The Carolingians were not renowned for oceangoing ships. They traded with lands overseas, but the carriers were most often foreigners such as the Frisians, who although technically part of the Carolingian

Empire saw themselves as separate. The Frisian cogs and hulks, both cargo-carrying ships of short, wide stature, plied the North Sea and carried goods between the Carolingian Empire and England and Scandinavia. Ports along the Frisian coast as well as the Flanders and Normandy coasts were active in overseas trade. The ships of the Carolingians and Frisians were not nearly as seaworthy as the ships then constructed in the Muslim world and in China. The European boats were clinker built, where the boards that form the sides were overlapping planks riveted together like the siding of a house. This requires more wood and yet makes for a rigid structure. They were pointed at both ends, much like the Viking boats of the same era. The ships were open decked and used a single mast carrying a large square sail. A single large steering oar near the stern acted as the rudder. The Muslims were building carvel construction, where the planks are edge to edge on a preconstructed frame. Holes were bored in the planking near the edges, and the planks were bound with fiber twine inside over stringers or long thin pieces of wood. The seams between the planks were caulked with pitch or resin, although the Muslims had the advantage over later European carvel-built ships in that they had teak and coconut wood available from Southeast Asia. These woods, once cured or aged, would not split, crack, or shrink like the woods used in the Carolingian ships. This made the Muslim ships lighter and tighter than the Carolingian ships. The Muslims were also using a triangular or lateen sail that allowed the ships to sail far closer into the wind than square-sailed ships. That meant that Muslim ships were far more maneuverable than Carolingian ships.

Canal Project

In 793, Charlemagne began a major canal-building project that he had dreamed of for years. It was to connect the Rhine and the Danube via several tributary rivers. If this project had been accomplished, it would have connected the two largest waterways of the empire and would have completed a route by inland water from the North Sea to the Black Sea and Constantinople. Militarily this canal was to provide movement into the Avar territories to the east that Charlemagne was in the middle of conquering. Equipment could have been moved up the Rhine and then down the Danube. Charlemagne understood the importance of commerce moving into the region once the Avars were subdued. A vast workforce was assembled, and work began on the canal. Archaeological evidence corroborates the *Royal Frankish Annals* that at least 4,000 feet of canal, 300 feet wide, were dug between the two tributaries in the summer of 793. According to the *Annals*, because of continuous rain and the fact that the land was naturally swampy, all that the workers dug out during the day filled back in at night, and the project was abandoned. Charlemagne was also distracted from the grandiose project by two major rebellions late that year, one by the Saxons and one by the Saracens; the Saxons had been engaged in an ongoing decades-long conflict, while the Saracen rebellion was a foreshadowing of the invasions that would eventually destroy the Carolingian Empire.

Seaports

In 811, Charlemagne traveled to the port city of Boulogne to inspect the fleet that he had ordered to be constructed the year before. While he was there, he ordered the restoration of the lighthouse that had been constructed long before and had a fire lit on its top at night to direct ships coming into the harbor. There had been an expansion of the Channel ports in the seventh century, but some of these must have fallen into decline by the late eighth or early ninth century. Charlemagne understood their value and was concerned about their renovation. In the second half of the ninth century, as the Viking incursions increased, it was the Channel ports that were among the first to be lost. Charlemagne had enough trouble trying to expand the empire and maintain its territories. He had never been able to commit enough resources to control the seas, so consequently the Carolingian merchants tended to remain land based and left most of the overseas trade to others such as the Frisians, the Anglo-Saxons, and the Muslims. Both the contemporary Muslims and the Chinese seemed to understand better that they needed to have some control of the seas. Charlemagne seemed to comprehend that overseas trade was important, but not that building a fleet that could control the seas around his empire might ensure its continued existence.

6

THE CHURCH: RELIGION, MONASTICISM, AND EDUCATION

RELIGION

Christianity had become the official religion of the Roman Empire in 394. With this official endorsement and ensured defense, Christianity spread fairly rapidly throughout most of the empire. Asceticism was one of the attractions, but in an era of social decline the morality of Christianity was also attractive. In many areas of the empire, the spread of Christianity had the same power and ruthlessness as the later spread of Islam. Pagan idols were destroyed, and people often felt compelled to convert to Christianity. By the end of the fourth century, Christianity had become the majority religion in the empire.

The Germanic tribes that had entered the western half of the Empire in the third to fifth centuries were not Christian. Some tribes converted, often halfheartedly, to Arian Christianity, which was a widespread belief within Christianity that the Father and the Son were not co-eternal and not of precisely the same substance, in essence, that the Father and the Son were separate entities, not different forms of the whole. This belief made more sense to the non-Greco-Roman mind of the Germanic tribesmen. The idea that the Trinity was three independent and distinct entities that were also one and the same was a difficult concept to accept. However, the Church at Rome had declared Arianism wrong and heretical. In other words, a true Christian could not believe it.

The Franks, as latecomers to the Roman Empire, judiciously avoided the pitfalls of the other German groups and also carefully balanced them-

Utrecht Psalter, University of Utrecht, Ms. 32, fol. 15r. The church's design shows apses and crossing, but looks more Mediterranean than Carolingian. Notice the army tents in the foreground, both left and right.

selves against the remnants of the Roman aristocracy. In doing so, Clovis, king of the Franks, in 500 converted to orthodox or Catholic Christianity. His conversion gained for the Franks the automatic support of the Church, the only Europe-wide superstructure left after the fall of the Roman Empire in the West, and gained for the Church the support of one of the powerful Germanic kingdoms that had established itself within the realm of the former Western Roman Empire.

When Clovis converted, he had 5,000 of his warrior nobles convert with him. This started the Franks down the path of mutual admiration and competition with the Catholic Church. Christianity became the source of Romanization, the source of literacy and education, and the source of acceptance by the old Roman aristocracy and by the Byzantine Empire, which was the continuing eastern half of the Roman Empire.

Paganism

In many ways, Christianity had become Romanized by the end of the fourth or at least the fifth century, only to become barbarized by the end of the seventh. Animistic and magical practices had become the norm for many who claimed to practice Christianity, including many of the clergy.

Christianity, however, did not immediately gain acceptance among all of the Franks. Paganism died a hard death, hanging on in many ways for centuries. Customs that had been pagan were often absorbed into Christianity to make the new religion more palatable. Pagan gods were turned into saints. Pagan celebrations such as the winter solstice were combined with Christian holy days so that the birth of Jesus, a date that was not known nor of much concern to Christianity, became Christmas, celebrated remarkably close to the old pagan celebration.

As late as 740, a handlist was made of pagan practices, probably by a church official. This included sacrilege (stealing or desecrating sacred things) at the graves of the dead and over the departed, swine feasts in February, sacred rites of the woods, rites upon stones, sacred rites of Mercury and Jupiter, sacrifices, incantations (the use of spells or charms), auguries (foretelling events from omens) from dung or sneezings of birds, horses, or cattle or from animal brains, diviners and sorcerers, and worshiping eclipses, storms, and idols of dough or rags or wooden feet and hands. In a life filled with the entire night of darkness where one had no idea what might be happening beyond one's abode, surrounded by thick unknown woods, where life was always on the edge with illness, injury, and death, as well as fire, flood, and starvation, people looked for a religion or occult that could help to provide some sort of explanation and control. If divining bird sneezings (which were interpreted from the pattern) or the content of dung could provide an explanation for the otherwise unexplainable events around one, it was useful. If worshiping stone or wooden idols seemed to provide control over the massively overwhelming odds of the world, then it was done. Christianity had to compete with these superstitions. If Christianity could not provide explanations, edification, and consolation at the same level as the pagan practices, it would not replace them.

But Christianity did become of utmost importance to the Franks and especially to Charlemagne. He wanted very much to strengthen it and renew it to its old Roman luster. For Charlemagne, the Roman Church was the Roman Empire. It still echoed the administrative structure of Rome, being urban based, with its bishops residing in all the major cities, or at least what remained of former major cities. The Church spoke the language of the Roman Empire and could read the literature of the Roman Empire. But when Charlemagne came to power in 768, even the Christian Church was in decay.

Clergy were not always educated. There are records of masses and baptisms said by clergy who did not really know Latin, and questions were raised whether these masses and baptisms were valid. Communications throughout Europe had broken down, and regional churches were developing substantial differences. For instance, the Church in Ireland and northern England calculated the dating for Easter in a different way than the rest of the Church. This was resolved at the Synod of Whitby in northern England in 663. The viability of a universal church was being threatened.

With the Carolingian conquests east of the Rhine, there were additional problems in that most of the new German territories were pagan. Boniface (born Wynfrith in England circa 675, d. 754; renamed Boniface by Pope Gregory II) cut down the great sacred oak tree of Geismar just as Charlemagne in his conquest of the Saxons felled the Irminsul, the great tree worshiped by the Saxons as the upholder of the heavens. Charlemagne had to legislate against the worship of forest gods and the practices of the pagans. In 785, the Saxons were ordered that anyone caught cremating the dead would himself be condemned to death. Charlemagne went on to prohibit worship of springs, trees, or forests.

Superstition

It was certainly not just the pagan Saxons who held these superstitious beliefs. Many people throughout the Carolingian realm believed strongly in magic, superstition, astrology, sorcery, divination, and charms. Women in particular were suspected of participating and more often did participate in superstitious activities. It was women who were most often the herbalists, making remedies for illnesses. When things went well and even more when they did not, the woman was suspected of collusion with evil spirits or the devil. Women were also the midwives, and again when something went wrong, it was easy to accuse the midwife of evil dealings. The monthly menstrual cycle of women was not well understood by men and was therefore feared and suspected. Women were probably more often suspected of *maleficia* or evildoing because they spent more time apart from others in the house or garden, whereas the men were more often together or out in the open fields where their activities could be seen. When a person's grain did poorly or a cow got sick, it was easiest to accuse the neighboring woman.

The problem with widespread superstition, as far as the government was concerned, was that it was not Christianity. The two existed side by side, but as long as people believed in both, they could not be considered true Christians. By the eighth century, there was a crisis in the Church caused by the widespread lack of conformity to true Christianity and the widespread superstition and lack of proper belief and ritual. The Christian Church was supposed to be a universal church, a church with beliefs the same everywhere and a liturgy (the public rites and services of the Church) that was uniform.

Need for Uniformity in the Church

In any kingdom, there is the need for some form of unity to hold the people together. In a vast empire such as Charlemagne's, there was an especially strong need for unity. Charlemagne understood these issues and believed that a universal church that was literate, with schools for training clerics as well as laypersons, and with ties to the universality of the past Roman Empire, was a very useful instrument. It could provide a commonalty for all the various peoples of the empire. It could provide a clear structure of morality and order in which the people were mollified and subdued. It could provide literate administrators. It could provide a hierarchical superstructure throughout the empire for administering the king's wishes and commands. It could provide order to the empire.

Saints' Relics

It was not until the sixth century that the title of "saint" became commonly associated with the dead whose cult was publicly celebrated in the churches. Originally these were the illustrious Christians, usually martyrs, and then church fathers and other leaders of the Church or performers of miracles.

Commemoration of the lives of holy people (saints) was as old as Christianity itself (see "Death and Burial" in chapter 4), but the Roman tradition that saints' bodies should remain intact and in the place of their original burial was strongly defended. In the ninth century, the same current of interest in the knowledge of Christianity and in Roman Christian liturgy on the part of the Carolingians and the interest in extending its authority on the part of the Church in Rome that sent a flood of books northward also started a flow of saints' relics northward. Relics are bodies, parts of bodies, or objects owned by individuals who have been deemed saints. The body or objects were venerated, and it was believed that through this veneration miraculous benefits could be gained. During the pontificate of Paul I (757–767), saints' bodies were exhumed from peripheral churches around Rome and taken to St. Peter's to exalt the importance of the papacy. Consequently, during the ninth century, with the attempts at unifying the Church and strengthening Christianity in Francia, the bodies of saints or pieces of them were sent from their original resting places in Rome to churches and monasteries in the north to establish importance for new foundations or for renewal at old ones. Shrines were established and churches were constructed or renovated for the display of these relics. Relics became prestigious items to acquire and could establish a church as an important pilgrimage site. Bodily

Saint-Germigny-des-Prés Church (France). A typical Carolingian-era church with apses and central crossing. [M. Clausen.]

relics became so valuable that a trade in stolen body parts existed in the Carolingian age.

Need for Church Reform

If Charlemagne was to build a unified empire, he needed a reformed Church. The papacy was willing to allow Charlemagne to take the lead on reforms because the papacy needed Charlemagne's protection, and the Church knew that it needed reform. Pope Gregory I had called for reforms long before, but only with Charlemagne was there the coercion to bring about the reforms.

Charlemagne began to reform the Church in numerous ways. In his General Admonition of 789, Charlemagne demanded that priests have good manners and lead a just and fitting life, as commanded in the gospel, so that by their example people would be led to the service of God. In a capitulary from 803, it was ordered that priests not be ordained without examination. At the councils of Tours in 813 and Mainz in 847, it was recommended that priests be able to preach in the local language of their parishoners—the vernacular. This was sometimes a problem when priests from the western part of the empire were moved into churches in the eastern regions of the empire, but the more common problem was that the priests knew little more than the vernacular. Only through the knowledge of Latin could the priest be a part of a universal Church, while use of the vernacular connected the priest to the people.

There were Greek-Latin glossaries, so some were even able to learn Greek to read church fathers and commentaries from the eastern Mediterranean, but this was rare indeed.

Charlemagne was willing to exhort the people by stating his own beliefs, probably laid out, in actuality, by his leading clerics. His doctrine included the basics of Christianity: belief in one God, the Trinity of Father, Son, and Holy Spirit, knowledge that God's son Jesus was begotten of the Holy Spirit out of the Virgin Mary, and that for humans' salvation Christ suffered death and rose from the dead on the third day, ascended into heaven, sits at the right hand of God, and will come to judge the living and the dead. His statement goes on to assure that baptism saves people from their sins, that there is eternal life, and that confession, repentance, and forgiveness relieve one of daily sins. People should be loving, humble, and kind and care about the poor and downtrodden.

Enforcement of Unity

The religion of the day was maintained with real enforcement. If one committed a sin, one had to be contrite, admit the sin, and make some payment for rectitude. As in the old Germanic law codes, a payment had to be made to the wronged. In the case of sin, the wronged was God, and therefore a payment of some sort had to be made to God. The penitentials were manuals compiled for the guidance of priests in assigning appropriate penalties or penances for sins. Laypeople were to confess their sins at least once a year, clerics more often, and at the confession the priest would assign the penances in a graded scale appropriate for any sin. If a priest committed a sin such as drunkenness, the penance was different from that assigned to a lay individual. The penance for a cleric might last for months or even years for a heinous offense such as murder. While one was doing penance, he might be required to abstain from most foods and observe a diet of bread and water, and even to abstain from intercourse.

Merit and Penance

In the eighth and ninth centuries, the concept of purgatory was not fully developed, so if a person died before completing the assigned penance, there was no method of paying for the sin, as there would later be by spending time in purgatory. The sinner would thus be damned to hell. Hence people took their religion seriously and feared the committing of sin and even more the appointment of the penance, for it was often a penalty they were unable to fulfill. This is also why the transmission of merit from one individual to another was important and why the prayers of the priests and monks were important and valuable. Establishing or endowing a monastery provided merit by having given the gift and further provided an endless source of merit through the intercession of the prayers of the monks. This also explains the Carolingian monastic reforms in that monks living proper lives and saying proper prayers were more beneficial than corrupt illiterate monks.

The eighth and ninth centuries saw a number of other reforms instituted or confirmed. Charlemagne reestablished the system of metropolitans or bishoprics each headed by bishops or what came to be archbishops. This structure had evolved in the late Roman Empire following the structure of the Roman imperial government. Each major city had been a seat of Roman government for its territory, and within the Church each metropolitan ruled ecclesiastically over its surrounding territory. For the Carolingians, this provided not only a clear hierarchical structure for the Church, but also a governmental structure for the king, since all clergy, including archbishops, were answerable to the king. By the ninth century, the offices of bishops or abbots were considered benefices granted by the king and for which the bishop or abbot owed fealty and military service to the king. Each cathedral (seat or cathedra of a bishop) had an administration that was expected to carry out the ecclesiastical and imperial legislation. The bishop and his administration were willing to do so, for they owed their material well-being to the king. Each diocese was generally endowed with vast domains granted from the king. The Church's hierarchy and system were more effective in administering a region than the nobility, for they had a more extensive and more literate officialdom and were more malleable, for the Church could put up little or no military resistance. The system was even more effective since Charlemagne put his own relatives and friends in the positions of authority such as bishops and abbots. He did this especially with monasteries since they often held sway over larger amounts of land and because the abbot did not have to be a clergyman to function as a leader.

To tighten control over each diocese, each bishop was required to travel to each church in the diocese on a regular basis. Since this did not happen every year, in some cases not for a number of years, it became standard practice to baptize all those who had not yet been baptized. In this way, infant baptism became the norm. Confession was required on a regular basis, and Communion at least three times a year. Work was forbidden on Sundays and other holy days (holidays) (see "Agriculture" in chapter 5). All of these developments from purgatory to infant baptism, confession, and forbidding of work on Sunday drew the people into the structure more uniformly. Individual spirituality was not as much the concern as were order and control. Purgatory encouraged uniformity of belief by providing a Christian version of a negative netherworld that had been an important part of superstition. Purgatory became the evil element of Christianity, encouraging positive Christian responses. Infant baptism provided uniformity by turning an elective religion into a universal religion of which all were made members. Confession forced all members to accept the same body of sins and to admit them to the overseers of the spiritual society, the clergy. The prohibition of work on Sunday was, on the one hand, attractive to participants because it gave them a reprieve from work, but more important for uniformity it ensured that all would attend church services and hear the admonitions and advice for the people coming from the pulpit.

MONASTICISM

The Monastery

The day began early in 801 at the monastery of Centula, the Monastery of the Holy and Indivisible Trinity. As one of the great monasteries of the Carolingian Empire, it had many duties and responsibilities. Before dawn, the novices appointed to keep watch of the time by sand dials awakened the three hundred monks and one hundred novices for vigils. They would arise, dress, and fold their bedclothes. Silently moving from the monastic dormitories in one direction and the novitiate dormitory in another, both groups drowsily trooped to the main Church of St. Salvator (Holy Savior), St. Maria (Virgin Mary), and St. Richarius. It was a long walk, for Centula was an enormous monastic complex, built in the form of a giant triangle one thousand feet long on each side, a triangle to symbolize the Holy Trinity. At each corner of the great triangle was a church: the main Church of St. Richarius, one dedicated to St. Benedict, and one to Notre Dame (Our Lady).

In the choir of St. Richarius, around the altar at the west end of the church, one hundred of the monk novitiates (those in training) stood. The main altar was above a crypt that held the most precious relics of the monastery, of St. Richarius, which made this altar even more special than most. The shrine of St. Richarius was decorated in the most glorious fashion with many doors of silver and gold. Before the altar were six columns covered with gold and silver work and seventeen arches of gold. Underneath these arches were bronze images of birds, beasts, and men. But because of the great numbers, this church had three altars, one at the west end, one in the middle, and one at the east end, and the monks often divided into three choirs of one hundred monks plus novitiates for services. All three altars were made of marble and were covered with gold, silver, and precious stones. Bronze statues stood on columns around the altars. Over the altars were canopies of gold and silver, and from each hung a crown of gold decorated with crosses and with precious stones. In each church was a lectern of marble, silver, and gold. The walls were covered with fresco paintings of the major biblical

Utrecht Psalter, University of Utrecht, Ms. 32, fol. 73r. Monasticism is represented in the upper scene with a baldachin over the altar, a lectern or manuscript stand with a scribe on the right, and another scribe with a scroll on the left.

stories, and stucco carvings of biblical characters reminded all those present what their purpose was. Altogether there were thirty reliquaries made of ivory, gold, and silver, seven circular chandeliers of silver, seven of gilded copper, and many crosses, candlesticks, and other costly items throughout the churches at Centula. One gospel book that had been given to Centula by Abbot Angilbert was written entirely in gold and was contained in a silver box covered with gems and precious stones.

Prayers were said standing and in the form of sung chant with each of the three choirs on a different timing so that the chants resounded throughout the vast building like a round. After the prayers, the men returned to their dormitories and lavatories to wash their hands and faces, comb their hair, and prepare for the next prayers, matins, at dawn. Baths were only allowed at Easter and Christmas. The other two churches were used by some of the monks for certain prayers. The Church of Notre Dame was a large rotunda with a central altar surrounded by twelve altars dedicated to the Twelve Apostles. There were thirty masses said daily at Centula at the different altars, and innumerable processions. Both Notre Dame and the east and west ends of St. Richarius were surmounted by round towers flanked by smaller towers containing spiral stairs to enter the churches. The great sides of the triangle were covered walkways and enclosed an area so large that all activities of arts and labors could be executed within the boundaries of the monastery. There was even a river that flowed through the middle of the monastery and provided water for all purposes within.

The Plan of St. Gall

The reform movement that created Centula stirred up a great deal of thinking about the design of monasteries. The most famous example of this design reform was the plan of St. Gall. St. Gall, in Swabia (now Switzerland), was one of the prominent monasteries founded in the early seventh century by Irish followers of St. Columban, in this case, a priest named Gall. By the ninth century, St. Gall had become one of the great monasteries of the kingdom. Saint-Germain-des-Prés near Paris had 39 great estates and 340 smaller ones with more than 7,300 peasant families supporting 150 monks. Fulda had approximately 15,000 peasant families, and St. Gall approximately 4,000.

During Charlemagne's life, there were repeated attempts and many successes in reforming and unifying monastic function and performance. After Charlemagne's death, his son Louis the Pious continued this movement and to effect reform called nearly back-to-back synods (ecclesiastical councils) in 816 and 817 at Aachen. Out of the second synod came an official proclamation known as the Monastic Capitulary. This document is believed to be the source of the plan of St. Gall. The capitulary called for many reforms, including dormitories for visiting monks, separate workshops, separate kitchens for monks and visitors, an abbot's house, a school, and baths. The plan takes all of these items into account and more. There is a vegetable garden, a medicinal herb garden, an orchard, a scriptorium, brew and bake houses, a henhouse, a granary, a mill, infirmaries, a guesthouse, and houses for shepherds, goatherds, cowherds, and other servants. There is a monks' dormitory, a privy, a laundry, a bath, a refectory, and a cemetery. Very little was not thought of in this plan. The plan was never put into effect and never became a completed construction, but the ideas that were laid out in the capitulary and in the plan began to appear in some monastic foundations. The plan of St. Gall probably provides an excellent example of the ninth-century ideal of a monastic facility.

Prayer

To the original seven offices of the day provided for in the Benedictine Rule were added by Abbot Angilbert several other sets of sung prayers,

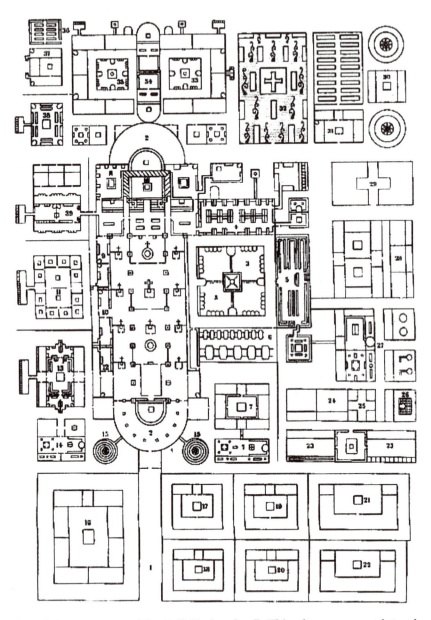

Plan of the monastery of St. Gall (Switzerland). This plan, never put into effect, represents the ideal monastery of the ninth century. [From Shepherd, *Historical Atlas*.]

A nineteenth-century rendering of a Carolingian soldier, clergymen, and petitioner. Braun & Schneider, *Historic Costume in Pictures*, Plate 11, Dover Publications, Inc., 1975. Reprinted by permission.

the thirty masses, processions to all the altars of the three churches, prayers for the dead, and numerous private prayers said by individual monks or whole choirs. The original plan of the Rule to balance prayer with work and study was heavily shifted to prayer. Much of the day at Centula was spent in sung or private prayer.

The purpose of the prayers of the monks of Centula was asking for pardon from punishment for sin of the souls of those living and dead. When Charlemagne granted the rebuilding of Centula, he expected to merit pardon for his sins through the prayers of the monks and thereby help work toward salvation. The medieval belief was that the merit that accrued to an individual through prayer and good works could be transferred to others, both living and dead, through prayer for that individual. Since salvation was determined by merit through good works that one accumulated, this transfer of merit was a useful aid in gaining salvation. Charlemagne also believed that the prayers might help to provide stability to the kingdom and that the establishment of Centula would give assistance when necessary to the kingdom. This assistance might come in the form of military assistance, monetary assistance, or any number of other forms. Furthermore, by establishing a monastery, a noble family gained an outlet and safe haven for surplus family members. Even though the Carolingians did not follow primogeniture, for many of the noble families it was imperative that younger sons and daughters find a suitable setting to live their lives comfortably and respectably without marriage, which required committing shares of the family estates. Retiring to a monastery provided this setting with a reduced financial and land commitment. In fact, the Carolingians often appointed family members to head the monasteries. Centula's abbots included one son-in-law and three grandsons of Charlemagne. One of Charlemagne's daughters became the abbess of the convent of Faremoutiers. Centula's chronicler even boasted that every nobleman in the entire kingdom had a relative at the monastery. Other monasteries prided themselves on the fact that they excluded anyone who was not of noble birth.

The Scriptorium

Between the prayers, work was accomplished, but again silently. Some of the monks worked in the scriptorium. Only those who were literate and who had fine handwriting were chosen for copying in the scriptorium, although there were other jobs to be done. There were dyers if the parchment was to be dyed, most commonly purple, for an extravagant manuscript. The parchment had to be prepared, cut to size, folded, and stitched into gatherings, and individual pages had to be marked for lines of writing. This was done with a piece of lead or carbon and a straightedge drawing light horizontal lines on the pages, by using a stylus with a metal tip to leave indentation lines in the parchment, or by using a pin and a straightedge to prick lines. The advantage of pricking lines was that a pin could be driven through all the pages of a gathering, hence marking lines on all pages at once. In the Carolingian age, most manuscripts were ruled with drypoint or indentations. After the writing of the manuscript was completed, binders tied the gatherings together to form the codex.

Copying was the most important job and was done by placing the parchment and the prototype on stands or sloped tables to hold them upright for easier access and because the pens worked best if they were held at a right angle to the page, but only slightly slanted. The copier sat in a seat with a high upright back.

Pens and Ink

Pens were crafted by each scribe from large wing feathers (quills) or from reeds. They were cut to provide a point that was then split and squared off at the very end of the point with a sharp knife. The point of a quill or reed pen also has to be constantly sharpened, so a knife (penknife) was kept in the left hand (if the scribe was right-handed) to quickly sharpen the pen or to scrape away mistakes. The quill or reed pen, because of the narrow tube, naturally draws ink into the chamber when it is dipped in liquid. Even so, it has to be dipped frequently into the ink when one is writing a page, and a ready pot or horn of ink had to be always at hand.

Ink was generally of two types: carbon ink and iron-gall ink. Carbon ink was made from any carbon substance such as lampblack, the black substance that collects on a surface near a fire, or from charcoal. The carbon had to be mixed with gum to produce a usable liquid consistency, but primarily to provide an adhesive. Iron-gall ink was made from oak galls, a vegetable tumor on oak trees, that provides a cocoon for gall wasps. Once the insect had departed, the tumor, rich in tannic and gallic acids, was crushed and soaked. This solution was mixed with copperas (ferrous sulfate). A chemical reaction caused the mixture to turn black, at which point it was mixed with gum to thicken it, and the ink was ready. Since quill and reed pens work better on a downward stroke than upward, most letters were formed with a series of downward strokes. An *o* might be formed with two curved, downward strokes. An *m* was three downward strokes. Because of this, it is sometimes difficult to distinguish between letters made from a series of similar strokes such as *m*, *in*, and *ni*. Once a manuscript was completed, it was checked for errors and corrected either by erasing the mistake with a knife or pumice stone or by crossing out the error and filling in a correction.

More prestigious than the copiers were the illuminators, who painted images or decorated letters in bright colors in the books. This required great skill. Most books were not illuminated. Only the extremely important and therefore extremely rare books were illuminated, and this took a high level of skill (see "Illuminated Manuscripts" in chapter 9).

The Library

Related to the scriptorium was the library. Centula had one of the largest libraries in the empire by the ninth century. Library catalogs known to us via the monastic chronicles indicate that the library in 831 was large enough to divide the books into sections of biblical texts, books by Jerome, Augustine, and Gregory I, and then various authors such as Isidore, Origen, John Chrysostom, and Cassiodorus. The catalogs also list grammarians, classical texts, and liturgical texts.

Other Jobs

Another job was the maintenance of the clothes required by all the monks and novitiates. Each monk was equipped with a set of clothing made from local materials such as wool, linen, and leather. Each monk received a pair of drawers, socks, a long robe, a cape, a winter pelisse (cloak) with a hood, shoes, boots, gloves, and a belt. To keep all of these supplied and in repair was a substantial job.

In addition to these jobs at Centula was the care of the sick and of pilgrims. Monasteries had specially built infirmaries to keep the sick separated from the well and sometimes even separate quarters for the contagiously ill. It is clear that the monks recognized the needs of those suffering from illness. The ill were fed especially well, including more meat than the other monks, and were kept warmer than the others. The infirmarian was knowledgeable about herbs and medicines and kept the monastery herb garden, which was often grown just outside the infirmary. Separate from the monks and the infirmary were quarters for visitors and especially for important guests where the abbot could hold audience in a hall by the main gate to the monastery.

Meals

There were two meals a day at Centula. Neither included meat, which was forbidden by the Rule, although fowl was not considered part of the prohibition. Exceptions were made, as for the infirm and during holy seasons when nourishment was needed between the extensive fasts. Gruels of cooked grain and vegetable dishes were served. Fish was common on feast days. Wine was served, but in moderation.

The monastery was a royally supported institution. In 790, Charlemagne appointed Angilbert as abbot, and a great building program began that was completed in 799. Angilbert was one of Charlemagne's favorites, despite the fact that he had a child by one of Charlemagne's daughters before he married her. He was renowned as a scholar and poet and was sent on several missions by Charlemagne to the papacy in Rome. Angilbert's appointment may have been a way to remove him from Charlemagne's daughter without loss of status.

The Monastic Complex

Outside the vast complex of the monastery was the holy city of Centula. It had a population of around 7,000, making it one of the larger towns in northern Europe. It was well laid out and divided into wards, some for crafts and trades, and a marketplace. There were five churches, including one for the knights of the town who owed military service to the monastery. Outside the city were the suburbs, with seven villages that took part in liturgical processions approximating the seven stations of Rome. The town was where many of the workers and servants of the monastery lived. In fact, 2,500 of these people owed the abbot of Centula payment either in kind or in work obligations, so there was always free labor available to Centula. Stonemasons, blacksmiths, gold- and silver-smiths, bakers, brewers, candlemakers, and all the other craftsmen lived and worked in the town. The town of Centula depended upon the monastery, while the monastery depended upon the emperor and the emperor, depended upon his conquests to provide the wealth to support the building and maintenance of Centula. The importance of the military was even echoed in the order and discipline preached at the monastery.

History of Monasticism

Monasticism, from the word "monos" (alone), originated with individuals living alone. The movement began in the Middle East, in Egypt and Palestine, toward the end of the third century C.E. It was a way for individuals to remove themselves from society to pursue ascetic, spiritual, godly lives in solitude as hermits. But as these individuals and their feats of holiness began to attract followers, monasticism soon developed into communities. By the fourth century C.E. the desert to the west of the Nile and the wilderness in Judea were scattered with small communities of monks. Most monks at that time were not priests but laypeople who wanted to live the most spiritual life possible and found these remote colonies to be the most effective way.

In the fourth century, the ideas of Eastern monasticism were transmitted to the West. Stories, both oral and written, of the desert hermits of the East attracted individuals from the West to go and experience that life, and also some of the ascetics left their enclaves in the East to move to the West. Several "centers" of monasticism were established; one at Tours, founded by St. Martin, was among the earliest in the West, twin centers, one for men and one for women, were established by Cassian at Marseilles, and others soon began to crop up. Although the tradition had been one of individuals isolated, but living near one another, in the West it was found that the community worked better. In the early stages of monasticism, the training for the monks worked better to have them living together—what is known as cenobitic life. This became so much the norm that the word *monasticism* is used to describe what is really cenobiticism. The Western monk wished not so much to flee the world as to give an example to society of a life of simplicity and godly living that one gained through self-denial.

Benedictine Rule

As these communities grew in size and in number, there was a growing need for organization. Several monastic plans or "rules" gained widespread acceptance, the Rule of St. Basil, the Rule of St. Columban, and the Rule of St. Benedict. The Rule of St. Benedict became the dominant rule followed by monasteries in Europe throughout the Middle Ages. St. Benedict of Nursia (c. 480–c. 550 C.E.) founded a monastic community at Monte Cassino in Italy and wrote his rule for that community. The Rule of St. Benedict (or Benedictine Rule) spread to other monasteries, although the earliest extant (still-existing) copy is only from the eighth century. A copy of the Rule, presently at the monastery of St. Gall, in Switzerland, was made at Charlemagne's capital at Aachen in the late eighth century from a copy requested by Charlemagne in 787 from Abbot Theodemar at Monte Cassino. The copy sent to Charlemagne from Monte Cassino was itself copied, we believe, from Benedict's original. This means that the codex at St. Gall is twice removed from the original, making it an extremely valuable codex, and also that we have something so close to the original that we can be quite certain of its accuracy.

Benedict wrote his Rule following a prototype that already existed, but Benedict's Rule was not only better organized, it was kinder and gentler. Instead of the autocratic tone of other rules, Benedict's called for even the abbot to rule with love and to take the views of all of the monks into account. It was careful to ensure that those who joined were appropriate by insisting that the individual wanting to join knock at the door for several days before being admitted and that when admitted, the individual spend one full year as a novitiate before being asked to take vows for life.

The Benedictine Rule set out the daily and annual schedule for a group of monks living as a family, sharing work, food, prayers, and living. The emphasis was on prayer and manual labor. Each monk was required to perform several hours of daily labor because sloth and idleness were considered disobedience to God and "the enemy of the soul." Prayer, however, was the most important element, and each monk had times allotted for personal prayer or meditation and seven periods of communal prayer. Included in these periods of prayer was the chanting of psalms, which developed into sung chant later known as Gregorian chant.

The Rule has chapters on obedience, silence, and humility, as well as on the divine offices (prayers) and how they are to be said at night, during the summer, and on Sundays and mornings during the week. It includes chapters on work, prayer, punishment, excommunication, the officers of the monastery, how to treat boys in the monastery, food and drink, the sick, labor and crafts, and how visitors are to be treated.

Monastery Design and Organization

Since the earliest monasteries were generally in Italy or southern Gaul and were often led by individuals who were descended from the old

Gallo-Roman aristocracy, the design of monastic buildings was similar to the old Roman villa, with a patio or square around which the buildings were placed. This provided room for a community of people with enough separation for different activities. For the monastery, this became the cloister. All of the support systems of the villa, such as kitchens and gardens, were essential for a community, and so they found their place in the monastery. Each monastery became a self-contained unit, able to provide all of its own worldly goods as had the villa (see the illustration of the plan of St. Gall).

Monasteries, according to the Rule, should be overseen by an abbot who acted as father of the monks and whose rule and decisions were to be strictly obeyed. The abbot was meant to be a benevolent autocrat, the earthly manifestation of God or at least the Christ of his disciples. What this meant in the Age of Charlemagne was that the abbot of a monastery was a powerful and influential figure, especially if the monastery was a large and wealthy one.

Monastic Literacy and Discipline

Because of the need to read the Bible and the Rule and to chant psalms, it was essential that monks be literate, and therefore monasteries became centers of literacy and education. Even as early as the fifth or sixth centuries, it was becoming clear that the Roman level of literacy was disappearing. Monasteries became refuges for learning.

By the beginning of the seventh century, the Frankish Church was growing in power and wealth. The Merovingians supported the Church with donations of money and land and exemptions from taxes. When St. Columbans, the Irish missionary, arrived on the Continent around 585, there were approximately two hundred monasteries already in existence. His missionary work paid enormous dividends, as new monasteries began to appear all over. Between 610 and 650, a flood of new foundations were established, and by the end of the seventh century there were well over four hundred monasteries across Europe.

Charlemagne was obsessed with monastic discipline. Decrees and capitularies constantly reiterated the need for order and discipline and demanded that abbots follow the Rule. Charlemagne was apparently convinced that the Benedictine Rule provided the best possibility of strict order for a monastery and encouraged its use in place of the any earlier rule or especially in place of the lack of a rule. Charlemagne tried to ensure that all monasteries followed the Benedictine Rule, but it was not until his son Louis the Pious's reign and under the direction of St. Benedict of Aniane (c. 750–821) that the Rule was zealously forced upon nearly all the monasteries of the kingdom. It is ironic that the Rule that Benedict of Nursia created to maintain order and provide independence would become enforced from the outside as an act of state. These monasteries, then, in Charlemagne's time were the clerical equivalent of Charlemagne's armies and provided order and security for the region in which they were located.

These monasteries became the front line, the shock troops, of the war on illiteracy, ignorance, and paganism. In the General Capitulary for the Missi from 802, all bishops, abbots, and abbesses were ordered to strive to surpass their subjects in upright behavior and love and not oppress their subjects with harsh rule or tyranny. Abbots and abbesses were to live with the monks and in accordance with the Rule, with canon law, and with the law of the land. Those doing otherwise were to be disciplined. Monasteries were to provide protection and support to the poor, the widowed, the orphaned, and pilgrims (those on religious journeys such as to sites of veneration).

Corruption

Traveling monks and other travelers were a constant burden to the monastic system. According to the Benedictine Rule, monasteries were to open their doors to travelers, probably on the assumption that they would be pilgrims. However, many travelers were instead on business or merely wandering, and yet monasteries were required to take them in and feed and house them for several days if necessary. Not only was this a financial burden on the monastery, but the presence of outsiders could be very disruptive to the orderly workings of monastery life.

It is important to remember that most monasteries were not like Centula with its 300 monks and 2,500 lay dependents. Most monasteries in the Merovingian and Carolingian eras would have had a few dozen monks or fewer. Most monasteries were modest, humble, austere operations. Instead of having an obligatory workforce, the average monastery required the monks themselves to perform some of the work. That was an integral part of the Rule of St. Benedict. Prayer, study, and work were supposed to hold equal value in the monastery, and monks were to experience humility, not extravagance. As previously mentioned, Charlemagne's son, Louis the Pious, encouraged the standardization of the Benedictine Rule in monasteries, and through his agent, St. Benedict of Aniane, a synod or council of the Church in 817 approved the promotion of the Rule for all monasteries. This encouraged the more balanced approach of prayer, study, and work and a simpler life. The monastery of Aniane, where Benedict went to live in 779, was indeed a humble affair with plain walls and the roofs covered with straw. The ciborium (a vessel for the eucharistic wafers) and chalice (a vessel for the eucharistic wine) were made of wood. This humble background shows through Benedict of Aniane's movement away from excess and decadence.

It was rumored in the ninth century that monks committed fornication and other sins, including sodomy, although Charlemagne ordered them not to do so and told monks to protect themselves from these evils. Charlemagne also threatened that if these specific sins became known to the court, there would be severe punishments.

Monastic women were ordered not to be allowed to wander about, but to be constantly guarded. No man was allowed to enter a convent, except for the priest to celebrate the Mass and to minister to the sick. Although convents were not as common as monasteries in the Carolingian world, they were not rare, and some of these convents became important intellectual centers and even produced important scriptoria. But there was always concern about the risk of corruption by having groups of women or of men together.

The great wealth of the Carolingian monasteries, built up by land and monetary endowments from the Carolingian nobility, also provided a tempting source of land for a monarchy that was always in need of land to distribute to loyal followers. This was the reason for the creation of the polyptychs or inventories of all that was held by the monasteries of the Carolingian realm. They listed all lands and movable property for a purpose similar to the English Domesday Book of the eleventh century. Only by knowing exactly what was held could the monarchy know what might be taken away. This wealth was always suspect by those outside the Church, but was also always eyed by these same people.

EDUCATION

Before Charlemagne

Education in ancient Rome was of extreme importance. By the time of Marcus Terentius Varro (d. 27 B.C.E.) education was defined as the liberal arts and included nine subjects. These would later be refined as the trivium and the quadrivium, or the three subjects and the four subjects. The trivium was composed of grammar, rhetoric, and dialectic, while the quadrivium was composed of arithmetic, geometry, astronomy, and music. Grammar included not only grammar in the modern sense (as: "English grammar"); but literature and interpretation of language and literature and was considered the primary subject of study that had to be mastered first.

By the fourth century, the seven liberal arts were the essential form of education, and the state-supported schools of Rome used it universally. First, students studied the trivium and later, after gaining some grasp of these subjects, moved on to the quadrivium to develop a more disciplined mind through the study of mathematics. Astronomy enabled one to understand the cosmic relationships of heavenly bodies to the earth as laid out in the Aristotelian universe. Music was seen as both refinement and mathematics in the relationship of notes and in the meter of the rhythms.

Augustine

Augustine (354–430) was thoroughly trained in this form of education and even began writing treatises on each of the seven subjects, although most of the treatises were lost during his lifetime. Born of a Christian mother and highly educated, Augustine converted to Christianity in 386, was baptized by Ambrose, and returned to his native North Africa to become a bishop. Through Augustine and his extremely influential theological works, the emphasis on the trivium and the quadrivium was absorbed into Christian culture in the Roman Empire. Augustine believed that a boy should study first the seven liberal arts, the trivium and the quadrivium, before going on to the study of theology or divine wisdom. Also in North Africa was Martianus Capella (before 400), who wrote a treatise titled *The Marriage of Mercury and Philology*. In this allegorical wedding, the bride is presented with a gift of the seven liberal arts. This work was held in high esteem as an encyclopedia or textbook for the ages that followed, especially later among the Irish and Anglo-Saxon scholars who would come to have a strong influence on the development of education in the Carolingian Empire.

Jerome

Jerome (d. 419), another one of the great church fathers, helped to incorporate late classical education of the seven liberal arts into monasticism. Jerome was also highly educated like Augustine and was concerned with education. Both were themselves experienced teachers. Jerome had been educated at Rome and there spent some time as a teacher of upper-class women who took a form of monastic vows. Jerome's ideal for monasticism was of a formal rigorous education. However, through Cassian, also of the fourth century, monasticism received its skepticism of education. After all, one of the points of monasticism was a certain denial of the earthly gifts, and education was one of these. Jerome had struggled with this issue and concluded that education, including the use of some pagan literature, was useful for the advancement of the Christian spirit. For most of the Middle Ages, secular learning and literature, even when encouraged, would be regarded as a means to an end—a better understanding of the divine.

Cassiodorus

With the Rule of St. Benedict in the sixth century, education, of at least a limited sort, was required of all monks. It was with the educational program laid out in encyclopedic fashion by Cassiodorus (c. 490–c. 585) that education was firmly ensconced in the monastic routine. Cassiodorus was born of a noble family and held high political offices. To understand theology thoroughly, one had to be educated, and Cassiodorus combined the two cultures of the pagan ancients and of Christianity into a new curriculum. Under this curriculum, a monastic library was essential, and therefore copying of books became one of the most worthy forms of work as required in Benedict's Rule. The otherwise isolated monk was fighting a worldly battle against the devil in transmitting knowledge. For the sixth, seventh, and eighth centuries, the monastery became nearly the sole repository of education in the West.

Anglo-Irish Monasticism

Yet even monasticism and its educational regime declined in these centuries to a point of dilapidation where education was nearly defunct. Only in Ireland and Anglo-Saxon England had the rigors of monasticism and education been maintained. As missionaries were sent out from these islands to the Continent to carry the Word of God, they also carried the knowledge and demands of an education that still incorporated the seven liberal arts. As monks reformed monasteries or established new ones, one of the fundamental elements of that reform was education to enable monks to understand their own religion and theology. Even Pope Gregory I, who was not enamored of the past, recognized that educational reform was essential to clarify and unify the Church. He supported the missionary movement from Ireland and England and encouraged the reform of monasteries on the Continent.

Education in Charlemagne's Time

Education as it existed (when it existed) at the time of Charlemagne's accession to the throne was reduced to a limited study of grammar and, for clerics, a small sampling of theology. Even grammar was beyond most clerics and monks. The reading and writing ability of those who were not entirely illiterate was extremely weak to the point where their poor knowledge of Latin made it impossible to formulate a proper sentence, let alone a proper document or the performance of a proper church service. The seven liberal arts were at this time an educational scheme rarely followed, for there were few qualified instructors and few schoolbooks for training. The most accessible form of the liberal arts was through Isidore's *Etymologies*, which during the reform movement was copied extensively. Only at the end of the eighth century did manuscripts of Cassiodorus's *Institutions* begin to circulate. With the advent of Irish missionaries, the work of Martianus Capella entered into circulation and reestablished a curriculum of the seven liberal arts. Only with the reintroduction of grammar could the Church hope to establish a uniformity of service and a literate and functioning clergy. This is why libraries of the Carolingian era have their largest holdings in grammarians, liturgical texts, and writings by Augustine and Jerome. It was this demand for material in the seven liberal arts in the libraries and the demand for qualified instructors that resulted in the educational reform under Charlemagne often known as the prominent feature in the Carolingian Renaissance.

According to Einhard, Charlemagne zealously cultivated the liberal arts and held those who taught them in great esteem and conferred great honors upon them. He revered learning so much that at dinnertime someone present was expected to read to the others. Charlemagne studied grammar under Paulinus and Peter of Pisa, both of Italy, and under the tutelage of Alcuin of England. Although he had a good mind, he was never successful in learning how to write. He apparently kept wax tablets under his pillow in bed to practice when no one was watching. We have, in what some believe to be Charlemagne's own handwriting, the word *bene* (good) on some documents, but he might not have been able to write much more than that.

Educational Reforms

The educational reforms that were initiated by Charlemagne brought about a number of real changes and some considerable contemplation about possible changes. Alcuin's handbooks on rhetoric and dialectic were among the most useful and influential works on the liberal arts in the Carolingian era and made the study of these subjects more accessible. If a student moved beyond Alcuin's work on rhetoric, the next step was the Roman rhetorician Cicero. On dialectic, which was thought of as synonymous with logic, if students were to move past Alcuin, they had to go to his original sources, commentaries on Boethius (born circa 480 of a senatorial family). In addition to Alcuin's works, compilations of Bede and the grammar books of Donatus (a Roman grammarian who flourished in the 350s, taught St. Jerome, and wrote the widely used *Ars Grammatica* [Grammatical arts]) and of Priscian (a grammarian who flourished in the 540s and was the second most popular after Donatus) were used for the more advanced student. These were the standard texts of the day, although probably the most common "text" used for students was a compilation derived from these grammars and others that the instructor had drawn together for teaching. As with teaching at any time, the best teachers would draw what they considered the best examples from a number of different places to present to the student.

Charlemagne tried to expand the influence of the reform movement by his General Admonition of 789, which ordered that schools be established in every church and monastery so that boys might learn to read. In his letter on the cultivation of learning, probably written sometime in the 790s, Charlemagne instructed that in order to practice Christianity properly, education was necessary. The letter encouraged all clerics and monks to study diligently to better transmit the Christian beliefs through proper writing and speech. Although the most numerous schools were established at the parish level by rural priests, we know very little about these. They have left few records. The schools that have left traces are almost all cathedral or monastic schools.

Whether at a parish, cathedral, or monastic school, a boy would first begin the study of the seven liberal arts with the trivium. Grammar began with texts written on the Bible, or extracts of the Bible books, so that a child learned to read and at the same time learned the basic elements of Christianity. There was some memorization, especially of the Psalms. Grammar texts or extracts from grammar texts such as those by Donatus or Priscian might be used. At a slightly more advanced level of education, pagan literature was used to teach a more highly refined grammar. As this level was reached, rhetoric and dialectic could be taught through the pagan works such as those of Cicero, but also through Christian authors and the multitude of commentaries and compilations that appeared in the eighth and ninth centuries.

An additional type of book that became very common was the dictionary or glossary. Dictionaries and glossaries were both used in teaching and a product of teaching. Glosses were explanations of the meaning, origin, and implications of specific words. Often a student would be instructed to produce a glossary as a learning tool. Since the definitions were usually derived from early texts, the glosses became more and more removed from the original sources and consequently more and more inaccurate. The very best of these dictionaries, however, were useful tools, part dictionary, part encyclopedia. One of the best of all was produced as part of the Carolingian Renaissance—the *Liber glossarum* (Book of glosses). It was derived from Virgil, Isidore, Augustine, Ambrose, Jerome, and others.

Mathematics

Beyond the trivium, there was interest in mathematics, but only at a somewhat more advanced level of learning. The major purpose of mathematics for the Carolingians was computing the dates of holy days and festivals in the Christian calendar. Therefore, computing incorporated some mathematics and some astronomy, and a large body of literature concerning this developed in the ninth century, although most of it was derived from Boethius, Martianus Capella, Isidore (560–636, bishop of Seville, author of *The Etymologies*, an encyclopedia of the liberal arts and sciences), and Bede (c. 673–735, author of *A History of the English Church and People*). Proper computations were essential for uniformity in the Church; hence Charlemagne's emphasis on this in his 789 General Admonition. Charlemagne also convened an assembly of scholars in 809 to study the possibility of reforming astronomical computations in use for determining movable holy days. In 810, they produced an illuminated astronomical handbook with a series of constellations that were quite accurate. The study of astronomy for the purpose of actually understanding the movement of the heavenly bodies was of little concern to the Carolingians, and geometry was never of much interest because they could not see how it pertained to or advanced the understanding of Christianity.

Musical Education

Musical education was an integral part of the monastic and cathedral training because of its importance in the liturgy. Prior to the ninth century, most Roman chant, often called Gregorian chant, was memorized and transmitted orally and not in a fixed unalterable form. Under Charlemagne, there was a commitment to replace the Gallican liturgies in Frankish territories with Roman usage. This concerted effort to transform the liturgies, combined with the rapid expansion of monasteries and churches with the same need for a fairly uniform chant, overextended the ability of trained professionals to memorize. In the ninth century, writing down chant melodies was the only way to ensure that the proper form was being used. Consequently, we have the first large number of musical manuscripts from this period. Whereas previous musical notation had been little more than a reminder to the performer, it became a nearly complete form of expressing the music, although one quite different from ours today.

It is not known precisely which of the Gregorian chants of this period were borrowed from Roman chant and which were composed in the ninth century. Some were already very old, but were transformed in the Carolingian age, and many more probably originated in the ninth century. Almost all of what is known to us today as Gregorian chant comes via the Carolingian world of the ninth century. There were few important individual music texts of the Carolingian age. The most important was *Musica enchiriadis* (Music manual), written probably at the very end of the ninth century. This text established the use of the first seven letters of the alphabet for the notes of the octave (although it probably did not invent it) and discussed harmony and polyphonic music.

Other Subjects

Other subjects such as history, geography, and natural sciences were not unheard of in Carolingian education, but texts were rare. Classical pagan authors still provided the best studies in these subjects and were one reason that the pagan authors were not entirely rejected for Christian authors.

Study of the Bible

Ultimately the highest subject of study was that of theology or at least of the Bible. Only students who had mastered or reached a level of proficiency in grammar, rhetoric, and dialectic could begin the study of the Bible, although the Bible would have been used as the literature in the study of grammar. Therefore, a working knowledge of the Bible was assumed by any student at this level. The traditional method of study was to read the interpretations of books of the Bible that had been written by the church fathers such as Augustine, Ambrose, and Jerome.

Schools

The model school was the palace school. Not a particular place or curriculum, the school at court was a model for all church and monastic schools in a number of ways. It drew together the greatest teachers of the Christian West. Men such as Paulinus, Peter of Pisa, Paul the Deacon, and especially Alcuin were scholars and teachers. The palace school collected manuscripts to use in teaching and copied them for further distribution. The manuscripts, as they were copied, moved out from the palace school to the churches and monasteries, as did the students once they were trained, and eventually so did the masters themselves as each one "retired" by becoming an abbot of a monastery and sometimes inspired these institutions to reach new heights. St. Martin at Tours developed a preeminent scriptorium after Alcuin retired to become abbot there.

To be educated, a boy would be sent to a cathedral or, more often, a monastic school. Although Charlemagne's General Admonition ordered that schools were to be provided for all boys at every church and monastery, a universal education was far from possible. But this did at least establish a kingdomwide policy of education. However, this policy barely outlived Charlemagne, as his son Louis the Pious in 817 ordered that only those who were oblates, or vowed to take orders, should be educated in the monastic schools. Repeatedly in the decades after Charlemagne, there were pleas that education was deteriorating. But during Charlemagne's reign, a limited number of boys from aristocratic families joined small numbers from free or even servile backgrounds in the monastic schools. The numbers were never large, but it was consistent growth over what had existed before. In the smaller monastic communities, the boys who entered were probably assumed to be trained as monks or clerics, but in some of the larger communities there were facilities to train boys who were not intending to stay as monks. The two groups were usually kept separate in two different locations at the monastery, as at St. Gall, although it is not known how common the two-school setup was.

The great plan of St. Gall discussed earlier, when examined and pieced together with other information, tells us something about the ninth-century mentality about children and their education. Male children could be donated to a monastery, a practice called oblation, starting normally at age six or seven. This provided a major means of recruitment into the Benedictine monastic system throughout the Carolingian era and through the eleventh century. These novitiates, or oblates, as they were usually called, formed a highly malleable educable core of prospective monks. Their training and education were important for the entire future of Carolingian culture, for these boys would become the future monks, scholars, and administrators for the empire. These boys, from age five or so until age fifteen, were seen as a valuable asset. The plan of St. Gall, although it was never carried out, provides us with the ideal design of a monastery.

The boys had their own section of the monastery, carefully separated from the rest of the monks by walls, with only one access gate that required a considerable walk to reach it. Within this region of the monastery, there was a separate cloister, although it was designed at one-quarter the scale of the adult cloister. That took into account the reality of the difference in size of people, especially for the youngest boys, five to ten years old. The distances that the boys had to walk during the day for all of their activities were substantially reduced. The oblate realm was also planned to be near the infirmary, probably just to economize by sharing part of the building structure for the two respective chapels. The boys lived in a communal setting that was in most ways identical to that of the monks, but where the boys were kept separate from all adults except for the masters, the abbot, and the prior. There were watches at night to ensure that no one, including the monks, sneaked into the oblate quarters. There was continuous fear of homosexuality within the institution of monasticism. In 802, one of Charlemagne's capitularies denounced all "fornication, abomination, and uncleanness" among monks, pointing out that the monks were the very people to whom everyone looked for guidance.

To help protect them from outside intrusion, the oblate quarters were at the far end of the monastic complex and next to the cemetery. Putting the quarter next to the cemetery was presumably to discourage anyone from approaching from the outside, such as a parent trying to retrieve a child or a kidnapper, since child slavery was a lucrative business in the Carolingian Empire. Young boys were the principal casualty of slavery. In fact, Verdun, in the center of Frankish territory, was the center of slavery of young boys who were castrated and exported to Spain and other Mediterranean regions. The cemetery location would also discourage any of the boys from trying to escape, especially at night, the most likely time, for it was not uncommon for boys in adolescence to try to leave a monastery to which they had been given.

In addition to the safety of the location of the oblate quarters, the dormitory was located next to a large warming room that contained an oven and also next to the fireplace of the infirmary. A fireplace would not have been wanted in the dormitory because the smoke produced would have interfered with sleeping, since chimneys were not a regular feature of construction in Europe until the eleventh century. But building the dormitory abutting the two sources of heat, together with the body heat of many boys, would have kept the temperature bearable. The fire of the heating room was also used as a secondary bakery to produce the morning bread for the boys. A heated room was a special provision or privilege of the children in recognition that children were not merely smaller adults.

That children were given separate quarters, designed for smaller bodies, well protected from outsiders, where they were under constant supervision and provided with more heat and more food indicates a caring and understanding of children. Historians have sometimes claimed that children were not really understood as distinct beings, different from adults, until the Enlightenment of the eighteenth century. The evidence from the plan of St. Gall would suggest that some of that distinction and the need for special treatment were understood in the ninth century.

Teaching Methods

The actual teaching method in the ninth century can be discerned from Alcuin's teaching manuals. They are mainly in dialogue form of question-and-answer. They are written with either Pepin and Alcuin or Charlemagne and Alcuin as the speakers, and in different sections of the manuals the speakers reverse roles as to who is asking and who is answering the questions. By modern standards, the method is pedantic, but it worked and trained many great scholars. Alcuin himself taught Einhard (the author of the *Life of Charlemagne*) and Hrabanus Maurus (the greatest teacher of the next generation). Even the grammar books of Donatus and others used the dialogue form of question and answer such as "What is a noun?" with appropriate definitions. These dialogues, along with reading and memorization of the Psalter, were among the most common methods. The Psalms was the best known of the books of the Bible, for references to it appear throughout the writings of the Carolingian authors. For beginning lessons in reading and writing, psalms were selected that contained all twenty-three letters of the alphabet (*i* and *j* were one and the same letter, as were *u* and *v*, while *w* did not exist). Students practiced writing their letters on wooden tablets inlaid with wax. Once the wax surface was filled with letters, it could be smoothed by rubbing or by warming by a fire and was ready again for use. These same wax tablets were sometimes used by monks to write notes to one another to maintain silence in the monastery.

These methods were almost certainly used in many of the schools throughout the Carolingian Empire. Except for the very youngest boys, Latin was spoken at all times in the monastery. Lapses into the vernacular (local language) were severely punished. Discipline was very severe, and floggings and other physical punishments were not uncommon, although the monasteries probably treated the boys better than they would be treated outside. A ninth-century writer about the Carolingians, Notker (c. 840–912), was noted for his leniency at St. Gall, for he dispensed with the use of the birch rod as an aid to teaching.

It is not known what class of society many of the students came from. Although Charlemagne ordered that all boys be educated, it is not clear what the social background was in most cases. There are a few instances where we know that a highly educated person started out as an orphan or poor, just as we sometimes know that the individual was from an aristocratic background. But in some cases, the origin of such persons is not known.

It is also important to remember that it was not merely monks who ran schools. Nuns could also run a school, even for boys. In fact, it is known that some schools had both girls and boys, probably at a young age, for one well-known scholar suggested that that arrangement should be stopped. Nuns also performed renowned work as scribes and produced a number of extant manuscripts.

Education for Girls

Education for girls varied according to class, as it did for boys. Lower-class girls would be trained to do the same activities as their mothers, such as cooking, cleaning, gardening (for food, not for pleasure), and needlework. Needlework was not only essential to produce all the clothing necessary in a family, but was a point of pride for women. Charlemagne insisted that his daughters be trained in needlework, especially the finer types such as knitting, spinning, weaving, and embroidery, so that they would learn to do something productive and not become lazy. Girls of the aristocracy were trained not only in needlework, but in household management because they would grow up to run great households of multiple serving people. It was the woman's responsibility to run the household, and this was one area where the male of the house would probably not interfere.

Among the aristocracy, girls were occasionally educated to read. Charlemagne's own daughters not only could read, but were educated in the same liberal arts as his sons. Those who joined convents, where literacy was useful and encouraged, were often highly literate. Charlemagne's sister Gisla and daughter Rotrud wrote to Alcuin and pleaded for him to write them a commentary on the Gospel of John to be used for their studies. However, the evidence seems to suggest that even for aristocratic females, education was permitted for the purpose of participating in the Christian religion, but rarely beyond this to the true level of scholarship. Even among those women who were copyists, and therefore quite literate, we have very few who wrote their own creative tracts.

There are numerous examples of individuals who prove that the Carolingian Renaissance's reforms in education were successful. We move from an era before 750 when few were educated, and those often poorly, to an era one hundred years later in which literature flourished and some individuals were highly educated. Walahfrid Strabo (c. 808–849) is an example of this success. He began his education at the great monastery of Reichenau as a young boy, studied at another of the foremost schools at the monastery at Fulda under Hrabanus Maurus, the brilliant disciple of Alcuin, and returned to Reichenau to become abbot. He kept a notebook from 825 for most of his short life. This notebook proves that Walahfrid studied mathematics. There are extracts from Bede on a variety of standard subjects as well as on calendars, agriculture, and natural science. There are literary creations, including a poem about Walahfrid's own garden. This example can be repeated in the notebooks of others and illustrate the wide-ranging education that was available in the Carolingian world. It is true that the average person was probably no more affected by education in 850 than in 750, but an enormous change had taken place in both the number of people who were educated and especially in the quality of the education that was possible in 850. A priest could be expected to know enough Latin to understand and perform the Mass properly, but also to make mathematical calculations for reckoning of calendars as well as other everyday needs, to know some of the writings of the ancient Romans, and to understand theology. This distribution of learning among a larger group of people with a deeper knowledge meant that there was the possibility of survival for classical learning.

7

SCIENCE AND MEDICINE

SCIENCE

Science and medicine reached a low point in Western civilization in the period 500–1000 C.E. Humans have always tried, in a variety of ways, to understand and deal with the "natural" world around them. They have sometimes imagined it as governed by benevolent or hostile forces that could be influenced by gifts or actions. They have developed elaborate mythologies or tried to understand it by interpreting revelations or dreams of inspired individuals or actions or forms of nature, for example, by reading palms or examining the innards of animals. They have tried through magic or religion to control the natural world. What we know as science today, called natural philosophy throughout most of the Middle Ages, originated with the ancient Greeks, who used reason to study the physical world around them and tried to understand how it functioned. Although they rarely ran actual experiments, they tested their conclusions mentally with great success and established a coherent, if not entirely accurate, understanding of the universe. However, by the eighth century, natural philosophy had taken a back seat to religious beliefs. Scholars of the eighth century regarded the earth and its objects not as an independent reality that needed to be studied, but as a part of God's creation that had to be studied to better understand its creator. However, it is important to know the origins of some of the "scientific" knowledge, the knowledge of the natural world and how it functioned.

View of the Universe

Aristotle (384–322 B.C.E.) conceived a cosmological universe (patterned after even earlier Greek models by Pythagoras, Philolaus, and others) as a finite sphere with the earth as a stationary sphere at the center and a series of concentric spheres surrounding the earth, in which were carried all the other objects of the heavens. This universe was comprised of nine concentric spheres containing the moon, the planets, and, in the outer-most sphere, the fixed stars. According to Aristotle, the universe was ordered by two sets of laws, one for the perfect incorruptible heavens composed of ether beyond the moon and one for the earth, which was clearly imperfect. On earth, all things were composed of the four ele-ments earth, water, air, and fire, which were constantly undergoing transformation into one another. Hence the earth's incessant change, gen-eration, and decay.

This understanding was passed on to the Roman Empire. However, the Romans, although they were impressed by Greek scientific accom-plishments, were not interested in the theoretical and abstract concepts of science. Roman science emphasized authorities, often Greek, who could organize knowledge. A man such as Pliny the Elder (23–79 C.E.) was an amateur in the sense that he did not "do the science," but merely collected and wrote about what others had said or done.

The first three centuries of the Christian era (common era) produced some very good science and mathematics. Hero of Alexandria (c. 50 C.E.) wrote on pneumatics, mechanics, optics, and mathematics, Nicomachus wrote on Pythagorean arithmetic (and influenced the West through later translations and interpretations), and most important, Claudius Ptolemy (fl. 127–151 C.E.) wrote the *Almagest* on astronomy and other works on optics and geography. The *Almagest* remained the most important and influential work on astronomy until Copernicus's *On the Revolutions of the Heavenly Bodies* in 1543. Also of great importance was Galen (129–99), whose work on human anatomy remained the standard in the West until Vesalius's *On the Fabric of the Human Body*, also of 1543.

Yet these works, typical in Greek culture, were not as influential in the western half of the Roman Empire, both for lack of interest and because all were written in Greek, not Latin. The Romans preferred to provide a simple synopsis of a scientific or mathematical treatise, and so they gath-ered and disseminated Greek science through handbooks and manuals, somewhat like reading a study guide instead of an actual novel.

Christianity and Science

By 500 C.E. very little original work was being done in natural philos-ophy. Most of the great minds, and there were very few in Europe at that time, were drawn to the Church. Christianity had long struggled with pagan learning and was often suspicious of Greek natural philosophy. There is an inherent problem in merging Christianity with natural philosophy in that Christianity believed in a universe created by a superior, powerful, and intensely personal being who manifested himself in diverse ways, including overriding any laws or rules of nature, for example, in the occurrence of miracles. For natural philosophy, the emphasis is on the universe as observed, with patterns or rules being essential. Even the question that each system asks is entirely different. Christianity, with its assumption of God's purposeful creation, asks "why," a question of purpose. Why is the sky blue, or why does the mandrake plant resemble a human in shape? Science asks "how," a question of structure. How is the sky blue, or how does human blood flow? Some of the church fathers, such as Tertullian (c. 160–240), were completely hostile to natural philosophy, while others such as Augustine (354–430) believed that some pagan learning, especially that of the Greek Plato, could be useful in the education of Christians. Augustine was one of the most influential of the church fathers and emphasized the liberal arts that from the time of the Greeks had included the subjects of geometry, arithmetic, astronomy, and music. However, geometry at that time was more akin to our geography, and arithmetic was handicapped by the sole use of Roman numerals, which make innovative mathematical thinking difficult. To make matters worse, in his later life Augustine turned against the liberal arts, and his writings would influence thinking and education for centuries.

Encyclopedias

In the Carolingian era, what passed for natural philosophy were encyclopedias. These were actually collections of knowledge, hearsay, and tradition in the form of scholarship. Often the information in an encyclopedia was lifted directly from a previous work. Those most influential in the eighth and ninth centuries were by Boethius, Cassiodorus, Isidore of Seville, and the Venerable Bede. Boethius produced one of the best of the encyclopedias with sections on all of the four sciences of the liberal arts. Cassiodorus (c. 490–c. 585) wrote about all of the liberal arts, including the sciences, in his *Introduction to Divine and Human Readings*. Isidore of Seville composed *The Etymologies*, a vast encyclopedia of twenty books. It was comprised of fantastic derivations of terms that were intended to provide the reader with some better understanding of the object. Isidore believed that the earth was only a few thousand years old and was shaped like a wheel, with the land encircled by oceans, and also believed that it was all soon to perish. Isidore did pick up the idea of concentric spheres from the Greeks and incorporated it, but with the addition of a final sphere as the abode of the heavenly creatures. Unfortunately, Isidore's work remained popular for centuries, misleading generation after generation on the structure of the universe. Isidore was much better on medicine. The Venerable Bede was extremely intelligent and may have been the only one of these writers to actually do any examinations or calculations himself. He was concerned with the construction of calendars and the calculations of movable feasts such as Easter. Bede also worked on tide timetables and determined that tides, although regular, vary slightly from place to place on the coast, and that timetables must be set individually for each location.

Much of the encyclopedic knowledge, however, was useless. The encyclopedias were collections of unrelated, inaccurate, incorrect facts, suppositions, and definitions. Even the sections lifted from classical works were often copied so carelessly or placed so out of context that the information was rendered useless.

This same approach was used in the construction of herbals. In theory, an herbal should be designed to provide the reader with a useful manual, as a modern bird guide or wildflower guide would do. However, in an age of handbook knowledge merely copied from its source or predecessor, herbals became formulaic in illustration and symbolic in interpretation. Plants were not examined directly and drawn from nature, but illustrations were copied from previous works. After this was done through many copies of copies, the image of the plant would have very little resemblance to the plant itself. The text that should have supplied a description of the plant and its medical or pharmacological uses instead provided the symbolism of the plant or its constituent parts.

Astrology was well known and highly revered in the Age of Charlemagne. In the *Royal Frankish Annals*, there are examples of the importance of astrology. In 807, the entry begins with a discussion of an eclipse of the moon on September 2 and tells what degrees of Virgo and Pisces the sun and moon stood in. The *Annals* goes on to describe Jupiter passing the moon, an eclipse of the sun on February 11 at noon, another two eclipses of the moon, and the position of Mercury and of certain stars. There was certainly a good deal of close observation of the heavens and their movements involved in this, yet it was entirely interpreted in astrological, not scientific or astronomical, terms. When a comet was observed to travel across the skies in 817, the interest was in its meaning rather than its existence.

MEDICINE

Medieval medicine was a very mixed bag. First, there were many different individuals involved in what we might call medicine: the *medici* (physicians), *rhizotomi* (herb gatherers), *pharmacopolae* (drug or herb dealers), *unguentarii* (salve dealers), *obstetricae* (midwives), and numerous other shadowy figures who specialized in poisoning, abortions, or the like. By the eighth century, medical literature consisted of various letters and pamphlets of medical interest, some as remnants of Greek or Roman medicine, that were read by lay individuals who practiced medicine, but who were not fully trained and apprenticed physicians as in the later Middle Ages.

The Church and Medicine

As far as the Church leaders were concerned, the structure and function of the human body illustrated the wisdom and goodness of God, and its study was considered to be of real importance. Benedict of Nursia, whose Rule for monasteries was discussed in chapter 6, ordered that the sick be carefully attended in all monasteries. Care of the sick was reasonable and humane, with special infirmaries for the sick, extra food portions, greater cleanliness, and resident herb gardens and monks skilled in the use of the herbs. Although the monasteries, in their care for the sick, probably knew as much about medicine and the human body as anyone in the Early Middle Ages, their purpose in knowing this was to do God's work and to glorify God, not for the sake of knowledge. The Church was willing to accept the Greek Galen's concept of localization of emotions, but oversimplified it: joy in the spleen, carnal love in the liver, knowledge in the heart, and anger in the bile. Illness was as often as not seen as God's punishment, and so its cure was not in human hands.

Augustine (354–430) was the most influential of the church fathers and was very prolific in his writings. He never wrote any works specifically on medicine, but mentioned things such as three cerebral ventricles, respiration, and the gastrointestinal tract. Augustine also took a stand against both abortion and contraception. The most important medical knowledge, however, came from Isidore, bishop of Seville.

Isidore of Seville was born around 560. Little is known of his life, but he produced a prodigious amount of writing, including one of the most influential works in the Middle Ages, *The Etymologies*, discussed earlier under "Science," which acted as a major transmission of information from the classical world to the medieval one. Isidore had clearly read widely and critically and was interested in scientific and medical knowledge even though his primary interest was language, hence the title of the book, which mainly focused on demonstrating the etymologies or origins of words. In doing so, however, he produced an encyclopedia of knowledge intended for the educated public, a very small group. Isidore also wrote about educational and school reform. He died on April 4, 636. His medical writings were some of the best medical knowledge available to the Western world in the seventh, eighth, and ninth centuries, yet they were not meant for physicians but for the educated public.

Isidore's medical information was meant to be useful to anyone. In his discussion of disease, he says that it is an imbalance and is best managed by diet and lifestyle. He held very reasonable thoughts about health and was influenced little by superstition or magic. Isidore absorbed the ancient belief that all matter, including the human body, is composed of four qualities: heat, cold, dryness, and moisture. The health of the human body depended on a balance of these, and disease was a disturbance of that balance. These qualities were also viewed in relation to earth, air, water, and fire, and Isidore discussed the human body as correlating: flesh to earth, breath to air, blood to water, and vital heat to fire. Even though he believed that diet and lifestyle were of utmost importance, he also wrote about diseases that were best treated by drugs or surgery.

Four Humors

The four humors of black bile, blood, yellow bile, and phlegm were also matched to the parts of the body, and knowledge of all of these factors had to be carefully considered in assessment of the patient and the patient's disorder. Even the season of the year, prevailing winds, local rainfall and temperature, sunlight, and other such factors were taken into account. Disease could be caused by a disturbance or imbalance of any of these elements. Acute disease (where a crisis will be reached and the patient will either recover or die) arose from an excess of blood or yellow bile. Chronic disease (ongoing or even permanent) was from an excess of phlegm or black bile. Only in a few cases did Isidore recognize that disease might come from a specific cause originating outside the body.

Isidore believed in the twofold existence of mankind, body and soul, but unlike many Christian writers, did not denigrate the body. He argued that humans are both body and soul, and therefore the body must be cared for through medicine. He did not argue that disease was caused by sin.

Isidore wrote about mental disease in a way that was remarkably free from superstition. He discussed epilepsy and pointed out that it is not demonic possession. He described mania as a disordered and disturbed mind and distinguished it from depression. He even mentioned several herbal drugs that induce mental changes, including hellebore and henbane, and described the stupefying effects of opium.

Nervous and Cardiovascular Systems

Isidore understood the anatomy of the human body rather effectively, describing the nervous system, the spinal cord, the importance of the brain, and the function of the skeleton, tendons, and cartilage. He described accurately the anatomy of the hip joint. The cardiovascular system was probably the least accurately explained, for until the seventeenth century, arteries and veins were not distinguished, and the circulation of blood was not understood. However, he included a description of the two chambers of the heart and explained that both contain blood, but one contains more of the vital spirit. Isidore's description is not terribly far off from our modern understanding. The purpose of the intestines was understood, but not fully the purpose of the liver or kidneys.

Pregnancy

Pregnancy was believed to be caused by the mixture of semen and menstrual blood. The fetus nourished in the womb through the umbilical cord was understood, as was the fact that the heart was formed in the fetus very early and that the fetus was in the complete form of a human by the fortieth day. This was understood by examining aborted fetuses.

Surgery

Isidore did not cover surgery in great detail except for amputation and cauterization (the burning or scarring of tissue). He did point out that although a patient with cancer cannot be cured, and drugs are ineffective, he may live longer if an amputation of the affected limb is performed.

Isidore also described the use of bandages, compresses, salves, expectorants, enemas, and snake antivenoms. He discussed roundworms, fleas, and lice and mentioned leeches and how they become attached to the human body; but never mentioned their medical use for bleeding or any other purpose.

Herbals

Herbals were intended as practical works. The Greek Dioscorides had written one of the most renowned herbals in the first century C.E. as a practical guide to medicinal herbs. It provides descriptions of the herbs, including the plants' characteristics, habitat, and pharmaceutical use and preparation. This herbal and its variations were intended for use by practicing physicians, but quickly over the years of the Early Middle Ages the illustrations as they were copied became less and less like the original and therefore less useful in finding the plant. In addition, the descriptions gradually were altered, especially as confusion arose over what plant was really meant in regions where there were different plants from those known by Dioscorides.

Contraception

The common people knew little about formal medicine and never saw physicians or even herbalists. People cared for their illnesses with home preparations from herbs and other substances. For contraception, there were herbal potions. For inducing abortions, there were others. Fern roots, willow leaves, rue, and gillyflower seeds were believed to be effective. The Church was strongly opposed to the use of either contraception or abortion and considered them homicide, although if they were done because of poverty, the Church was less harsh in its penalty.

Science and medicine had deteriorated since the Roman Empire to become little more than derivative formulaic descriptions, handbooks of general knowledge, or collections of word definitions or useless random esoteric information. By copying without understanding, the images, of which there were few, and descriptions were so far removed from nature that the actual object would have been almost unrecognizable. The collections no longer were connected to concepts nor had any conceptual purpose. In a world that did not comprehend a naturalistic or scientific approach, small glimpses or hints at science left over from the ancient world made little sense. In its place, these remnants were fitted into a world of mysticism, religion, and symbolism where they were studied for their intrinsic value.

8

LEISURE AND GAMES

Around the year 800, the Abbasid caliph Harun al-Rashid sent as a gift to Charlemagne an albino elephant named Abu al-Abbas in honor of the Abbasid dynasty's founder, the elephant having been sent to Baghdad as a present from an Indian king. The elephant had traveled from India to Baghdad, then overland to Syria, and then by ship from Beirut to Malta and Rome. Finally, after waiting out the winter south of the Alps, in spring the elephant traveled overland again from Rome to Charlemagne's court in the north, arriving in 802. It seems to have been kept mainly for entertainment. The elephant survived until 810.

ENTERTAINMENT

The occurrence of entertainment was not an everyday expectation in the eighth and ninth centuries. Life was hard and very infrequently fun. Most entertainment would have occurred around Christian or pagan celebrations. Holidays (literally holy days) were intended by the Church for religious observations, but the populace often combined the religious observance with a more corporeal celebration. This was especially true in the eighth and ninth centuries because Christianity was often new to the people of the Frankish empire or only vaguely and superstitiously understood by them. The people loved to dance and sing, and the Church tried to work with this by having liturgical singing. However, the people would have taken the entertainment to sacrilegious levels outside the church building with folksongs that were ribald, even profane. Since the Church was newly enforcing Sunday as a day of rest, the populace surely took this as an opportunity to entertain themselves with singing and dancing.

For the rich, minstrels to sing or tell stories and jugglers or puppeteers might brighten the evenings of otherwise long winter nights. There were animal acts, and as we mentioned at the beginning of this chapter, the mere appearance of strange and exotic animals would have provided entertainment for the rich.

For the royal court, there was clearly much more opportunity for entertainment. In the *Royal Frankish Annals,* there are numerous references to luxurious gifts that were meant for pleasure. In 807, the *Annals* tells of a marvelous clock brought to Charlemagne by the envoy of the king of Persia. It was a water clock made of brass that marked the course of twelve hours with twelve brass balls that dropped onto a cymbal to ring the hours. On the clock there were also twelve horsemen who at the end of each hour stepped out of a window and closed the previous window. According to the *Annals,* there were many other features of the clock too numerous to mention.

Time was normally measured by the sun. This meant that a day was twelve hours of sunlight, which in turn meant that an hour was variable according to the time of the year. One hour was one-twelfth of the daylight, whether in the winter or the summer, so an hour was much longer in the summer when daylight was lengthy than in the winter. To measure off uniform units was not necessary for most people; rising when the sun came up and going to bed when the sun set or soon thereafter were good enough. Generally it was only the monks who needed to keep track of time to perform their prayers according to the Benedictine Rule. For a monastery, water clocks, although not elaborate ones such as that mentioned earlier, or sundials, or sand clocks would have provided the measurement of time. All forms have their disadvantages. Sundials only work when there is visible sun, and in northern Europe there are many days when that is not the case. Water and sand clocks require constant attention to replenish the water or sand. In other words, if a sand glass or other container is not turned over immediately upon its emptying, the measurement is thrown off. So even if the measurement is a full hour, there has to be someone assigned to watch the clock so that at the end of the hour it can be restored.

Music

The *Royal Frankish Annals* contains a reference to an organ that was a gift from the emperor of Constantinople. An organ builder from Constantinople was escorted by the royal treasurer to Aachen, presumably to reconstruct the organ, which probably traveled in pieces. Even today that is precisely how an organ is sent to a distant location. The instrument is originally constructed in the shop of the organ builder, then deconstructed, transported, and reconstructed on location. In all likelihood, the organ builder became the court organist since no one else would have known how to play or maintain the organ. Although the organ was intended for liturgical purposes, it would also be entertaining for those who would have the opportunity to hear it in the royal chapel.

Church music in the Carolingian world was predominantly chant performed by monks, rather than hymns sung by a congregation. Early church music was predominantly monophony (a single line of music with no harmony), but by the Age of Charlemagne polyphony (two or more musical lines being sung simultaneously) was common in chant, known as Gregorian chant (Gregorian chant is modal or in a different arrangement of the eight diatonic tones of an octave and therefore sounds unusual to the modern ear). Chant for the Carolingians was emulated from the Christian Church in the Roman Empire. The problem with trying to emulate this music was that the Carolingians did not really understand the form and had to re-create an understanding of liturgical music, since the Romans never recorded their music in writing. The Carolingians, in fact, were the first to record their music in manuscript. Some of that music is extant, although the notation, unlike modern musical notation, provides mainly the rhythm and nuances rather than the pitches. Music, however, was clearly an important part of the Church liturgy. Whether one could call this entertainment or not is arguable, but in an age without any other professional form of music available to most, the chant of the church would have been the most commonly heard form of formal music.

In the Age of Charlemagne, the lyre was more common than the organ. Even so, any refined instrument such as a lyre was rare and expensive, and few would know how to play it. The wooden case provided resonance, and the strings were plucked, not bowed. Earlier lyres had three or four strings, but by the ninth century these had been expanded into six-, seven-, or eight-string instruments. The four-string or tetrachord lyre when doubled became a double-tetrachord or octave instrument able to produce music similar in sound to modern Western music, but may have been tuned to the Gregorian or another mode.

Drinking as Entertainment

For the poor, entertainment was probably never considered on a daily basis, although contrary to what historians used to claim about the peasants of the Middle Ages, they did have entertainment and did play games and sports. Drinking would have been the most common form of entertainment for rich and poor, but even drinking to excess was not an everyday occurrence since ale, wine, or any of the other fermented drinks were somewhat costly and essential for one's survival. If they were indulged in too readily, the supplies might run out. We know that Charlemagne considered himself a moderate drinker, consuming only four goblets of wine a day, although it turns out that the goblets were probably around a quart in size. Drinking containers varied widely in size and material, from animal horns and wooden goblets to metal cups that were sometimes highly decorated. Wine was usually mixed with water before being drunk, almost as moderns might do with whiskey. Even so, large quantities of wine would be intoxicating. However, those who wrote about Charlemagne said that he rarely overindulged in alcohol, and Charlemagne himself spoke against drunkenness, not for religious reasons, but rather for the sobriety needed to personally run a state.

It is important to remember that the Church had no restrictions or even reservations about drinking. The Church sometimes spoke against drunkenness, but not against drinking of alcohol. After all, alcohol was what one drank once one was weaned from one's mother, so there would not have been complaints by anyone about its consumption. The modern concept of the Church's prohibition against alcohol is nineteenth and twentieth century in origin and almost solely American as well. We know from the records that men and women drank ale or wine for entertainment since life was hard and consumption of alcohol would temporarily ease the pain. Under these circumstances, people sometimes drank far too much. The records only tell us when fights occurred and laws were broken because of drunkenness, rather than about normal everyday consumption. Even the clergy were well known for having drinking bouts, getting drunk, and getting into fights.

SPORTS

Sports and games, as opposed to mere entertainment, were not unknown. Children certainly played games, but we have little documentation of them. We know that little girls have always liked dolls, and simple ones could be constructed from almost any natural material—a stick or straw, for instance. Boys seem to have always imitated elders, especially warriors, and we know that they would have played soldier, riding a pretend horse with a pretend sword. In fact, this was a favored activity, seen as preparation for actual military training. At one time, historians thought that noble boys started training to be warriors at about age seven. This may have been extrapolated by historians from the ancient Spartans. Modern historical research suggests that the boys may have played at soldiering, but that formal training only began as a young adult and that there was less overall training than originally believed. The Carolingians frequently sent their young adult sons off to train under someone else such as an uncle, this was a common practice for training, for the young person would take instruction better from someone other than the parent. Much of the training may have been literally "in the field," meaning on the battlefield. Aristocratic boys would certainly have learned to ride at an early age, possibly as early as five or six, and then to use weapons for hunting. Charlemagne expected his sons to learn these skills very early. The equivalent training for girls was to learn sewing and embroidering as well as spinning and weaving. However, for the average peasant boy, the bulk of the day would not have been spent out playing soldier, but working alongside his father or mother since mere survival was always in question, and that was everyone's business.

Children also played ball games. We do not have details, but from evidence later in the Middle Ages the games appear to have resembled baseball and soccer. Children also played leapfrog, tag, and hide-and-seek and engaged in tumbling, wrestling, swimming, running races, jumping, and stone throwing. All of these could easily be turned into actual competitions for individuals or teams.

Many of the same activities were done by adults. Wrestling, running races, jumping, and stone throwing have been common in nearly all societies. Swimming was done as a leisure activity by both men and women, and where there are swimmers, there are bound to be swimming races. Charlemagne himself was an excellent swimmer, according to Einhard. Another water sport was ice skating. Wherever there is regularly frozen water, as in northern Europe of Charlemagne's day, there are people figuring out ways to slide on it. Pictures from much later times show people with skates of bone, deer horn, or wood. Any hard surface might slide somewhat on ice, but the real point of ice skates is to provide an extremely narrow surface touching the ice so that under pressure from the weight of the person the blade forces the frozen water to return to liquid and the blade slides along this thin layer of water. This, like swimming, would be a leisure sport that could turn competitive at any time. Another water sport was boating. From the records we know that both men and women went boating. Fishing also was common, but with nets and line and hook. We also know that the Carolingians went night fishing. Fishing was both a necessity and a sport, one practiced by both rich and poor.

Hunting

More common among the nobility were riding, hunting, archery, hawking, and simulated combat. Generally only the well-off had horses, but for them riding was both a necessity and a pleasure. Charlemagne, again according to Einhard, was an excellent rider. For those who could ride, hunting was very much a sport.

Hunting was performed by many people at all levels of society, but for the poor, hunting was more of a necessity. That does not mean that it was not enjoyable or not even seen as entertainment, but for the rich, who could have others supply them with their food, hunting was more purely sport. Both stag hunting and boar hunting were popular, and each had its challenges. Stags, or male deer (also called harts in the Middle Ages), were swift and powerful. To chase a stag and bring it down with a lance or with a bow and arrow was a difficult and skillful job. Boar hunting was as difficult and more dangerous. Boars, which ranged through the oak forests of Europe, were very vicious and intelligent. If a hunter was not skillful, a herd of wild pigs could actually surround, attack, and kill him. Hunting dogs were used for both stag and boar hunting, but the dogs had to be particularly smart to hunt boars and not get killed themselves. A safer, if not less difficult, animal to hunt was the beaver. Beavers were prized for their beautiful soft pelts, but they were also hunted to help keep waterways clear of the beaver-constructed dams that flooded lands and made it impossible for boats to course the waterway.

Hunting was clearly a sport for the nobility, for they jealously guarded their favorite hunting grounds. Charlemagne had special hunting regions that were protected by law and by royal foresters who roamed the royal forests looking for poachers. The nobility also developed special hunting dogs that resembled greyhounds for their speed. Special officials were in charge of the royal hunting dogs.

Wolf hunting was both sport and necessity. Wolf hunting was even ordered by Charlemagne to keep the wolf population down and make it safer to farm and to travel through the vast forests. Special dogs were trained for wolf hunting, and all methods were used. Wolves were shot with bow and arrow, trapped, and poisoned. Charlemagne ordered that in May wolf cubs be located and killed and the pelts presented to him. In 813, wolf hunters were sent into every region of the country to destroy the animals, but to little avail. In 846, a wolf even entered a church during the Sunday mass and terrorized the people.

Archery

Archery as sport was very popular, and not merely among the nobility. The Frankish bow, as mentioned in the section on the military in chapter 3, was of a simple construction that could be made by almost anyone. For the nobility, archery was important, and boys grew up practicing archery as a sport in preparation for warfare. For the common folk, archery was probably even more important since its success meant the difference between eating or not. This would certainly have led to competitive archery among the common people.

Hawking

Hawking was generally a noble sport since it took a great deal of time to train the hawk. A properly trained hawk could be sent out to hunt other birds or small game and return them to the owner. From much later times, but certainly unchanged from the Carolingian era, hawking was viewed as hunting and as a sport similar to modern model-airplane flying, watching the hawk soar and dive.

Tournaments

One of the most popular Carolingian sports with modern readers and historians is the tournament. The Carolingians did not have the large spectacle performances that the Romans had with circuses, large-scale combat for entertainment, or mock naval battles, all of which were held in nearly every major city in the Roman Empire in great coliseums. The grandest display in the Carolingian world was the tournament, and even this was not what moderns think of with their images from fifteenth- and sixteenth-century tournaments such as those put on by the Order of the Golden Fleece. Carolingian tournaments were merely simulated combat for practice and fun. In a tournament in Charles the Bald's time, in 842, warriors charged on horseback with lances leveled, but did not strike one another. Certainly there must have been times when by accident or by competitive tension the lances did not miss and men were injured or killed. But only through such rigorous and intense "games" would the men have been prepared for real combat.

Board Games

There were some games that did not require physical performance. The Carolingians played board games. Chess, probably very similar to the game we play today, was popular, and another board game that probably resembled backgammon was played. We know that later in the Middle Ages chess was played by women as well as men and that men and women even played against each other. One can only surmise that this may have been true in the Carolingian age. There was also some form of dice-tossing game among the Franks.

Needlework

Another form of leisure for girls and women was needlework. Even though it was an essential activity to produce clothing, needlework in the Carolingian age, as today, was used as a leisure activity. Knitting and embroidery could be done at the slow times of the day such as evenings when all other work was done, or during gatherings and celebrations while the men took part in other activities such as drinking or sports. Needlework could be taught to girls as young as four years old, yet with age, experience, and coordination the needlework could become more and more elaborate. Needlework was a source of pride and even competition for women, to see whose needlework was the finest. For the aristocracy, needlework was an essential component of refinement.

9

THE CAROLINGIAN
RENAISSANCE

The Carolingian recovery of learning and renewed interest in scholarship, books, and art, especially the recovery of art and learning from the Roman Empire, has been referred to as the Carolingian Renaissance since Jean-Jacques Ampère coined the phrase in 1839. Modern textbooks typically include the "Carolingian Renaissance" as the most important phrase for the Age of Charlemagne and claim it as the most important contribution of this era. Some of the latest scholarship, however, has called the Carolingian Renaissance into question and challenged the belief in it as a conscious attempt on the part of the Carolingians to cause a rebirth of Roman learning.

One challenge is that the Carolingian Renaissance was not so much a revival of classical art, which may in fact have continued to exist through the seventh century, but was merely a more thorough understanding and reproduction of classical art at a level that would not be equaled on a large scale until the fourteenth-century Renaissance in Europe. It has also been argued that a "renaissance" cannot occur if there is a continuum from previous eras; that if one examines closely, one will see there was reform in the sixth and seventh centuries, and not just in Francia, but in Italy, Visigothic Spain, and Anglo-Saxon England. What is missed in these arguments is that a "renaissance" is not dependent upon a complete lack of previous examples of revival or reform, but upon the amount and intensity of change. There was indeed some continuity with the past, but a dramatic and distinctive break from the immediate past centuries occurred around 800 in the Frankish empire through a conscious attempt to reform it by reviving ancient Rome and the Church as a model. This view is supported by Charlemagne's sending for books from Rome or Monte Cassino, by the Franks building in imitation of architecture from Rome or Ravenna, by the creation of whole schools of art that worked in a renewed style of natural illusionistic techniques, and by the explosion of texts that filled new libraries.

REFORMS BEFORE CHARLEMAGNE

The models of Rome and the Church were not selected out of antiquarian interest. The models had practical purposes—to reform learning would bring about a more vibrant and thorough Christianity and more unified laws of the empire—but the reforms still brought about a rebirth of classical form and ideas. The reforms can be traced back to Pope Gregory the Great (590–604) with his desire to unify and strengthen the Church and his subsequent influence on the Anglo-Saxon tradition that remained vibrant still in the early eighth century, as witnessed by Bede (d. 735). This tradition of reform was brought to the Continent from England by the missionary Wynfrith, renamed Boniface by Pope Gregory II, and a stream of disciples. Boniface spent thirty-five years in lands east of the Rhine spreading and reorganizing the church. One of the major elements of his reform was to improve church discipline and discourage laxity of observance. In his efforts to reform the Church, Boniface also founded or reformed numerous monasteries and nunneries. Boniface was in contact with Charles Martel and, after Charles's death in 741, with his two sons Pepin and Carloman. Carloman, who resigned his secular role and took monastic vows in 747, was very supportive of the expansion and strengthening of the Church by Boniface. Pepin saw the advantages of having an organized and orderly territory east of the Rhine. In many ways, because of these efforts, the Church in Germany was more unified and had a more literate clergy than in Gaul or even England. When Pepin became king of the Franks in 751, he understood the benefits of the reform movement for the unity of his kingdom.

King Pepin was also handed a golden opportunity when in the same year that Pope Zacharias died and was replaced by Stephen II, the Lombard kingdom began movements of expansion and tried to gain lordship over Rome. Pope Stephen looked to Pepin for help against the Lombards and began cooperation between the Church and the Franks that would become beneficial to both sides.

REFORMS UNDER CHARLEMAGNE

When Pepin's son became king as Charlemagne in 768, he not only understood the benefits of reform as developed by his father, but merged the reform movement with his desire for expansion and consolidation into a true secular and clerical alliance. Not only was the reform movement capable of integrating the East into the existing Frankish empire, but it provided a means of unifying the rest of the empire, as well as a supply of literate clerics who could function as administrators in the government. Without a system of taxation, the need for literacy within the secular realm had disappeared with the Roman Empire. Only through a literate clergy could literate administrators be produced. This also produced a natural bond between the Carolingians and the papacy. This was the real origin of the Carolingian Renaissance.

Charlemagne began immediately to appeal to bishops and abbots to reform their organization, liturgical integrity, and educational standards. From 769 onwards, writing centers began to multiply across the empire. Each had a distinct script (style of forming letters) that enables us today to identify it, but all of these scriptoria were using the relatively new Caroline or Carolingian minuscule. Most of these writing centers, separated by vast distances of the empire, were in touch with one another, a clear indication that there was a self-conscious movement under way— a reform or renaissance. The leading twentieth-century scholar of Carolingian scripts, Bernhard Bischoff, was convinced that the common thread connecting these writing centers and driving a concerted reform movement was a court scriptorium even before the court settled at Aachen. This gives fairly strong support to the long-standing claims that the renaissance was driven by Charlemagne himself.

Education

Charlemagne was interested in educational reforms not merely from an altruistic belief in the importance of education, but because it would benefit the kingdom. Charlemagne's travels and conquests around Europe had brought him a heightened reputation, but also an awareness that there was more to the greatness of an empire than military prowess. He saw in Lombardy, both in his original conquest in 774 and after his suppression of the rebellion in 776, the richness of the art, architecture, and scholarship. (In 776, he even took some of that architecture back to Francia with him.) In Spain, he witnessed much the same. In both places, Charlemagne experienced a culture still maintaining direct connections to the ancient glories of Rome that no longer existed in Francia. Among the many Anglo-Saxon scholars and missionaries, Charlemagne saw what knowledge and learning could provide. Especially, Charlemagne saw the magnificence, albeit faded, of Rome itself and gained a respect for Rome present and past. He understood that scholarship could enhance the reputation of his realm by creating a more learned clergy and by producing clerics for his court. He also understood that education and scholarship had deteriorated since the Roman Empire and in comparison with these other civilizations around him. Advancing the arts and learning would not be a simple task.

Recruitment of Scholars

Beginning shortly after his conquest of Lombardy in 774, Charlemagne recruited the best scholars who could be discovered anywhere in Europe. The first was a man named Paulinus from Italy. Peter of Pisa, a noted scholar at the Lombard court in Pavia, arrived at the Carolingian court shortly after 774. Paul the Deacon, also from Italy, arrived at court soon after 776, attracting Charlemagne's attention by writing a letter asking for the release from prison of his brother. It seems more than a coincidence that these men, as well as two other Peters from Italy, all appeared soon after Charlemagne's conquest of Lombardy. Some may have been brought to court as hostages, but more likely they followed the source of influence and money, since all scholars need patrons. The most influential of all the scholars brought to court in Francia was a non-Italian, Alcuin of England (c. 735–804), whom Charlemagne met for a second time at Parma when he was returning from Rome in 781. Then there were Dungal from Ireland, Theodulf, a Christian from Spain, who decided to move to the Carolingian court after the military expeditions of 778, and the native Frankish noble Angilbert. These were men with varied abilities. Paulinus was a great poet. Alcuin had few scholarly achievements before he arrived at court, but was a brilliant teacher who inspired several generations of scholars in his nearly twenty-five years at court. Alcuin wrote books on grammar, rhetoric, dialectic, and spelling. His most important achievement beyond training teachers was the corrected version of the Latin Bible that he produced at Charlemagne's charge. This became the standard text of the Bible for much of the Middle Ages. Paul, although he was only at court for seven years, influenced it by the strength of his literary skills. Dungal was an expert in astronomy, one of the subjects of the quadrivium. Theodulf brought with him a familiarity with late classical antiquity that survived in Spain more than elsewhere. Sometime around in 780, Charlemagne brought to court a scribe named Godescalc from Italy. He was commissioned to produce a set of Gospels for court chapel use. This was to be a royal project to demonstrate the importance and sophistication of the Carolingian court. The Godescalc Evangelistary was the beginning of the production of a number of luxury illuminated texts at court for court use in the royal chapel or to be given away to popes or other important individuals.

Charlemagne as Inspirer

At the center of this circle of scholars was Charlemagne himself, never a good scholar even under Alcuin's tutelage, but an admirer and appreciator of learning who discussed, debated, and encouraged all the scholarly activities. According to Einhard, Charlemagne kept a writing slate under his bed for times when he could not sleep. Under the influence of these scholars, the king became even more aware of the great heritage of the ancient world that was slipping away and needed to be salvaged. The circle of scholars, actually of teachers, was referred to by Alcuin as the court school. Alcuin once called them "the crowd of scribes." Much has been made of this, although there is little evidence of any organized school, especially after the court was established at Aachen in 794. By school, Alcuin almost certainly meant that many scholars and teachers had been gathered together in one place.

However, by the late 780s, the renaissance was clearly under way, and Charlemagne was conscious of it as a reform movement. Charlemagne's General Admonition of 789 ordered that schools be established so that boys of all conditions might be educated to read and that all psalms, writings, songs, calendars, and grammars might be corrected. A letter by Charlemagne on the cultivation of learning instructed that churches and monasteries be zealous in this cultivation. It pointed out that many of the letters being received at court were full of errors and poor writing and that poor writing was often an indication of lack of knowledge and understanding. Texts for use in the Frankish kingdom were to be correct and uniform and edited with care. The emphasis was on producing correct and authentic texts.

By 803, Charlemagne sent out a capitulary ordering that priests must pass an examination before they were ordained and another that laypeople learn the creed and the Lord's Prayer. This reform was intended to be widespread and influential, not merely a gathering of dilettantes at court. In 809, Charlemagne gathered a group of scholars at Aachen to produce a uniform and authentic astronomical and computational handbook, which they did by 810. Texts sometimes left the court school with a note that they had the authority of the king or emperor behind them.

Many of the court scholars went out to lead monasteries and churches that became important centers of learning and scholarship. Many of these became the leading centers of book production, including Lorsch, St. Martin at Tours, St. Richarius, St. Wandrille, Saint-Denis, and Fleury.

Looking Back to Rome

As for the debate on whether this movement involved a conscious looking back to ancient times, it seems clear that there was a self-conscious attempt to renew the arts in light of changes that had taken place in the Church and in Byzantium. Charlemagne ordered the *Libri Carolini* (Caroline books) to be composed as a response to the Seventh Ecumenical Council held at Nicaea (second Council of Nicaea) in 787 when the cult of images (the use of images to express the ideas of Christianity, which had been questioned as "worship of false idols") was restored, being defined as veneration, not adoration, of images. The *Libri Carolini* denounced the council's and Byzantium's position on images, but at the same time attacked the council's narrowness and laid out a defense of pagan arts by listing a whole catalog of mythological subjects including the Argonauts, the Chimaera, Medusa, Pegasus, Perseus, Prometheus, Vulcan, and others. The knowledge of Greek and Roman mythology and the poetry of Rome can also be seen in a poem written by Theodulf of Orléans, one of the most learned men at Charlemagne's court. He eulogizes an antique silver bowl given him that contains reliefs depicting the labors of Hercules. Familiarity with the arts of the ancients is dramatically apparent in the Carolingian copying of the Roman architectural books of Vitruvius and in the reliquary commissioned by Einhard to imitate a Roman triumphal arch or in the building of the Torhalle, or Gatehouse, at Lorsch as a northern version of the Roman triumphal arch (this building is discussed in greater detail later in this chapter).

In the sixth century c.e., what was left of the greatness of the Roman Empire, and even of classical Greece, gave way in the West to a period of intellectual decline. This used to be called the Dark Ages, but in a modern avoidance of derisive names, many textbooks now refer to this as a period of transition. However, the sixth and seventh centuries were "darker" in that literacy declined quite severely from the days of the first- and second-century Roman Empire or even the fourth or fifth century. With this decline in literacy came a comparable and associated decline in written texts. When books are not read, they may be kept for their intrinsic value or for their aesthetic value or for prestige, but eventually these books will deteriorate and disintegrate if they are not kept in optimum conditions. If books are not kept safe or replaced by new copies, they disappear. Without books, literacy suffers, and so a vicious spiral of scholarly and intellectual decline spun out of control in the sixth and seventh centuries. With this, cultural life declined nearly to the point of extinction. Fortunately, most of the concern for education and the care of books and cultural life had passed into the hands of the Church, the only Europe-wide superstructure and the only living institution with ties to the ancient past. However, most Christians, even Christian scholars, were hostile to the pagan literature of the Greeks and Romans. Without some recognition of the importance of this literature, it could very easily have disappeared without a trace and left the modern world without a number of great classical works.

Remnants of Scholarship

There were developments even in the sixth century that helped to maintain some remnants of scholarship and eventually influenced the

Carolingian Renaissance. In the 540s, Cassiodorus founded the monastery of Vivarium in southern Italy, endowed it with one of the greatest of contemporary libraries, and established a tradition of learning and scholarship that endured and spread to other monasteries. Vivarium was renowned for its scriptorium or copying center, although it never emphasized classical works. More important was the establishment of the monastery of Monte Cassino in 529 by Benedict of Nursia. As mentioned in the section on monasticism in chapter 6, Benedict had an enormous influence on monasticism by the working out of his Rule, which came to be known as St. Benedict's Rule for Monasteries or the Benedictine Rule. This became the standard rule for monastic life in the West. Although the Rule had no specific provisions for intellectual pursuits other than reading, reading was included in the chapter on daily manual labor, and so scholarship and copying of texts came to be recognized as an acceptable labor for monks. After all, reading could not be accomplished without books, and since they were not readily available, copying them became a necessity. Nearly all monasteries had libraries of at least a few books essential for the performance of the liturgical year, and since the monks held almost a monopoly on education, the copying of books came to be one of the more important provinces of monasteries.

Scrolls versus Codices

Prior to the second century C.E., most written documents were rolls or scrolls. These were made of papyrus, which was constructed by cutting thin strips of reed that originally grew in the Nile. By laying one set of these strips that had been soaked in water over another layer set at right angles and then pressing them, a sheet was formed. Then sheets were glued together into long strips and rolled up. Papyrus makes a very good writing material, in fact, better in some ways than parchment, but it is only practical in locations where the reeds are readily available, and it is cumbersome for storing and retrieving information. It is only practical to write on one side of papyrus since it is rolled and the outside receives enough wear that the writing would be worn off. That means that a very long roll is required to contain a document of any length, or multiple rolls must be used. To read a scroll, one unrolls with one hand and rolls up with the other the portion already read. That requires a rerolling before it can be read again. The entire process is so unwieldy that scholars tended not to search for a reference in a document but simply to try and recall it as well as possible from the original reading. In addition, the storage of rolls is not very efficient since their shape wastes a lot of space within the centers of the rolls.

To overcome some of the drawbacks, writing tablets of wood filled with wax were sometimes tied together with a leather thong in the Roman Empire. But for legal documents and Christian documents that needed to be reexamined frequently, parchment leaves tied together produced a codex (plural codices), which could be easily flipped to a needed section. These were occasionally used by the second century and were common by the fourth century. Parchment was made from processing skins of sheep or goats into a smooth white surface (see the section on parchment in chapter 5). If kept dry, parchment can last almost indefinitely. It also can easily be written on both sides with no deleterious effect (except in the rare instances where the sheet is so thin that the writing shows through to the other side). By binding together sheets, as long a document as necessary can be put into one codex. Additionally, codices store very efficiently, stacked side by side, and they can be easily identified by marking or titling the bindings. Pages can be numbered, so referencing specific points in a codex is quite simple, whereas doing so in a roll is difficult.

Carolingian Script

One of the greatest Carolingian innovations solved another problem for Roman and medieval scribes, the script itself. Roman script was in capitals. If it was done well, this was a clear script, but very time consuming to produce and very space consuming on the surface of the writing material. Rustic capitals were a little more fluid, but still slow and large and a little less clear. In the fourth century, a script known as uncials, or large rounded letters with some characteristics of capitals and some of minuscules, appeared. In the eighth century, a new script was developed that has become known as Carolingian or Caroline minuscule. This was a beautifully clear script developed from cursive, the everyday script of late Rome, of smaller separate regular letters in a calligraphic style that could be written quite quickly. It also separated the individual words for clarity and speed of reading and used majuscule letters to set off sentences, titles, or headings. It was so superior that it became the standard script throughout the Carolingian Empire by the beginning of the ninth century and spread to become the standard script of Europe by the twelfth century. In the Renaissance, scholars were so impressed by the beauty and clarity of this script that they were convinced that it was Roman imperial script. Therefore, they replicated the script and made it the primary script of the Renaissance. Through this route it became the basis of printing as it appeared in the fifteenth century and indeed of modern print today, especially Roman font. Although this script appeared too early to have been created under Charlemagne's direction, it was his scholars and the schools established under his leadership that spread the Carolingian minuscule. It was perfected, possibly at Corbie, around 780, and through the Carolingian Renaissance it rapidly was disseminated to all the major writing centers in the empire.

Manuscript Correction

In Charlemagne's General Admonition of 789, when he called for correcting books and manuscripts and careful copying, especially for the Gospels, the Psalms, and other liturgical texts, it was the Carolingian minuscule that made it possible to carry this out. It made possible the extraordinary expansion of codices, for copying could proceed at a more rapid pace, and the codices in Carolingian minuscule could be easily and clearly read. Abbreviations were kept to a minimum, and the confusion of letter strokes or where the words broke was eliminated (previously the words had all run together, and the reader had to figure out what the divisions were; for example, "betwomen" could be "be two men" or "bet women"). It was the Carolingian minuscule that made the rapid expansion of the Carolingian Renaissance and the explosion of copying of books possible.

Spanish Influence

Spain influenced the Carolingian Renaissance primarily through Isidore of Seville, who was a prolific writer, renowned especially for his *Etymologies*, the encyclopedic work on numerous subjects discussed in chapter 7. Isidore contributed immensely to medieval education through *The Etymologies'* sections on the trivium and quadrivium even though the work is filled with as many erroneous bits of information as accurate facts. It drew upon ancient Roman literature and science, although it is quite clear that Isidore only knew these works second- or thirdhand.

English and Irish Influence

England and Ireland had much greater influences on the Carolingian Renaissance. When nearly all of Europe slid into an intellectual abyss, Ireland was approaching its zenith. While the Western Roman Empire declined and cities waned, Ireland was little affected, for it never had any cities. The Church in Ireland was never urban based and consequently survived in a more vibrant state than elsewhere. By the sixth century, there was an enormous enthusiasm for learning among the Irish monks and a proselytizing or missionary zeal that sent out numerous monks from this extremely sparsely populated land. In 563, Columba founded Iona on an island just off the western coast of present-day Scotland. This became the center of an Irish missionary movement to Scotland, England, and then on to Gaul to convert, educate, and inspire. Columban (c. 543–615) (not to be confused with his contemporary Columba) set out on a mission with eleven other Irish monks around 590 and crossed the seas to Brittany and onward to Burgundy. They were driven by a zeal to take Christianity to heathen lands and to reform and strengthen Christianity wherever they found it. They founded a monastery that attracted such numbers that they were encouraged to found two more in Merovingian Gaul. Columban was eventually driven out, probably because of his uncompromising commitment to monastic discipline and possibly because of the inherent conflict between an Irish monk who believed in monastic independence and the Merovingian bishops who would have wanted to control the monasteries. Columban traveled around, eventually settling in northern Italy, where he founded the most famous of all his monasteries, Bobbio.

Modern scholarship since the Renaissance has focused on the revival and survival of classical literature, and for this survival the Carolingian age has received a great deal of credit. There were cases in which a single copy of a classical author survived into the Carolingian period to be copied and thereby saved from extinction. Many things worked against the survival of classical texts. The first was that in a stridently Christian era many people did not read the classical authors because they saw them as superfluous. Many more thought that the classical authors were unacceptable and should be destroyed. Books that were necessary such as liturgical texts and Psalters were copied. More often, through neglect, mere aging, dampness, mice, and reuse for writing material (or lighting material for a fire), manuscripts disappeared. Some classical authors disappeared forever, but Carolingian scholars were interested in classical texts, and as the revival in learning spread and more libraries were being built up, classical texts were located, copied, and disseminated around the empire.

Law and Reform

An additional driving force of the Carolingian Renaissance, beyond the need for literate administrators and a reformed and strengthened Church, was the need for unified laws. The Carolingian Empire was built, and built very rapidly, by welding together many different nations and peoples with widely differing laws. Some of these peoples had clearly defined and codified laws, while others, especially east of the Rhine, had only customary laws. To conquer vast tracts of land and call them an empire is difficult enough, but to forge them into a unified whole that can be managed by a central administration is much more difficult. All great empires, including the Romans and the Chinese, have faced this problem. The Carolingians were confounded by the additional problem of limited literacy even at the central administration. To build a true empire, Charlemagne would have to work on both problems at the same time.

The only place to begin was with the education that the Church could provide. But by the time Charlemagne had become Roman emperor in 800, he had begun the process of attempting to unify and codify the laws of the Franks and all the other peoples within the empire. This was seen as part of Charlemagne's responsibility to "correct and amend," the responsibility of an emperor in the tradition of a Constantine or Justinian. Einhard stated that once Charlemagne was emperor, he noticed many defects, gaps, and discrepancies in the legal codes and hoped to have them rewritten. There is other corroborating evidence that in the year 802 Charlemagne assembled his dukes and counts and had copies made for them of a set of laws known as the *Lex Salica*. This text has survived in a large number of copies, indicating that it was very widely distributed and suggesting that a real attempt was made to disseminate a unified set of laws. The attempt was continued even after Charlemagne's death by his son Louis the Pious.

The Carolingian Renaissance needed not only learned clergy to correct the problems and discrepancies in the Church, and learned scribes to produce the manuscripts for the Church and for the law codes, but also learned men out in the field so that each count could know the law code to enforce it in his county. This was an ongoing process. Constant changes appeared through the capitularies, and these were expected to be put into effect immediately. Each church, monastery, duke, and count had to receive a copy and be able to have it read. This required a large number of literate individuals at court as well as in the counties, and this required that manuscripts be uniform and that the script be legible.

ART

Function of Art

Art in the Age of Charlemagne performed several functions. The average person would have seen little or no art beyond local folk craft, and the architecture, as well, would have been local, rudimentary, and relatively unchanging. In a culture with such little exposure to artificial visual expression, when art was experienced, normally in a church, the impact would have been enormous. The art of Christianity within the church, such as wall painting, metalwork, wood carving, and illuminated or decorated manuscripts, was intended for edification for the nonliterate and also to inspire people to work toward a heavenly reward. In addition, art and architecture in any setting, spiritual or secular, would induce respect for the power of the authority that could patronize such a creation. Buildings that were larger or more splendid than average, gold and silver work, carved ivory, and illuminated manuscripts all demonstrate the importance and power of the owner. It is for these reasons that the *Libri Carolini* defended the use of art while recognizing that art itself could easily come to be worshiped, and that Charlemagne supported and encouraged the production of the arts, though not their worship.

Carolingian art experienced the same sort of renaissance or renovation that learning did, but whereas scholarship had the obvious notability of a circle of scholars drawn from all over Europe to the court in Francia, art and especially architecture could not be as easily disseminated from a central point of origination. However, the court at Aachen did become a focal point where great art and architecture were produced that would be copied or used as inspiration throughout the empire.

Merovingian Art

The Merovingians left some of the better evidence of their arts in Frankish aristocratic graves. The Franks had a custom, not uncommon with Germanic groups, but not adopted by the Franks until their conversion to Christianity, of burying symbols of wealth and status with the body. This practice, illustrated in the 1959 discoveries at Saint-Denis and Cologne mentioned in chapter 2, has provided clothing, jewelry, and highly decorated weapons. However, by the mid-eighth century, the custom of burial with possessions or status symbols had disappeared. This eliminated one rich source of artifacts for modern archaeologists and art historians. The Merovingians left little architecture that has not subsequently disappeared or been severely altered.

Portraiture and Wall Painting

The Carolingians left a great deal of art in monumental architecture, sculpture, painting, and crafts. Art historians have debated whether the Carolingian art appeared "out of nothing" or was merely derivative (the same debate over continuity versus noncontinuity). Most recent work has concluded that it neither appeared out of nothing nor was entirely derivative. Carolingian art was as creative as any area of Carolingian life. Whereas the scholarship and especially the literature was derived from classical or Byzantine motifs, the art, although gaining its inspiration from others, went on to create new styles and combinations that were entirely Carolingian. The Carolingian Renaissance was an understanding of classical motifs. Portraiture, the art of producing a likeness of an individual, had declined during the sixth and seventh centuries, but was restored in the eighth and ninth centuries, only to be lost again for the next several hundred years.

Wall painting in the Carolingian churches was the equivalent of books for the transmission of information about Christian belief, especially for the nonliterate. Wall paintings provided essential biblical stories in pictorial form. Many of our extant examples of wall painting have come to light only in the past fifty years as restoration work on buildings has uncovered Carolingian wall paintings from centuries of overpainting or plastering. Evidence, including literary evidence, indicates that what currently exists of Carolingian wall paintings is just a small fraction of what once existed. Many Carolingian churches had their walls completely painted in biblical Old Testament and New Testament scenes. Some of these wall paintings provide us with excellent examples of the ability and direction of Carolingian art. The aim of the artistic classical revival in late-eighth- and ninth-century Francia was the renewal of perception of the three-dimensional figure and its portrayal two-dimensionally by using illusionistic techniques. In locations where exemplars from ancient Rome still existed, this naturalism was more common and more derivative. In locations to the north and east where less was known of Roman art, the forms were cruder and more symbolic, less naturalistic, but also often more original.

Illuminated Manuscripts

One of the greatest arts of the Carolingian Empire was manuscript illumination. Manuscript illumination in the Roman Empire was not common, and during the sixth and seventh centuries there was very little done on the Continent. The Irish and the Anglo-Saxons were the great innovators in this field. The first decorated letters were done in England in the eighth century. The quantity and quality of illuminated manuscripts in the Carolingian period are outstanding. (It is important to remember that the overwhelming majority of manuscripts were not illuminated. Only those of extraordinary importance were illuminated.)

In 781, Charlemagne traveled to Rome with one of the court clerics, Godescalc, where they witnessed some of the grandeur of the ancient remains of the Roman Empire and some of the contemporary grandeur of the papacy in Rome. On their return to the court in the north, Charlemagne ordered Godescalc to produce a gospel lectionary, or evangelistary (passages taken from the Gospels for liturgical use in the church service), that was completed sometime between 781 and the end of April 783. This was the first luxury manuscript produced at court (it is now housed in the Bibliothèque Nationale in Paris). Although Godescalc was presumably a Frank, judging from his name, the manuscript was produced in a method related to that used in England and Ireland. The fine vellum leaves were soaked in dye to turn them purple. The writing on the leaves was done in real gold and silver. The manuscript writing was in two types, an old-fashioned and very formal uncial and several pages of the new style of small minuscule that would become known as Carolingian minuscule. The arrangement of the manuscript followed the usage of the Roman Church. The manuscript was made to celebrate the

**British Library, Harley 2788, fol. 11v, Gospels, canon
tables. The curly columns are derived from columns
at the altar of St. Peter's in Rome. By permission of
the British Library.**

baptism of Charlemagne's son Pepin at Rome at Easter in 781. The ded-
ication has references to Charlemagne that use ancient Roman terms such
as *consul* and *fasces*, clearly taken from some model in Rome.

In this manuscript, we see a number of features of the Carolingian
Renaissance. The momentum of the movement seems to have picked up
after 780. There were influences from England and Ireland in both the
writing and the art, but they were touched by a much more powerful
influence, that of classical and papal Rome. All of these influences came
together and soon evolved into a new creative form that was distinc-
tively Carolingian. The art may have begun with emulation, but moved
to innovation. The initial encouragement and patronage came from the
court, promoted by Charlemagne himself.

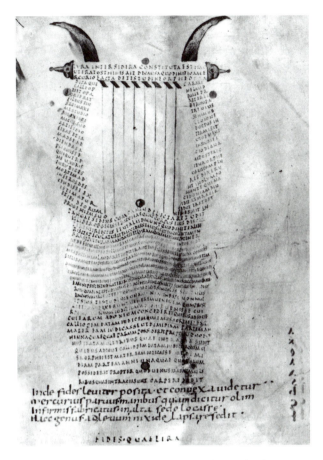

**British Library, Harley 647, fol. 5r, lyre. The lyre was
a classical instrument still used in Charlemagne's
time. By permission of the British Library.**

Soon other luxury manuscripts were to follow. They were intended as gifts, such as one produced in the late 780s by Dagulf, a royal court scribe, for Pope Hadrian I that has decorated letters, or for use in the court and royal chapel to express the importance of the court and the continuity with the glories of Rome, both pagan and Christian. Many of these connections with Rome are quite clear, as in the use of specific models such as the curly vine-covered columns from St. Peter's in Rome, or the modeling of figures and draperies, and the perspective used in painting of architectural motifs. The Harley Golden Gospels, produced in the last years of the eighth century or around 800, contains canon tables that are extraordinary. Instead of the usual canon tables' design of straight lines or straight classical columns separating the lists, this manuscript incorporates the curly columns that were known to have existed at St. Peter's as part of an altar screen (the actual columns were later rediscovered and inspired Bernini's baroque seventeenth-century baldachin in St. Peter's in Rome), although the artist may not have copied directly from the original columns, but from a Roman gospel book painted from the columns themselves. Even so, this illuminated manuscript demonstrates the Carolingian knowledge of Roman ideas and also an understanding of illusionistic techniques to reproduce the look of twisted columns.

As the Carolingian period wore on, the development of manuscript illuminations clearly progressed. They became more realistic or naturalistic in their rendering, with more perspective in the framework or background, although they remain predominantly medieval in their emphasis on symbolism, not realism. Along with the emulation of Roman models, there was considerable innovation. The artist or artists of the Coronation Gospel Book (in the Kunsthistorisches Museum, Vienna), the book said to have been on Charlemagne's knees when his grave was opened by Otto III in the year 1000, used a model of classical style to produce illuminations that are classical in inspiration, in their simple settings, in their harmony, and in their naturalism.

In two other illuminated manuscripts can be seen elements of the Carolingian Renaissance. The ninth-century Carolingian world copied Aratus's treatise on the stars. Aratus was a Greek poet of the third century B.C.E. who wrote on astronomy. Many Roman Latin writers borrowed from Aratus even though astronomically Aratus was of little value. The Carolingian copies incorporated the Roman style of painting typical of Roman wall painting. Most of these copies are sophisticated renditions of their Roman exemplars, with figures of gods and constellations or text in a special shape, as in the British Library manuscript with the text in the form of a musical lyre. The lines of text even flow in wavy lines to simulate wood grain such as that in maple wood (it has recently been claimed that this was to imitate alabaster, but a lyre would not have been made of alabaster, as the sound chest had to be hollow and resonate as in a modern guitar). This basic design is similar to the seventh-century Sutton Hoo burial lyre (a reproduction) where the horns of the Carolingian illumination become vestigial metal decorations on the wood. The playfulness in the Aratus manuscript, both in using the script to form the image and the wavy script to imitate wood grain harkens back to the gospel canon tables, where the illumination portrays curly or twisted columns as if the artists were enjoying their ability to create such art.

An illuminated manuscript from the period shortly after the life of Charlemagne, around 830, the Moûtier-Grandval Bible, demonstrates many of the important themes of the Age of Charlemagne. One is that this is an illuminated Bible, not merely a single book of the Bible. The

British Library, Add. 10546, fol. 5v, Moûtier-Grandval Bible. Each band tells a different part of the Genesis story, from the creation of woman from man's rib to the expulsion from the Garden of Eden and the labors of man and woman afterwards. By permission of the British Library.

Carolingian minuscule and the encouragement of the court school enabled the regular production of single-volume Bibles, really for the first
time. Alcuin was concerned with a pure text for the Bible, but under his
successors the text was felt to have been resolved, and elaboration in the
form of illumination was added. Full-page illuminations as frontispieces
often provided extended Bible stories by breaking the image into multiple horizontal bands to convey successive portions of the story. The
Moûtier-Grandval Bible has four full-page illuminations, before Genesis,
Exodus, and the Gospels and after Revelation. Folio 5v depicts the Creation and the Fall of Man. The uppermost band contains the creation of
Adam and Eve, the second is of Eve presented to Adam and God's prohibition of the fruit of the Tree of knowledge, the third is of the temp-
tation of Eve and of Adam and God's rebuke, and the fourth is of the
expulsion from the Garden of Eden and the labors that befell mankind
after the expulsion. Eve is nursing Cain, and Adam is tilling the earth,
which is covered in thorns and thistles. The form of the illumination is
somewhat formulaic with the atmospheric background bands, the scene
divisions of trees, and God, who is haloed (as are the angels) and always
turned toward the right.

Manuscript Illustration

One of the most imaginative artistic productions was manuscript illustration such as that in the Utrecht Psalter (ink sketches, rather than
colored illuminations; several pages are reproduced in chapters 3, 4, 5,
and 6). Now called the Utrecht Psalter because it is held by the University of Utrecht Library, it was originally produced at the Benedictine
monastery of Hautvillers within the ecclesiastical region of Rheims. A
man named Ebbo became archbishop of Rheims immediately after the
death of Charlemagne (he had been librarian at Aachen under Charlemagne), partly because he was an intellectual and abbot of a nearby
abbey, and partly because he was a foster brother of Louis the Pious,
Charlemagne's son who followed him as emperor in 814 (Ebbo's mother
nursed her son and at the same time acted as wet nurse for the infant
Louis the Pious; such children are sometimes referred to as milk brothers). An illuminated manuscript known as the Ebbo Gospels was produced at Hautvillers sometime between 816 and 823. The Utrecht Psalter
seems to have been produced at about the same time, probably by the
same scribes and artists as the Ebbo Gospels.

Both of these works contain artwork that is in an entirely new spirit
with an impressionistic style that is more alive, with greater movement
than anything seen since classical Rome. The Utrecht Psalter has 160 pen-
and-ink drawings that are dynamic in their sketchiness. Whereas most
art, including drawings, had previously been static, flat, and lifeless,

these seem almost modern in their cartoon vibrancy, producing a violent motion that makes them come to life. It is believed that many of the illustrations were copied from an earlier model, but that alone cannot account for the illusionistic qualities produced here. From these illustrations, even taking the derivative origins into account, a window into life in the Age of Charlemagne opens. There are military figures with lances, bows, and swords, cavalry, agricultural workers with plows, plow teams, sickles, scythes, and axes, and craftsmen with sharpening wheels, forges, and scales. There are activities such as assembles, burials, and sowing. The purpose of the illustrations is to illuminate the psalms. Some of the illustrations are literal interpretations of points in the psalms, while others are abstract, almost comic illusions to the psalm in reference. To separate the multiple scenes on a folio, the artist took a contemporary technique of dividing scenes with wavy lines and transformed the lines into part of the scenes in the form of rocks and hills. This makes a much more cohesive naturalistic-looking collection of scenes than the very stark and artificial series of lines.

The Utrecht Psalter in many ways exemplifies the process of emulation and innovation in the Age of Charlemagne. It is widely accepted that there was an earlier prototype from which this was copied, yet the understanding of how to use the illusionistic techniques to produce something original with realism was a Carolingian innovation. The artists of Hautvillers expressed the new understanding of ancient ideas of illustrating naturalism in a two-dimensional medium. This manuscript is one of the most important, original, and exciting productions of the Carolingian Renaissance.

Ivory Carving

Ivory carving was another of the fine arts of the Carolingians. Ivory carving had nearly disappeared in Europe by the eighth century because the rise of Islam had cut off supplies of ivory from India and Africa. With the expansion of Carolingian trade and diplomacy, the ivory trade reemerged. Ivory carvings were used as covers for luxury manuscripts such as the Dagulf manuscript (now in the Louvre, Paris) and for altarpieces. In the panels of the Dagulf manuscript cover, David is seen in one selecting the poets for the Psalms and then playing his harp. Charlemagne was called "David" by those around him in allusion to King David for their similar inspiration. The carving is extremely skillful and naturalistic. Numerous other ivory carvings survive that bear witness to the highly refined artistic skill of the period. The cover from the Lorsch Gospels, produced about 810, is an important ivory work, showing such artistic ties to classical art that it has sometimes been considered as partially a Roman Christian carving. The Dagulf and Lorsch ivories were

Victoria and Albert Museum, Lorsch Gospels, ivory diptych. Ivory carving was one of the highest art forms in the Age of Charlemagne. Victoria and Albert Picture Library.

apparently used as models for other ivories produced at court. It is believed that many of the finest ivory carvings were produced at the Carolingian court or at major centers influenced directly by the court. It is also believed that the artists carving ivories worked from late antique, fifth-century exemplars similar to ones used by the illuminators.

Architecture

The most visible of the arts was architecture. Large-scale building programs increased under Charlemagne, starting around 780, and continued throughout his reign and into the reign of his heirs until about 845. During Charlemagne's reign, 768–814, there were approximately sixteen cathedrals and more than 230 monasteries constructed or reconstructed. Considering the time, the economic conditions, and the technology, this is an enormous outburst of monumental construction. Until after World War II, most historians had dismissed Carolingian architecture as insignificant. In the past fifty years, however, more evidence has been unearthed, uncovered, and were pieced together. The picture that is beginning to emerge is one of great creativity and distinctiveness. There were great innovations that affected the rest of the Middle Ages. New inventions that first appeared or innovations disseminated by the Carolingians included the double apses, westwork or western towers, the transept, the crypt, and the crossing tower. Many of these features became standard characteristics of Romanesque architecture two centuries later.

The stonework was often very fine cut ashlar (squared, not irregular) stone quarried from local sites mixed with stone harvested from antique Roman constructions. Marble columns, in particular, were better supplied from distant Roman sites and were transported in, often from great distances. When Charlemagne had his palace built at Aachen in the 790s, columns and capitals were shipped all the way from Rome and Ravenna. Large-scale architecture was always a monumental project. A master mason had to be employed and a crew of stonecutters gathered. Carolingian architecture used rubble construction on many of its projects, but cut stone was always needed. Scaffolding was built out of wooden poles as the building went up beyond reach. Wooden frames were built to hold and guide the construction of arches. Most of the construction took place roughly between April and October because the weather was too difficult in the winter to work outdoors and extreme cold interfered with mortar. Although lime and sand mortar was actually better in cold weather than modern portland cement because the lime slaked in water created heat, the mortar did not set up or solidify well in cold temperatures.

Charlemagne was quite aware of Roman church construction, having been to Rome and seen some, and having even provided materials for

**Corvey (Germany), abbey church, westwork. The dual
towers and elaborate western facade, typical of the
Middle Ages, were an innovation of the Carolingians.
[F. Muirhead.]**

the restoration of St. Peter's in Rome. Carolingian churches were often
copied from Roman models, and the basilica (rectangular central nave
with side aisles) design became the dominant type.

Double Apses

One of the unusual features of Carolingian churches was that many
constructed in the era from 790 onward were built with apses at both
the west and east ends. The ancient tradition was originally to "occident"

Corvey, abbey church, westwork interior. The westwork created a complex interior with new spaces previously not available. [F. Muirhead.]

a church (have the altar at the west end). This was copied by the Carolingians from Roman models, such as the Cathedral Church of St. John Lateran, as part of Charlemagne's conscious adoption of Roman liturgical practices. Yet the tradition to "orient" churches (point them eastward) had already become common. The Carolingians apparently hedged their bets by building their churches with altars at both ends, with the west end the more significant one, in the older tradition of Rome. This can be seen in the plan of the church rebuilt at Fulda in 794 and in the Church of St. Richarius at Centula built at about the same time. This new construction also benefited the new movement of saints' relics, from Rome and elsewhere to be displayed in Frankish churches. Having two altar ends meant that there was room for twice as many relics, providing greater drawing power to the church.

Westwork

What we call westwork the Carolingians called castling or towers. It is the high-towered west end of a church, typical of the Middle Ages, that the Carolingians first developed. The only Carolingian example to survive is Corvey, built between 873 and 885. It has two flanking towers and a projecting central porch. Internally the westwork provided an elaborate structure, on the ground floor of which there was a crypt for relics and an entrance to the main room, square in design. The side towers provided stairs to an upper chapel. At one time there was a central tower over the middle of the church so that the three towers of the external layout would have produced a similar silhouette to St. Richarius (Centula), which was probably among the first of this design (St. Richarius never had a true westwork, but had towers at both east and west ends). The purpose of the westwork was probably to replace the double apse and double altar of the Carolingian churches. With the liturgical focus redirected from the west end to the east end, Carolingian designers must have desired a reemphasis on the west end by producing a grand entrance, a crypt for relics, and a chapel or space for a choir.

Crypts

The Carolingian church also had a number of other distinctive features, such as a crypt (vaulted chamber wholly or partly underground constructed of barrel vaults or groin vaults—the intersection of two barrel vaults). Christians used the crypt for holding relics because the saints were buried and churches dedicated to them were often constructed immediately above the site. Consequently, to keep access to the subterranean relics, crypts were constructed beneath the altar, beneath the choir (the end of the church where the service actually takes place), or occasionally under the main structure of the church. In Carolingian churches, the relics were often kept nearer the level of the nave (the main rectangular body of the church), where they were less inaccessible, instead of dropping them beneath, as in the Roman churches. Therefore, Carolingian crypts were not always entirely below ground. At the Council of Mainz in 813, it was decreed that worthy individuals could be buried inside of churches, not only in the churchyard, and burials in crypts increased. Although groin vaulting was not invented by the Carolingians, it was used more effectively in these crypts. A crypt, by the original definition, was a hidden chamber, but by moving the crypt upward and opening it to a surrounding ambulatory (a walkway around the nave, usually set off by rows of columns), greater numbers of people could move through to worship the relics.

This was significant because relics were just then becoming popular and widespread. When Rome had been under attack in earlier centuries, the bodies of saints buried in the cemeteries of Rome had been exhumed and moved into the churches for safekeeping. Space was often dug out under the altar, and crypts were constructed. In 765, with the danger past, Pope Paul I had many of the bodies brought out of storage and

Corvey, abbey church, crypt. The crypt became very important as a repository for relics to be viewed. [F. Muirhead.]

distributed to churches around Rome. Gradually parts of the relics spread further, and the movement was expanded by the addition of illicit relics. The movement of relics was especially strong into the Carolingian realm. But without any threat to the relics, the need for the crypt to be a hidden chamber subsided, and the crypt could be moved to a more convenient location.

Transepts

When the monastery of Fulda built a new church in the 790s, it constructed it in the basilica plan with an east apse and lower crypt for relics. Only a decade or so later, a large transept (which in essence is another nave at right angles to the original nave) was added at the west end of the building with an additional apse, making a **T**-shaped design. This design was similar to that of St. Peter's in Rome and continued the Carolingian preference for emphasis on the west end. The Abbey of

Saint-Denis earlier copied the design of St. Peter's, and other churches followed, including SS. Peter and Marcellinus at Seligenstadt as late as 830. With the redirection of liturgical emphasis to the east end, however, and the development of westworks, transepts began to appear toward the east end, intersecting the nave and producing a central crossing leaving the eastern end of the ✝ shape as an enlarged apse and choir.

Crossing Tower

The crossing tower, over the intersection of the transept and the nave, was another Carolingian architectural innovation. When Saint-Denis was reconstructed between 755 and 775, a crossing tower was added. Any time that stone was hoisted high above the ground, it required greater technology and became expensive. The tower was to emphasize the location of the high altar, to furnish a location for bells that could be used in the liturgy and be heard by the surrounding countryside, and to provide a dramatic visual marker externally. The central crossing tower and the westwork towers were bold innovations that required risks in engineering, but produced a striking new look and accent to churches. They dramatically displayed the importance of Christianity in Carolingian society.

Vaulting

Instead of roofing the apses (the projecting part of a church building used for the choir or for chapels) in timber, which produced a fire threat, the Carolingians covered the apses, as well as the crypts, with barrel or groin vaulting made of stone. Barrel and groin vaulting was also used in the great westwork towers that were often constructed by the Carolingians. This was the beginning of what would become one of the most distinctive features of Romanesque architecture in the eleventh century. The Carolingians were the first in the West to use vaulting extensively for their churches because of its effectiveness in multistory towers and the need for the accessible storage of relics in crypts.

Royal Palace and Chapel at Aachen

The royal chapel at Aachen, which survives remarkably intact, was built as part of a royal complex starting before 794. There had been a royal residence here for many years because of the local hot springs, but it was Charlemagne who began construction of a new palace. This complex was meant to display the grandeur and importance of the king or a great kingdom and, after 800, to demonstrate his imperial power. It included a chapel, a meeting hall, a residence, a library, and a chancery, as well as work buildings, gardens, and even baths fed by the local hot

Fulda (Germany), St. Michael Abbey Church, crossing from southwest. The apse provided an interior space for an additional altar, while the crossing provided an exterior, as well as an interior, focal point. [F. Muirhead.]

springs. The largest of the baths, according to Einhard, could hold one hundred people, and presumably Charlemagne held gatherings in the bath.

Pope Leo III dedicated the chapel in 805, but it was completed some years earlier. It provides a good example of Carolingian emulation and innovation. The chapel was designed with a centralized plan and an octagonal dome, probably modeled after the sixth-century Church of San Vitale in Ravenna (from which columns were brought), which Charlemagne had visited. But it was in no way a slavish copying of any other building. In fact, that it did not precisely copy any other has bothered art historians for decades. They have tried to determine the source of its inspiration, looking to Ravenna, Rome, and Constantinople. The chapel is a complex double-shell construction with a sixteen-sided outer wall, but an octagonal center. From the throne room in the octagonal tower Charlemagne could look at the altar of Jesus below, the altar of the Virgin Mary above, and on high the mosaic in the dome of the Apocalypse with Christ in majesty. The designers used marble veneers to enrich the interior. The designed symbolism of the chapel, and probably of the rest of the complex, was to emphasize the connections with Christianity and with Rome, for the emperor was the protector of the Church and hence the leader of all Christians. In fact, the richness of the chapel was probably meant to be associated with an image of the Heavenly Jerusalem. It is here, as the center of the Christian empire, that Charlemagne chose to be buried. Aachen was so admired that it became the model for numerous churches all over Europe for centuries to come.

Also within the palace complex at Aachen, the great meeting hall of Charlemagne was based on Roman precedent. It formed the northern side of the palace complex and was 138 feet by 68 feet in the basilica design, but with no aisles and with three apses, one to the west and smaller apses off the north and south sides. It was similar to other royal Carolingian palaces like Paderborn and Ingelheim, but the three apses were in the tradition of Roman villa audience halls, a style revived in the eighth century in Rome for the papal palace. Other elements of the architecture are reminiscent of Constantinople via Constantine's hall at Trier. This would be logical, as Charlemagne was often seen as a "new Constantine." The chapel and palace, indeed, the entire Aachen complex, demonstrated Charlemagne's importance and his ties to Constantinople and especially to Rome—both imperial Rome and Rome as the center of the Christian Church.

Lorsch Gatehouse

Some of the great creativity and originality of Carolingian architecture, along with its emulation of Rome, can also be seen in the Torhalle or Gatehouse of the monastery of Lorsch. The date of its construction is uncertain, although it was probably built to commemorate Charlemagne's visit to Lorsch in 774 after his conquest of the Lombards and may have been built within the next twenty-five years. It is actually not a gatehouse at all, but a freestanding building with three arches, a chamber on the second floor, and stair turrets at either end. The three arches are supported by Roman-style piers and have attached columns. It seems to have been inspired by the Arch of Constantine in Rome, but the masonry of six-sided and diamond stonework in several shades of brown, along with the pilaster columns on the second floor, produces an imaginative example of architecture unlike anything from Rome. It may also

Lorsch (Germany), Torhalle (Gatehouse), front. The Gatehouse was actually a freestanding building reminiscent of the triumphal arch seen by Charlemagne in Rome.

have emulated the gateway to the atrium of St. Peter's, but that has been destroyed.

Sculpture

Stone sculpture in the ninth century has left few traces. The few pieces indicate an emulation of the ancients, although they do not match in any way the statuary of ancient Rome. The Carolingians used reliquary statues in the churches—a bust of the saint whose remains were venerated. The stone sculpture of the ninth century was the beginning of the great age of symbolic stone sculpture of the Middle Ages.

Metalwork

The Merovingians had been renowned for their metalwork. We have large amounts of their gold and silver work because they buried it with their dead, a practice that ended in the ninth century. The Carolingians, however, did not discontinue the beautiful metalwork, but simply did not bury it in graves for our discovery. The objects that do survive prove that there was still a remarkable facility in metals. It may have been the

Lorsch, Torhalle, detail. The alternating color and design stonework of the Torhalle was innovative, showing the creativity of Carolingian stonemasons.

Franks' finest medium. The elaborate gates that still survive at the Aachen palatine chapel were constructed at the palace complex. Jewelry,
altar fronts, reliquaries, and book covers all demonstrate their great skill
in metals. In relief sculpture, the metalwork equals the finest manuscript
illuminations and sometimes resembles the work of specific illumination
artists. Reliquaries, book covers, and jewelry show the Carolingian love
for decoration and color in their use of gems and pastes and inlays of
silver and niello or their use of cloisonné. The altar fronts must have
been the most glorious of all the metalwork, but unfortunately we have
almost none, for they were stolen or sold to be melted for the value of
their metal.

Carolingian art was a decisive intermediate stage between classical antiquity and the Middle Ages, just as Carolingian education was an intermediary in learning. Many of the remnants of classical art are "saved" in the naturalism, the perspective, and the harmony. But alongside these qualities are usually found rusticity, Germanic folk symbols such as representations of animals, and a lack of understanding of the models being used from the ancients. The Carolingians were often able imitators of the ancients, but the native input provided a burst of energy and innovation. This new synthesis of styles and techniques would by the eleventh century become known as Romanesque.

LIBRARIES AND LITERATURE

In the library of the monastery of Reichenau, activity commenced early. The day began with the usual predawn prayers, a wash in cold water, quick breaking of the nightly fast, more prayers, and a reading of a chapter from the Rule of St. Benedict. After a walk across the monastic grounds where there was a view of the mountains surrounding beautiful Lake Constance by which the monastery stood, it was off to work. Work was an essential part of the Rule of St. Benedict. Some of the monks went to the fields to till the gardens, some went to work repairing buildings or constructing tools. But several of the monks walked to the library and scriptorium. The library was kept in a room of shelves and tables. In the early ninth century, Reichenau's library had become one of the greatest in the empire, with nearly four hundred books. The library was large enough that there was need for a librarian to keep track of the books. In the mid-ninth century, Reichenau had a remarkable librarian named Reginbert, who kept careful records of the library, including four lists of book additions to the library. He referred to the three methods of acquiring books: copying in the scriptorium, gifts, and purchase. Some of the largest gifts of books to a monastery were from new abbots as they arrived, since they were often scholars. Reginbert was also a scribe and wrote in each of his books:

> Dulcis amice, gravem scribendi attende laborem;
> Tolle, aperi, recita, ne laedas, claude, repone.

[Sweet friend, observe the scribe's heavy toil; take, open, read, but do not harm, close, replace.]

Book Organization

The books were organized by category, and a catalog listed all the manuscripts. Reichenau, like many other libraries, put biblical texts first, then works by Augustine, Jerome, Pope Gregory I, and other church fathers, with laws, chronicles, and works by various other authors at the end of the catalog. The library was a place of tremendous activity. An order might come from the nearby monastery of St. Gall that it had no copy of Josephus and would like to acquire one from Reichenau. Usually St. Gall borrowed the original and had it copied in its scriptorium, but sometimes its monks were too busy with other manuscripts, especially when they were in the process of building up their library and Reichenau, only twenty miles away, was their best source. One could walk from Reichenau to St. Gall in one day, although it was a very long day. Reichenau's Abbot Haito, who was also bishop of Basel, was a strong supporter of Charlemagne's movement to strengthen learning in the empire and also a good friend to St. Gall.

The librarian would go to the shelves and withdraw the copy of Josephus and take it to the scriptorium, the area of the library with tables. There he might transfer it to a monk who worked as a scribe, working alone unless the manuscript required illumination. The scribe might be finishing a copy of Ambrose's *Exameron* for the library of the monastery at Fulda. When he completed that copy, he would pass it on to one of his brothers who did the binding. Then he could begin on Josephus. The process was long and arduous, for every word, every letter, had to be copied precisely so that no errors existed in the new copy. Occasionally the scribe might find an error in Reichenau's own copy and would alter the text to what he believed was the correct wording. The scribe had to be both careful and learned, for blindly copying strokes on a page was the quickest way to make errors that were then passed on to an entire community of monks.

After passing on the Josephus for copying, the librarian would have to return to work, for there would be other brothers waiting for books to examine. One might want to examine a liturgical text for Lent and preparations that needed to be made for changes in the chapel service. Another brother might want to examine an interpretation of a particular point in the Old Testament upon order of the abbot corcerning certain doubts that seemed to creep into the monk's mind during times alone at night. A novitiate might need a Bible to learn his Latin and to study further the Bible. The librarian would have to retrieve all these works, for the individual monks may not have been allowed to remove texts from the shelves themselves. This was the only way for a librarian to keep close track of such valuable goods. All three monks would also sit and read in silence in the library, for again the value of books at this time would have prevented lending books out even within the monastery. When a book was lent outside the library, such as to the monastery of Murbach, down the Rhine River, for copying, a text of equal value was often required from the other institution as security against the loss of the lent text. The monastic library could borrow books from the court library at Aachen. When the book was received, it would be passed to the scriptorium for copying and then carefully returned to Aachen.

Libraries as Study Centers

The library was constantly busy, for it was not a remote enclave of esoteric collecting, but a study center. The books were not museum pieces; this was very much a working library where books were handled and read and studied. The order of the catalog was an indication of which books were demanded the most. Those at the top of the list were most often needed: the biblical texts, Augustine, Jerome, and Gregory I. The Bible, of course, was necessary for the performance of the Mass, while the church fathers Augustine, Jerome, and Gregory I were also necessary for an understanding of the liturgy and proper performance of the church service. It was easy to tell what was read at Reichenau and what was less commonly viewed. The library was in many ways the center of the monastery.

The idea of a library was a Hellenistic invention. The great library at Alexandria in Greek Egypt was one of the marvels of the ancient world and was renowned throughout the known world. The first public library in Rome was established in 39 B.C.E., but was eclipsed by the famous Palatine Library, opened by Augustus in 28 B.C.E. as part of the temple of Apollo on the Palatine at the center of the city of Rome. This library had several thousand volumes divided into Greek and Latin divisions that were then subdivided by subject matter—poetry, philosophy, history, and so on. Libraries in Rome were important places, with instruction taking place just outside the libraries. The third and fourth centuries may have seen the height of Roman public libraries, and by the end of the fourth century there are said to have been twenty-eight public libraries in the city of Rome. But during the course of the sixth and seventh centuries, the last of the Roman public libraries disappeared.

Carolingian Expansion of Libraries

When Charlemagne came to the throne in 768, there were very few libraries within all of Western Europe, and they were small, with fifty books being a substantial collection. The great libraries of the Roman Empire had disappeared through neglect, raids by invaders, and pillaging of individuals taking one manuscript here and another there.

The use of papyrus had come to an end, and by the eighth century, works that were to be saved were transcribed from papyrus to parchment. Parchment was often reused by erasing the ink writing on the surface by rubbing it with pumice and writing over, producing a document known as a palimpsest. There are approximately 1,800 extant Latin manuscripts written between the sixth and eighth centuries, but for every extant work, many others have disappeared entirely or exist only in the form of a later copy.

Books had always been rare, but when very few people could read or write, there was little need for books and few opportunities to copy one. Producing a new copy of a book was a lengthy process, done entirely by hand. It was not worth the time commitment unless the book was going to be legible, so generally only trained scribes would be used to copy a book. In addition, a book was expensive, for a scribe was needed and the parchment for a book was extremely costly. Parchment was usually sheepskin, and depending on the size of the book, only about two pages could be made from one sheepskin. Therefore, many sheep would need to be killed to produce one Bible, for instance. Because the books were so costly, it is common to find marginalia (notes in the margins that are not part of the text) with comments, in Latin of course, such as "Wash your hands, hold the book gently, and turn the pages carefully." A note at the front of the text might say, "Whoever thinks of taking this book will burn in hell" or "If this book is not returned to its rightful owner, the thief will be damned in company with the devil."

The Anglo-Saxon missionary movement of the eighth century not only restored the physical settings of the Frankish monasteries and established new monasteries, but also renewed the emphasis on learning. The major purpose of Charlemagne's educational renewal was to restore or raise the level of literacy among the clergy and monks. This movement necessitated books for learning and encouraged the collection of books to build centers of education.

As monasteries renewed their interest in literacy, even if it was for spiritual rather than scholarly purposes, there was a new demand for books. In most of the monasteries, the libraries held little more than liturgical works and a few odds and ends. To increase the holdings was not a simple matter. Monasteries had considered manuscript copying a worthy occupation for monks and nuns for several centuries, and many monasteries developed renowned scriptoria. Each scriptorium often developed a fairly uniform script since scribes were usually taught from a single master at the monastery. It is this uniformity that enables modern scholars of paleography to trace the provenance or origin of extant manuscripts. It is also this uniformity of script, when it was carried by the Carolingian reforms, that spread the Carolingian minuscule across the empire and beyond. By the end of the ninth century, the Carolingian minuscule had become nearly standard, although minor distinguishing characteristics still separated scriptoria.

The model monastic scriptorium and library was the sixth-century establishment of Vivarium by Cassiodorus (c. 490–c. 585). Vivarium turned the scribe into the ideal of the Benedictine Rule's demand for manual work and the library into the heart of the monastic community. Cassiodorus left a partial list of the holdings of the library at Vivarium, and this list became the model for Carolingian libraries. Many of the libraries that existed in the sixth century were subsequently destroyed by pillaging in a less literate, contracting society, including the remaining Roman public libraries and the new monastic libraries such as that at Vivarium. Part of the great reform movement of Pope Gregory I included the circulation of books that survived, especially ones necessary for the proper functioning of the Church, for their copying. Books from Italy were sent to England or Spain.

Circulation of Books

The circulation of books, the need for the copying of books, and the establishment of new libraries were all part of the reform movement of the Irish such as Columbanus in the seventh century and the Anglo-Saxons such as Boniface in the eighth. The monastery of Bobbio, founded by Columban in 613, had a library by the ninth century with many books older than the monastery itself, proving that books were sent from other institutions around Europe, especially from Ireland and from Italy. We know that new monastic foundations often requested and received books from the papacy, sometimes biblical and patristic manuscripts of the fifth and sixth centuries. Two other Irish establishments became important Carolingian libraries: Luxeuil and St. Gall. Both played a role in the dissemination of books, so that today the recovery of Irish literature of the sixth to eighth centuries can only be accomplished through Carolingian copies. Luxeuil's script was influential over a wide area of the empire, especially among other Irish or Anglo-Saxon establishments. Many of these Irish or Anglo-Saxon establishments were among the leaders of the Carolingian Renaissance: Luxeuil, Bobbio, Fulda, Lorsch, St. Gall, and Reichenau.

Library Catalogs

The Carolingian Renaissance is usually revered for its rescue of classical literature, but for all the emphasis on classical texts, the library holdings were overwhelmingly patristic authors, not classical. These included authors such as Augustine, whose works far outnumber those of any other author, Jerome, and Gregory I. However, the Carolingian library inherited from the Anglo-Saxon tradition the ideal of a well-balanced library organized for study. That ideal, of course, emphasized the patristic and liturgical works, but also included classical works when they were thought useful. The Carolingian library was a working library, not a museum of lost works. This can be ascertained from the library catalogs that have come down to us.

There are twenty-five library catalogs, several only in copies, from the Carolingian age through the ninth century that tell us a great deal about Carolingian monastic libraries. Several of these are incomplete catalogs, while others are complete. They come from eight different monasteries (several monasteries have multiple catalogs from different dates): Bobbio, Fulda, Lorsch, Murbach, Reichenau, St. Gall, St. Richarius (Centula), and St. Wandrille. Since these monasteries are spread about the Carolingian empire, they probably provide a representative view of library holdings. The oldest of the catalogs is dated 742–747 from St. Wandrille and lists thirty-three titles. By the middle of the ninth century, there are catalogs from five monasteries listing more than three hundred titles each, two of which have more than six hundred titles. Many of the "titles" listed in these library catalogs were part of a single manuscript of multiple works by the same author or, in frequent cases, two or more works by different authors whose subject matter might be related, at least in the mind of the person who originally bound the works together. It is not uncommon to find books today from the Carolingian era in which several unrelated titles are bound together and for which it is difficult to find the logic.

Most of these libraries also had classical works and frequently Greek authors, although in Latin translation since very few people could read Greek in the Carolingian Empire. However, the number of classical pagan works in any of the Carolingian libraries was very small. Many of the libraries with several hundred titles might have four or five pagan works. Even the great libraries of Reichenau and St. Gall contained only a few pagan authors.

The library catalogs of the larger libraries were divided into categories that tell a great deal about the holdings and about the interests of the monasteries. Typically the catalogs would have the following order: biblical and liturgical texts, works of the church fathers, Augustine, Jerome, Gregory I, Leo, Cyprian, Eusebius, Hilary, Basil, and Athanasius. In some cases, such as the library at Murbach, there were even categories for contemporary authors such as Alcuin and Hrabanus Maurus and for histories, poetry, and medicine. Many of the catalogs ended with a category of grammarians. Since these were working libraries organized for study use, the grammarians were the equivalent of the modern reference section.

Court Library

Just as the court scriptorium led the reform of all cathedral and monastic scriptoria, the court library may have led the movement to build up library collections. Einhard's *Life of Charlemagne* claims that Charlemagne's will stated that "the many books he had collected in his library" were to be sold after his death. Consequently, it has been impossible to reconstruct the court library. It is known that Charlemagne liked to have read to him historical books and deeds of the ancients, and it is known from references that there was at court a wide range of works such as Augustine, Pliny the Younger, a copy of Benedict's Rule, the grammar of Diomedes, and a poem on medicine by Serenus Sammonicus, as well as contemporary theological treatises. It is extremely interesting to note that the donations of books to the court during Charlemagne's reign indicate a particular interest in rare literary works, not just practical books. The Carolingian Renaissance may have begun with practical aims in mind, but it took on a momentum of its own, and books were gathered to collect what could be collected. Just as Charlemagne gathered "classical" art from Ravenna as booty after the conquest of the Lombards, it is possible that the court library acquired manuscripts from Ravenna. This would have provided a wealth of sixth-century and older works.

Around 780, a clearly defined policy was put into place to build up libraries across the empire. Cathedral and monastic libraries were to acquire manuscripts that were produced in the fairly closely regulated scriptoria and to reorganize and expand. The reorganization and expansion did not happen consistently and evenly, but within a few decades it had spread across the entire empire, aided by the new Carolingian minuscule. The movement begun as a utilitarian effort to help provide learned administrators for the court and to educate monks and clergy to strengthen Christianity in the empire quickly broadened to preserve literary treasures of the past.

In 790, when the court library added classical Latin pagan works to its collection such as those by Cicero, Terence, Juvenal, and Horace, these works were quite rare and in some cases had been reduced to one extant copy. In some cases, of course, the situation was even worse, and there was no copy left in existence of a title by a Roman author referred to in other works. That often meant that the book was gone forever, unless in modern times a palimpsest of the lost title could be discovered and the text recovered through modern technology reading the underwriting that had been rubbed away. Although the classical works were often used in the schools for teaching Latin, they were also collected for their rarity. The monastery of Lorsch had works by Virgil, Lucan, Horace, Cicero, Seneca, and Pliny the Younger.

Grammatical texts were very common in all the Carolingian libraries, collected for their rarity, in the case of Roman grammarians, and for their usefulness in instructing students to produce a more learned clergy and administration. Grammar was the first of the seven liberal arts and the first step on the way to divine wisdom according to the late classical tradition. The most common texts were those of Donatus and Priscian.

Poetry was not quite as common within the library holdings, but certainly most libraries contained some, often for use in instruction in Latin and even in German. The Latin poet Virgil, for instance, was in most libraries because he was the first non-Christian author read by students in Carolingian schools. The larger Carolingian libraries had more substantial collections, especially of Latin poetry. More common were texts on meter for instructional purposes. Among these were works by Bede, Walahfrid Strabo, and Boniface. That poetry, both classical and Christian, was usually listed in the catalogs along with the grammarians is evidence that it was seen as having a primarily educational use.

Libraries of the Carolingian Empire are prime examples of both the cause and effect of the Carolingian Renaissance. The movement that was encouraged, expanded, and supported by Charlemagne witnessed its most tangible effect in the expansion of libraries. Libraries increased both in number and in size. Whereas the total holdings of libraries in the Merovingian Empire may have numbered in the hundreds, by the time of Charlemagne's grandsons there were individual libraries with holdings of more than a thousand volumes. Many works of classical antiquity were saved for posterity. More important, learning was revived. It may not have survived at this level for long, but its dissemination enabled it to survive another onslaught of destruction. Without the libraries and their store of knowledge, the process of reforming the learning of the clergy and the spread of education even among laypersons would not have been possible. That much of this expansion took place within a relatively short time, from 770 to 870, gives strong support to the claims of a Carolingian renaissance.

10

THE CAROLINGIAN LEGACY

On Christmas Day, 800, when Charlemagne was crowned emperor of the Romans at St. Peter's in Rome, all of Western Christendom, with the minor exceptions of the Anglo-Saxons and small bits of Italy held by Byzantium, was united under one ruler. This was the closest Europe would ever come to creating a political Christendom and the largest single political configuration to exist between the Roman Empire of the third century and the Napoleonic Empire of the early nineteenth century. However, it was neither a political nor an economic legacy that endured.

Charlemagne was conscious of the dignity that was bestowed upon him along with the title of emperor of the Romans. It thrust him into the same echelon as the Byzantine emperors and put him in a line, although broken, with the Roman emperors of old. That a German barbarian king who had inherited a large but relatively insignificant northern kingdom was now worthy of consideration as an heir to Augustus and Constantine was indeed a remarkable event.

The Carolingians were able to establish themselves and their empire as the political and military center of Europe and a recognized player in world politics, and by Western standards the empire became a major commercial center trading with Byzantium, the Muslim world, Anglo-Saxon England, and Scandinavia. Charlemagne understood the need for a stronger economy, although he had only limited ideas how to gain it. His reforms of currency were not only effective, but enduring as few other economic initiatives have been. In 875, when Charles the Bald was returning from his coronation in Rome, he met a group of Jewish merchants in Lucca. He invited them to return to Germany with him, they accepted, and soon Jewish communities were established at Mainz, Worms, Cologne, Trier, and elsewhere. This was the beginning of the German Jewish community that would grow and prosper and would become known as the Ashkenazic Jews (meaning German Jews, as opposed to the Sephardic Jews of the Mediterranean regions). This is proof of the importance of the Carolingian economy, but is also indicative of the enduring impact that Charlemagne's economic policies would have.

Before Charlemagne's death, he began to make arrangements for the empire. In 806, in a document known as the Division of the Empire, he decided that the empire would be divided between his three sons, apparently with no concern for the perpetuation of the unity of the empire that he had forged. Pepin was to have the East and Italy, Louis was to have southern Gaul and Aquitaine, and Charles was to have the heartland of the old Frankish kingdom. It is very possible that Charlemagne intended for the eldest son, Charles, to continue the role of emperor. That may explain why Charles was taken to Rome with his father in December 800 and why he was crowned by Pope Leo III in the spring of 801, before Charlemagne and Charles left to return to Francia. Initially, there was no word on the imperial title, and some historians have concluded that Charlemagne saw that title as one solely bestowed upon him and not heritable. The three were to rule their separate kingdoms as equals, and the title of emperor was to die with Charlemagne. However, in 810 Pepin died, and in 811 Charles died, leaving Louis as the sole son. In September 813, Charlemagne summoned to Aachen all the counts, dukes, and bishops and asked for their allegiance to his son Louis as emperor. The following week Charlemagne, in the chapel at Aachen, had Louis crown himself as Roman emperor. It was clear and significant that Louis was not crowned by the pope or by Charlemagne, but by his own hands. As they left the chapel and parted, they embraced, kissed, and out of joy began to cry. In January 814, after leaving the hot springs where he bathed, Charlemagne developed a fever and died. He was buried the same day in the chapel at Aachen.

During Charlemagne's life, there was only one pagan neighbor against whom he stood on the defensive, and that was Godofrid the Dane. He ruled a considerable northern kingdom to which some of the Saxon leaders had escaped during Charlemagne's Saxon campaign. Viking attacks began within Charlemagne's lifetime. In 810, Godofrid sent a fleet of two hundred ships to maraud the Frisian coast. Charlemagne ordered the construction and organization of naval fleets to defend the northern coastal regions, but the Carolingian navy was never able to take the offensive as the English navy would do under Alfred the Great. Within a few decades, the naval defense was abandoned in favor of land defenses along the coast. Port towns were defended and towns, especially those along the rivers, were once again walled as they had been in earlier centuries. None of the defenses were effective. Some towns tried to buy protection by paying off the Vikings, but this did little except encourage more interest by the Northmen.

As early as 890, Provence was described as a desert, destroyed by the Saracens. The Saracens attacked first the coastal regions and then inland and destroyed everything in their path, leaving the land uninhabitable. The only recourse was to flee the more exposed lands, which were usually the best agricultural lands, and head for the mountains.

There was a powerful political and geographic legacy from the Age of Charlemagne. The military expansion under Charles Martel, Pepin I, and Charlemagne defined and created modern Europe. It was tied together by universal coinage and a movement toward universal law. The military conquests ended by around 803, and from that point on the legacy shifted. The more important legacy that has endured is primarily intellectual. Charlemagne himself would have been proud of that. It seems relatively clear that by 800 Charlemagne was aware that it was the intellectual, not the military, successes of his reign that would establish it as one of greatness.

During Charlemagne's reign, there were some sixteen cathedrals and more than 230 monasteries either constructed or reconstructed (and another 200 monasteries within the next forty years). Many of these monasteries would remain major ecclesiastical, intellectual, and economic centers throughout the Middle Ages. There are approximately 1,800 manuscripts or manuscript fragments from the sixth to the eighth centuries of the Christian era, but more than 7,000 from the ninth century alone. It is not just the legacy of the 7,000–8,000 manuscripts for which the modern world is grateful, but the recovery, reform, and renaissance of learning that the 7,000 manuscripts indicate. What would have become of classical learning had the deterioration continued another century or two, no one can say. The thread upon which much of the ancient world's knowledge hung was already extremely precarious and in some cases had already snapped. Left untended and uncultivated, the ancient garden might have been entirely overtaken by weeds, never able to be recovered. The Carolingian Renaissance came in the nick of time and under astonishing circumstances. Who would have imagined that an illiterate king of a Germanic tribe with almost no connections to Rome or to civilizations of the Mediterranean and with only a marginal hold on Christianity would become the defender, reviver, and expander of the Christian faith, of classical learning, and of codified laws?

Almost immediately at Charlemagne's death, the idea of a golden age was created. Charlemagne was lamented as the father of all, the defender of Christianity, the most powerful, wise, and eloquent. Einhard wrote about Charlemagne to express the inadequacies of his heirs and successors, but in doing so, built up further the image that became the legend of Charlemagne. It is true that not long after Charlemagne's death the unity and strength of the empire began to falter. Some of that is because of the increased attacks from without, but some of the blame may appropriately lie with the heirs. Louis' three sons in 843 partitioned the once-united empire. But as late as 1095, when Pope Urban called for the First Crusade to liberate the Holy Land, he told men to rise up and remember the greatness of Charlemagne. To inspire men on this holy mission, the poem *The Song of Roland* was written, turning one of Charlemagne's greatest disasters into one of his glories.

Historians place such significance on the political structure that periods are usually determined by changes in dynasty, wars, and invasions. After the tremendously successful rule of Charlemagne, it is easy to look for a period change. With the invasions of the Vikings, the Magyars, and the Saracens of the ninth and tenth centuries, it is easy to designate a period change. With the partition of the Carolingian Empire and the disintegration of the Carolingian dynasty, it seems appropriate to indicate a period change. However, history is not simply political and military. The Age of Charlemagne is more importantly the revival of education, literacy, literature, theology, the arts, and music as well as the writing of history. The Age of Charlemagne was the revival of the Church and of Christianity in the West. These spheres did not stop or disappear after 814 or even after 888, the final partition of the empire. There was a continuity in them that endured in the West through the political disintegration and on into the recovery in the eleventh century.

Education may have deteriorated in the tenth century, but it never reached the nadir of the seventh century. Libraries were attacked and destroyed, but not all libraries were destroyed and books did not near extinction as they did before the Carolingian Renaissance. The Carolingian minuscule continued as the standard script throughout the tenth century and on into the High Middle Ages, to be revived again in the Renaissance. The organization or knowledge that was developed during the Carolingian era continued as the fundamental form throughout the Middle Ages. The Vulgate Bible as it stood in the Carolingian era became the standard Bible for the Middle Ages.

Although monasteries suffered a setback during the later ninth century, they never disappeared, and they began one of the greatest recoveries less than a century after Charlemagne's death with the Cluniac Reforms starting in 910. Yet the basic structure and organization of monasteries continued to be that developed during the Age of Charlemagne. The architectural forms of the Age of Charlemagne became the basic forms of the High Middle Ages, with the basilica design being renewed and features added during the Carolingian era, such as the western towers, the transepts, the extended chancel, the crypt, and crossing tower, becoming fundamental features of the Romanesque period.

The question of whether the Age of Charlemagne was a connection and continuum with the Roman Empire or a break with Rome and the beginning of Europe cannot be answered simply. In economics and in the history of towns and cities, there seems to be little doubt that there was a break and that a new form arose. In political and social life, the same was probably true, but the evidence is a little cloudier. Militarily the ties with Rome are weak, and certainly the military conquests of Charles Martel, Pepin I, and Charlemagne created something geographically reminiscent of the western half of the Roman Empire, but focused around the north, not the Mediterranean. In intellectual and artistic realms, the continuum with Rome is much stronger, although even in these fields there were originality and new forms. The Age of Charlemagne was a period of remarkable invention, emulation, and renewal in so many domains that it remains a period of wonder for its confidence and ambition as much as for the actual accomplishments.

GLOSSARY

Abbot	The head of a monastery with absolute authority over the monks and the workings of the community.
Ale	A drink of brewed and fermented grain without hops.
Apse	A projecting part of a church, often rounded and often located at one end.
Augury	Foretelling events from omens.
Basilica	Architectural form of a rectangular nave with side aisles separated by lines of columns.
Bifolio	A sheet of parchment folded and stitched at the center crease.
Bishop	The head of a diocese in the hierarchy of the Church.
Byrnie	A military covering made of small plates of iron attached to a vest.
Cathedral	Church seat of a bishop.
Chalice	The container in the Christian Mass used to hold the eucharistic wine.
Champlevé	Metal carved and depressions filled with molten glass.

Ciborium	The container in the Christian Mass used to hold the bread or eucharistic wafers.
Cloisonné	Artwork of glass in compartments made of wire on a metal backing.
Codex	A collection of pages bound together into a book (as opposed to a scroll).
Concubine	A woman who lives with a man without being his wife.
Corn	Any edible grain.
Count	The official responsible for a county for maintenance of order and ensuring appropriate military fulfillment. The office was not necessarily hereditary.
Crenellation	Indented battlements on a building.
Crypt	A vaulted area under the main room or apse of a church.
Duke	The aristocrat responsible for the military of an entire region.
Eucharist	The sacrament of the Lord's Supper in which the bread and wine are consecrated.
Exogamy	Marriage outside the immediate kinship group.
Fallow	A field left unplanted for a year to allow it to renew its nutrients.
Fief	Land granted in return for military service.
Ford	A place where a river may be crossed by wading.
Francia	All territories under Carolingian rule, but especially Neutria and Austrasia.
Gathering	A grouping of parchment pages in a codex.
Gospels	Books of the New Testament written by Matthew, Mark, Luke, and John.
Grammar	The study of grammar, literature, and interpretations of language and literature.
Harrow	An implement used to break up the clods of earth turned over in plowing.
Hauberk	A military covering made of interlinked rings of iron.
Illumination	Manuscript painting.

Incantation	The use of spells or verbal charms.
Manuscript	A handwritten document of any length.
Medium of exchange	Items like coins that provide a means to convert value of one item for another.
Minuscule	Script using lowercase letters developed from cursive. Carolingian minuscule was particularly clear.
Monastery	A community of men (monks) living under an organized rule.
Noncommercial payment	Taxes and fines requiring a standard form of payment, for example, coins.
Novitiate	A man, usually young, who was training to become a monk.
Nunnery	A community of women living under an organized rule.
Obverse	The front side of a coin.
Oxidize	To decay by rotting or rusting.
Paleography	The study of handwriting, from which a manuscript's provenance or origin can be determined.
Palimpsest	A parchment with the original writing erased and written over.
Papacy	The office of the bishop of Rome, from "pope," meaning father.
Parchment	Writing material made from the skin of a sheep, goat, or other animal.
Parchmenter	A person who produces parchment.
Penitentials	Writings to provide guidance to priests on penalties for sins.
Pestilence	Any contagious or infectious epidemic disease.
Primogeniture	Wealth and authority passing from father to eldest son.
Quadrivium	The study of arithmetic, geometry, astronomy, and music in medieval education.
Recto	Front side of a manuscript page.
Relic	The body, body part, or object of a saint that was believed to have special powers.

Renaissance	Rebirth, as of the ideas and knowledge of a previous era.
Reverse	The back side of a coin.
Sacrilege	Stealing or desecrating sacred things.
Saint	A person, often a martyr, whose godly life was to be emulated.
Scara	Professional palace or royal guard.
Scribe	Someone trained to write, often for copying manuscripts.
Scriptorium	A center of writing, as in a monastery.
Trivium	The study of grammar, rhetoric, and dialectic in medieval education.
Vassal	Freeborn man sworn to loyalty to a more powerful man.
Vellum	Parchment made from the skin of a lamb, calf, or kid.
Verso	Back of a manuscript page.
Villa	Estate and especially the house of a large landholder.
Wattle and daub	Building material of woven sticks plastered with mud.
Wergeld	Reparation payment for harm inflicted on another in the Germanic tradition.

For Further Reading

PRINT SOURCES

Alexandre-Bidon, Danièle, and Didier Lett. *Children in the Middle Ages: Fifth–Fifteenth Centuries*. Notre Dame: University of Notre Dame Press, 1999. Very little on the Carolingian era, but stronger on the later Middle Ages.

Bachrach, Bernard S. *Early Carolingian Warfare: Prelude to Empire*. Philadelphia: University of Pennsylvania Press, 2001. The most complete work on the Carolingian military, but biased toward establishing a continuum with ancient Rome.

Bischoff, Bernhard. *Manuscripts and Libraries in the Age of Charlemagne*. Translated and edited by Michael Gorman. Cambridge: Cambridge University Press, 1994. The premier scholar on Carolingian manuscripts and paleography. This is a superb book, but very scholarly and complex.

Bullough, Donald. *The Age of Charlemagne*. London: Paul Elek, 1965. Still the best introduction to art and scholarship in the Age of Charlemagne, with many illustrations, plates, and maps, by one of the greatest Carolingian scholars. Very readable for any level.

Bullough, Donald. *Carolingian Renewal: Sources and Heritage*. New York: St. Martin's Press, 1991. A lifetime of scholarship revealed by a leading scholar.

Burguière, André, Christiane Klapisch-Zuber, Martine Segalen, Françoise Zonabend, eds. *A History of the Family*. Vol. One. Cambridge, MA: Belknap Press of Harvard University Press, 1996. Contains only limited information on the Carolingian period.

Carter, John Marshall. *Medieval Games: Sports and Recreations in Feudal Society*. New York: Greenwood Press, 1992. A fairly thin study of games and sports, but one of the few available. Quite readable.

Collins, Roger. *Charlemagne*. Toronto: University of Toronto Press, 1998. The latest single volume by one of the leading current Carolingian scholars. Intended for university students.

Contamine, Philippe. *War in the Middle Ages*. Oxford: Basil Blackwell, 1984. One of the best books on war and warfare in the Middle Ages. Covers strengths and weaknesses of the Carolingian armies.

Davis-Weyer, Caecilia. *Early Medieval Art, 300–1150*. Toronto: University of Toronto Press, 1986. Primary sources and documents on art of the period, including a section on the Carolingian Renaissance, with minimal description and interpretation. No illustrations.

De Hamel, Christopher. *Scribes and Illuminators*. Toronto: University of Toronto Press, 1992. An easy-to-comprehend little book by one of the authorities on the subject.

Duby, Georges. *The Early Growth of the European Economy*. Ithaca, NY: Cornell University Press, 1974. Translated by Howard B. Clarke. A complex history on social relations and the economy in the Early Middle Ages that includes material on the Carolingians.

Duckett, Eleanor S. *Carolingian Portraits: A Study in the Ninth Century*. Ann Arbor: University of Michigan Press, 1962. Studies of individuals.

Dutton, Paul Edward, ed. *Carolingian Civilization: A Reader*. Peterborough, Ontario: Broadview Press, 1993. An excellent collection of Carolingian documents in translation.

Fichtenau, Heinrich. *The Carolingian Empire: The Age of Charlemagne*. Translated by Peter Munz. New York: Harper & Row, 1964. A standard work on Carolingian politics, scholarship, and the poor.

Fossier, Robert, ed. *The Cambridge Illustrated History of the Middle Ages*. Vol. 1, *350–950*. Cambridge: Cambridge University Press, 1989. An excellent overview. The place to begin a study of the Age of Charlemagne.

Ganshof, F.L. *The Carolingians and the Frankish Monarchy*. Ithaca, NY: Cornell University Press, 1971. One of the leading scholars, but somewhat dated.

Gies, Frances, and Joseph Gies. *Marriage and the Family in the Middle Ages*. New York: Harper & Row, 1987. A very readable book accessible to younger readers, but put together from good research. One chapter is on the Carolingian age. Contains many examples.

Herlihy, David. *Medieval Households*. Cambridge, MA: Harvard University Press, 1985. Scholarly, but approachable. Limited material on Carolingian Europe.

Herlihy, David. *Women, Family, and Society in Medieval Europe*. Providence, RI: Berghahn Books, 1995. A collection of essays published by this great medievalist from 1978 to 1991. Limited material on Carolingian Europe.

Hinks, Roger. *Carolingian Art*. Ann Arbor: University of Michigan Press, 1962. A rare monograph on Carolingian art; must be supplemented with recent scholarship.

Hodges, Richard. *Towns and Trade in the Age of Charlemagne*. London: Duckworth, 2000. The latest in archaeological contributions to the debate about continuity versus discontinuity. Argues for discontinuity in economics.

Hubert, J., J. Porcher, and W.F. Volbach. *The Carolingian Renaissance*. New York: George Braziller, 1970. The best collection of illustrations of Carolingian art and architecture. It also provides a very clear approach to understanding the significance of the creativity and inventiveness of Carolingian art, but filled with errors.

Hussey, J.M. *The Byzantine World*. New York: Harper & Brothers, 1961. Includes a nice section on everyday life for comparison with the Carolingian world. Very simple and readable.

Laistner, M.L.W. *Thought and Letters in Western Europe, A.D. 500 to 900*. 2nd ed. Ithaca, NY: Cornell University Press, 1957. Part III, "The Carolingian Age," is still one of the best works on Carolingian learning.

Lasko, Peter. *The Kingdom of the Franks: North-West Europe before Charlemagne*. London: Thames & Hudson, 1971. A brief and clear book covering the art of the early Franks before the Carolingians.

Lewis, Archibald R., and Timothy J. Runyan. *European Naval and Maritime History, 300–1500*. Bloomington: Indiana University Press, 1985. Very little on the Carolingian navy, for there is little to say. Good illustrations of Viking ships.

McKitterick, Rosamond, ed. *Carolingian Culture: Emulation and Innovation*. Cambridge: Cambridge University Press, 1994. An excellent work on the subject of culture by one of the greatest of current Carolingian scholars. The avowed theme is the legacy of Rome in Carolingian culture.

McKitterick, Rosamond. *The Frankish Kingdoms under the Carolingians, 751–987*. New York: Longman, 1983. An excellent political study by a leading scholar.

McKitterick, Rosamond. *The Frankish Kings and Culture in the Early Middle Ages*. New York: Variorum, 1995. One of the contemporary authorities on the Carolingians. Very dense but informative.

Metcalf, D.M. "The Prosperity of North-Western Europe in the Eighth and Ninth Centuries." *Economic History Review* 20 (1967):344–357. Reasserts the importance of coinage in trade.

Moore, R.I. *The First European Revolution, c. 970–1215*. Oxford: Blackwell, 2000. Finds the origin of Europe not in the Carolingian era, but in the tenth century.

Morrison, Karl F. *Carolingian Coinage*. New York: American Numismatic Society, 1967. A very scholarly study of Carolingian coins, a catalog of coins, and illustrations.

Munz, Peter. *Life in the Age of Charlemagne*. New York: Capricorn Books, 1971. A brief, but excellent book on life for most segments of society. Usable for high school.

Mütherich, Florentine, and Joachim E. Gaehde. *Carolingian Painting*. New York: George Braziller, 1976. A good introduction to the subject, with many color prints and brief commentaries.

Myers, Henry A. *Medieval Kingship*. Chicago: Nelson-Hall, 1982. A scholarly work on kingship with heavy emphasis on Germany, although not primarily early.

Nelson, Janet L., transl. *The Annals of St-Bertin*. Manchester: Manchester University Press, 1991. A published, little used, primary source on the Carolingians.

Nicolle, David. *The Age of Charlemagne*. London: Osprey Publishing, 1984. A very short, clear, and simple book on the military of the Carolingian age with numerous illustrations. Usable for high school or even middle school.

Reynolds, L.D., and N.G. Wilson. *Scribes and Scholars: A Guide to the Transmission of Greek and Latin Literature*. 3rd ed. Oxford: Clarendon Press, 1991. A classic, but still valuable as a guide.

Riché, Pierre. *The Carolingians: A Family Who Forged Europe*. Philadelphia: University of Pennsylvania Press, 1993. An excellent, thorough, and insightful study.

Riché, Pierre. *Daily Life in the World of Charlemagne*. Philadelphia: University of Pennsylvania Press, 1978. Excellent study of daily life.

Scholz, Bernhard Walter, transl. *Carolingian Chronicles: Royal Frankish Annals and Nithard's Histories*. Ann Arbor: University of Michigan Press, 1970. A very readable translation of two extremely important documents.

Stalley, Roger. *Early Medieval Architecture*. Oxford: Oxford University Press, 1999. A cogent explanation of Carolingian architecture, giving it its due credit.

Sullivan, Richard E. *Aix-la-Chapelle in the Age of Charlemagne*. Norman: University of Oklahoma Press, 1963. The best study of Charlemagne's capital and the argument for it as a second Rome. A very readable and entertaining book.

Sullivan, Richard E., ed. *"The Gentle Voices of Teachers": Aspects of Learning in the Carolingian Age*. Columbus: Ohio State University Press, 1995. One of the great Carolingian historians gathers essays by other prominent historians on Carolingian art and culture with an excellent revisionist introduction. Heavy reading.

Weinberger, Stephen. "Peasant Households in Provence: Ca. 800–1100." *Speculum* 48 (1973):247–257. One of the few studies of households of the Carolingian period. Very scholarly.

Wemple, Suzanne Fonay. *Women in Frankish Society: Marriage and the Cloister, 500 to 900*. Philadelphia: University of Pennsylvania Press, 1981. The best study of women in the Carolingian era. Lays out nicely the changes that took place between the Merovingian and Carolingian periods. Includes material on child rearing and childhood, marriage, and monasticism. Most of the coverage is of the aristocracy since that is where the sources are. Scholarly, yet approachable.

ELECTRONIC SOURCES

http://pages.prodigy.com/charlemagne   A simple site that introduces some Carolingian material and links to other sites.

http://www.chronique.com/Library/MedHistory/charlemagne.htm   A biography of Charlemagne from Will Durant's "Story of Civilization" from 1950.

http://www.fordham.edu/halsall/book.html   Fordham Medieval Sourcebook includes a number of Carolingian documents in English translation, including Einhard's *Life of Charlemagne*. A scholarly and very useful site.

http://www.kloster-lorsch.de   A close examination of one of the important monasteries of the Carolingian Empire.

http://www.wmich.edu/medieval/rawl/carolingian/index1.html The ultimate English language bibliography on the Carolingian era. Includes every work of any significance that has been published in English. Divided into useful categories such as primary sources, general histories, economy, society, and culture. Contains bibliographic citations of hundreds of books and articles.

INDEX

About the Author

JOHN J. BUTT is Professor of History at James Madison University in Virginia. He has published in the fields of Carolingian, British, naval, and agricultural history.